West Virginia

A History

West Virginia

A History

John Alexander Williams

West Virginia University Press
Morgantown

West Virginia University Press, Morgantown 26506
© 2001 by West Virginia University Press
Second edition 2001, reprint with additional matter
© 1984, 1976 by American Association for State and Local History
All rights reserved
First edition published 1976 by W. W. Norton & Co., Inc. under the title *West Virginia: A Bicentennial History*

Printed in the United States of America
10 09   5 4

978-0-937058-56-5 (paperback)

Library of Congress Cataloging-in-Publication Data

Williams, John Alexander. 1938-
    West Virginia: a History—Second edition
    p. map 21 cm
    Includes bibliographical references and index.
    Includes "Epilogue"not in earlier editions

1. West Virginia—History. I. Title
                                                        2001093429
                                                        CIP

Cover Painting *Blackwater River, West Virginia* by George Hetzel
West Virginia Historical Art Collection, WVU Libraries

Book design by Sara Pritchard
Printed in USA by BookMasters, Inc.

In memory of four from Pocahontas

Jack Williams

Ann Denison Fisher

Hud Crickard

Alice Rowan Waugh

and of their friend and contemporary

Louise McNeill Pease

Contents

West Virginia
A History

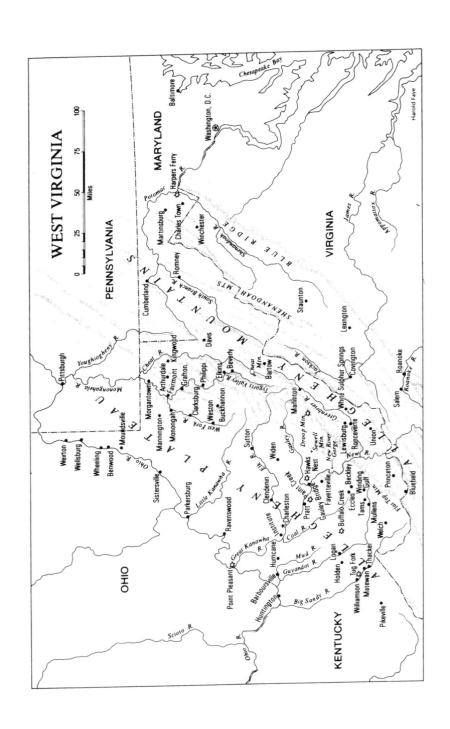

1

Point Pleasant

*T*HE battle of Point Pleasant, the climactic event in the history of colonial western Virginia,[1] was fought on October 10, 1774, a Monday, at the confluence of the Ohio and Great Kanawha rivers, a place whose "most agreeable prospect" gave the battlefield its English name. There an army of 1100 western Virginia militiamen commanded by Colonel Andrew Lewis faced a nearly equivalent number of Indian warriors representing several Ohio tribes united under the leadership of the Shawnee chieftain Keigh-tugh-qua, or the Cornstalk—"Support of His People." Both armies had expected to finish their work before breakfast. Instead, the fighting lasted all day, from first light until late in the afternoon when the Cornstalk, misconstruing a flanking movement ordered by Lewis for the arrival of reinforcements, withdrew his men from the field. Losses were heavy on both sides. Apart from their own losses and stories of

1. Before West Virginia became a state in 1863, the terms "western Virginia" and "West Virginia" were used interchangeably to describe the entire western half of Virginia, that is, all Virginia territory lying west of the Blue Ridge Mountains. The new state, however, took about two-thirds of this territory, which creates a problem of nomenclature when writing about present West Virginia in its prestatehood days. In this volume, "western Virginia" and "West Virginia" are used interchangeably, but only to refer to that territory now included in West Virginia. Traditional western Virginia (present West Virginia plus present west-central and southwestern Virginia) is called "transmontane Virginia."

3

valor, what stuck in the memories of white participants was the conduct of the Indians, whom few had ever met in pitched battle. Their bravery, wrote one observer, "exceeded every mans expectations. . . . Their Chiefs ran continually along the line exhorting the men to 'lye close' and 'shoot well,' 'fight and be strong.' " The Cornstalk's strong voice in particular rose above the "dismal Yells & Screams" of the Indians, some of which were rather more pointed than dismal: "they frequently Damn'd our men for white Sons of Bitches" and, referring to the fifes that colonial armies liked to tootle in less strenuous circumstances, asked tauntingly "why did not the[y] Whistle now. . . ." [2]

The battle itself amounted to a draw, but subsequent events turned it into a victory for Lewis's army. Menaced by the approach of another white army, this one from the north and commanded by John Murray, Earl Dunmore, the royal governor of Virginia, the Cornstalk retreated westward to protect the Shawnee towns of the Scioto Valley. Then, after the tribal council decided to discontinue the fighting, he turned to talk to Lord Dunmore. The governor agreed to keep Lewis and his men from falling upon the Indian towns (much to their disappointment). The resulting Treaty of Camp Charlotte formally ended what came to be known as Dunmore's War. Excepting only the destruction of the Indian towns, the treaty gave the whites everything they had fought for: the Indians surrendered all white prisoners, slaves, horses, and other captured property; they agreed not to hunt east of the Ohio and to trade with the Virginians on favorable terms; and they delivered hostages against the good performance of these obligations. The treaty ushered in nearly three years of peace on the Virginia frontier during the initial phase of the American Revolution.

As with most forms of bloodshed, a battle is easier to describe than to explain. Point Pleasant is no exception. The causes and effects of Dunmore's War have been debated for

2. William Christian to William Preston, October 15, 1774, William Preston to Patrick Henry, October 31, 1774, Orderly Book of William Fleming, October 10, 1774, in Reuben G. Thwaites and Louise P. Kellogg, eds., *Documentary History of Dunmore's War* (Madison: Wisconsin Historical Society, 1909), pp. 264, 292, 338, 342.

over two centuries. Perhaps the simplest way to cut to the heart of the matter is to say that the struggle was primarily a struggle for land—one word with two meanings. Land can mean property; it can also mean territory. At Point Pleasant men were fighting for both. The nature of the prize, and the ways in which the whites aspired to it, can tell us much about the impact of these Revolutionary years on the subsequent course of West Virginia's development.

Few persons better understood the complex significance of land in eighteenth-century western Virginia than the soldier-surveyor who camped at Point Pleasant just four years before the outbreak of Dunmore's War. George Washington traveled in 1770 from Mount Vernon to Pittsburgh, then down the Ohio and up the Kanawha to a spot fifteen miles above the future battlefield. He came in search of good land, both on his own account and on that of a syndicate of veteran officers, including Andrew Lewis, all of whom, like Washington, held warrants for free land by virtue of their service in the French and Indian War. Among his companions on this trip was Colonel William Crawford, fellow soldier, surveyor, land speculator, and Washington's principal western agent in land affairs. Four years later Crawford would play an important part in the march of the northern army in Dunmore's War, and in 1782 he would die a horrible death at the hands of the Indians in one of the climactic episodes of the Revolution on the frontier. But these events, along with Washington's more expansive destiny, lay in the future. In 1770 the Ohio could be traveled in peace. The party encountered rumors of murder, but it turned out only that an Indian trader had drowned while foolishly trying to ford the river at the wrong place. Washington met no Indians in force except for a hunting party led by one Kiashuta, who graciously entertained him with buffalo meat ''and Idle ceremony'' and also provided information about backcountry trails and types of land that the travelers could not spy out from their canoes.[3]

3. Entry of November 6, 1770, in John C. Fitzpatrick, ed., *The Diaries of George Washington,* 4 vols. (Boston: Houghton Mifflin, 1925), 1:430.

They floated down the river in autumn, taking advantage of those crisp, clear weeks between the completion of harvest and the first heavy snow. It was a good season for viewing the land. The display of fall leaves that Washington would have seen as he crossed the mountains was probably waning as his party moved southward, but the forest retained an abundance of clues for experienced land hunters. Beech trees, for example, their luminous, smooth gray branches crowned by wisps of pale-yellow leaves held late in the year, indicated soil that was rich, moist, but well drained. These trees were obstinate to the plow, however, by virtue of their wide, shallow root system "spreading over a large Surface of Ground and being hard to kill." White oaks, easily distinguished by their powerful broad branches holding withered cinnamon-colored leaves, warned against poor soil, as did the poplar or tulip trees, later the favorites of Appalachian lumbermen. Sycamores, their bent white arms prominently displayed against the drab November woods, defined the margins of streams and also offered in their capacious hollow trunks shelter for many a hunter huddling against the winter cold and rain. Washington found two giant specimens of this tree near Point Pleasant on November 3, noting in his meticulous way that one measured 45 feet in circumference "lacking two Inches"; the other was "31.4 round." [4]

It was not, however, such benevolent forest giants that the prospectors most eagerly looked for. Rather it was the trees of medium size—cherry, walnut, locust, sometimes hickory and "sugar trees" (maples)—that promised "the most luxuriant soil." Generally, as on the Kanawha lands that Washington picked out for himself, the "Bottom next the Water (in most places) is very rich; as you approach to the Hills you come (in many) to a thin white Oak Land, and poor; the Hills as far as we could judge were from half a Mile to a Mile from the River; poor and steep in the parts we see, with Pine growing on them." [5] Further conversation with Kiashuta on the return trip confirmed this estimate of the hills, which, as the Allegheny

4. Entry of November 4, 1770, in Fitzpatrick, *Diaries of Washington,* 1:429.
5. Entry of November 2, 1770, in Fitzpatrick, *Diaries of Washington,* 1:428.

Plateau, cover the western two-thirds of what is now West Virginia. The hills were generally thin-soiled and steep-sided, although here and there might be spotted exceptions that seemed to have good soils or a gently rounded ridge. But generally, in Washington's judgment, even the relatively low hills close to the big rivers were fit only to supply the bottomlands with timber for construction and fuel. The Indian told him, however, that close to the heads of the streams that drained the hills could be found tracts of rich, level land, a phenomenon that Washington later saw for himself in the headwaters of the Cheat and Youghiogheny rivers. These were the "glades" of the Alleghenies—wet, natural grasslands in the midst of the forest, the gift of erosion-resistant rock layers that slowed the spill of water out of the hills, and of countless generations of beaver that dammed the headwaters, then patiently moved downstream and started over each time as their ponds filled up with silt. Hunters, both red men and white, valued the glades for their abundance of game, especially bear and deer that came to feed at the margins of forest and meadow, but Washington was not much interested. Though he did pick up a piece of land that Crawford had found near the head of Chartiers Creek near Pittsburgh, such land could not be found in the quantity Washington wanted. Whenever he could get them, Washington wanted bottomlands. They were the kind that would sell. Consequently the lands he marked in the fall of 1770, and which Crawford surveyed in the ensuing summers, hugged the rivers closely, running over forty miles along the south bank of the Kanawha and for shorter distances along the Ohio, but rarely on either stream more than half a mile inland. The bordering hills were "generally so scraggy, steep, and rocky, that I could not survey it any further from the river than I have done," Crawford explained.[6]

The lay of the land presented serious problems to Washington and to others like him who hoped to find or improve their fortunes in western Virginia land. There was no trouble about what type of land to look for. They wanted it "high, dry, and level,"

6. Quoted in Roy B. Cook, *Washington's Western Lands* (Strasburg, Va.: Shenandoah Publishing Co., 1930), p. 43.

or, if not level, Washington wrote, "at least wavy, that is, in little risings, sufficient to lay it dry and fit for the plough." [7] There should be good timber and meadows, a place for a mill, and, ideally, access to a respectable road or a river without too much danger from floods. Western Virginia contained such land, but it was strung out in narrow ribbons along the larger watercourses, and it was even more narrow—if there was any at all—along the smaller rivers and creeks. Only in the Great Appalachian Valley just west of the Blue Ridge was the good land found in tracts large enough for land hunters to mark out their claims on the map without first inspecting the ground carefully. Elsewhere the slivers of desirable land would not fit into a neatly cornered boundary. As for "the Valley," as this fertile and beautiful basin came to be called, it presented problems of its own. For one thing, it was filling up by the 1750s; for another, its northern, or Shenandoah, end, containing the most attractive and convenient lands and the natural hinterland of Washington and other grandees who dwelt along the Potomac, fell into the domain of Thomas, Lord Fairfax, a resident English nobleman whose patrimony extended along the Potomac and its tributaries from tidewater to the top of the Alleghenies.

In many respects Fairfax, or more strictly speaking the ancestor who had originally secured his domain in the days of King Charles II, was the original of the bevy of land speculators and companies that sprang up on the Virginia frontier in the mid-eighteenth century. The idea was to get there first, as far as legal ownership of the land was concerned, and have the settlers come to you—either that or risk losing their cabins and fields through a defective title or nonpayment of rent. For Fairfax it worked. Starting with the German, Welsh, and Scotch-Irish immigrants who began the occupation of West Virginia's easternmost counties in 1726, most settlers paid Fairfax his due, both in the Shenandoah Valley and in the neighboring valleys along the upper Potomac that now comprise West Virginia's Eastern

7. "Memorandum for William Crawford," in John C. Fitzpatrick, ed., *The Writings of George Washington*, 39 vols. (Washington: U.S. Government Printing Office, 1931), 3:31.

Panhandle. Here settlements—and Fairfax's surveyors, among them the youthful Washington—began to appear in the 1740s.

Later corporate imitators of Fairfax were not quite so successful. These included the Ohio Company, organized by (among others) Washington's older brothers in 1748 to lay claim for Britain, Virginia, and themselves to that most desirable piece of transmontane real estate, the forks of the Ohio at modern Pittsburgh. The Greenbrier Company (1751), a project of Andrew Lewis and sundry of his relatives and friends, had designs on the southwestern frontier. The Loyal Land Company (1749) was a British venture associated with Dr. Thomas Walker, better known as the explorer of Cumberland Gap and the friend and neighbor of Thomas Jefferson. The Indiana Company (1768) was comprised of Pennsylvania traders who claimed land in northwestern Virginia. Not least in importance was the Grand Ohio or Walpole Company (1773), an Anglo-Pennsylvanian enterprise remembered in West Virginia lore as the promoter of "Vandalia," a scheme whereby the land jobbers hoped to escape the restraints imposed by Virginia and Pennsylvania governments by creating a separate jurisdiction, or "fourteenth colony," in the west. This last group had almost enough clout in London to bring off the project before the outbreak of the Revolution put an end to it. The other companies were heard from later, but with no more success. These corporate speculators came to grief over what were essentially matters of territory. The manifold contentions for control of the region between English and French, white and Indian, Americans and British, Virginians and Pennsylvanians, and state and federal authorities had all to be settled before the companies could have secured the legal rights to the land which alone would have made the grants profitable. The Ohio Company went ahead anyway, building facilities and selling land at strategic locations along the Potomac and Monongahela. It was the 1820s before the litigation that grew out of these transactions finally ceased.

The corporate land speculations made few people rich, but they played a large role in the initial English explorations of West Virginia and in the political and military history of the Allegheny frontier. In the end, however, it was individual speculators and settlers who provided the main contestants in the race to occupy the region. Very early in the frontier period many settlers had shown themselves unwilling to buy or lease land from large landholders, no matter how good their titles. The settlers pushed on instead to the nearest tract of attractive vacant land that they could acquire on their own either by direct purchase from the colony or, more commonly, through the process popularly known as "tomahawk rights" (so-called from the slashes made on the boundary trees) wherein they could acquire title to their land by virtue of occupying and improving it. The father of Andrew Lewis, for example, in company with a great number of fellow immigrants from Ireland in the 1730s, pushed up the Shenandoah past Lord Fairfax's boundary to the central Valley region drained by the James and New rivers. Twenty years later like-minded men were racing with the Lewises' Greenbrier Company surveyors to plant the first cabins in the Kanawha watershed. Similarly, squatters occupied out-of-the-way corners of Lord Fairfax's land in the upper Potomac region; when surveyors found them there, the squatters pushed over the divide into the Monongahela drainage. The men and women who extended the frontier in this fashion suffered many misfortunes during the French and Indian War and Pontiac's Rebellion, but the survivors tended to return when peace came in 1764. They could be equally stubborn in dealing with land speculators. Referring to an unusually large district of level land in the upper Monongahela watershed, Crawford wrote Washington in 1771 that "I do not much like running [surveying] any land in Tygart's Valley, as the people in general are very contentious there. . . ." [8]

There was no absolute distinction between speculator and settler, of course. Rather, these labels define a scale with many intermediate stops. Most settlers were speculators of a sort. Many speculators had been pioneers in the older frontier districts; Andrew Lewis and his relatives are cases in point. Perhaps the most appropriate distinction is between resident and

---

8. William Crawford to George Washington, August 2, 1771, in C. W. Butterfield, ed., *The Washington-Crawford Letters* (Cincinnati: Robert Clarke & Co., 1877), p. 21.

nonresident owners. The latter sought frontier land primarily as an investment. Whether the object of such investment was speculative in the strictest sense of the word is immaterial; most investors would have been delighted with bonanza profits, content with modest ones. Settlers, on the other hand, may be thought of as those who sought land primarily as a place to live and feed their families, although perhaps they expected also to gain from the land's eventual rise in price. One development that helped reinforce this distinction in a very practical way was the soldiers' bounty that granted land warrants to veterans of the earlier war. As issued originally by Governor Dinwiddie in 1754 and confirmed by the Royal Proclamation of 1763, the bounty distributed land on a British—and Virginian—model of society, giving the various ranks of officers from 2,000 to 5,000 acres of land; noncommissioned officers, 200 acres; privates, fifty. The purchase of warrants from fellow officers who preferred cash to free land enabled Washington to assemble a claim to over 30,000 acres under this bounty. The largest tract that he located in 1770 measured some 52,000 acres, or eighty square miles, and took in all of the Ohio river bottomlands from Point Pleasant northward around the "great bend" of the river to Letart Falls. This tract was subsequently patented to and divided by a group of nine officers who had helped to underwrite the cost of Washington's journey, among whom were some of the first settlers of Mason County. Any fifty-acre plots allotted under the bounty here would, therefore, have had to be taken from the "indifferent and very broken" ridges that Crawford so carefully excluded from the officers' tract. Thus whatever rough equality may have existed between these captains and their men in wartime or amidst the uncleared forest in the first days of planting new homes, this equality was hardly likely to have extended to their riper years, much less to the days of their progeny.

The unambitious settler was not without his advantages, however. There was a long delay between the proclamation of the soldiers' bounty and the drawing of those definitive territorial limits that would govern the location of the soldiers' land. Washington found the delay maddening. He correctly forecast that those provisions of the Proclamation of 1763 that prohibited white settlement west of the mountains would prove but "a temporary expedient," but there was still uncertainty about Virginia's border with Pennsylvania, together with the possibility that both jurisdictions might be displaced by Vandalia. The Pittsburgh district was filling up fast, he complained to Dunmore's predecessor, Lord Botetourt, in 1769, "and of course, every good, and fertile spot will be engrossed and occupied by others, whilst none but barren Hills, and rugged Mountains; will be left to those, who have toild, and bled for the Country." It hardly mattered, he added, that the settlers taking up the land had done so illegally, since removing them later would be "a Work of great difficulty; perhaps of equal cruelty, as most of these People are poor swarming with large Families, [and] have sought out these retreats on which perhaps their future prospects in like way wholely depend." [9] It took only one such squatter, set down in the midst of a fine stretch of bottomland, to ruin the commercial value of the tract. Settlers with more modest expectations could afford to do this, taking a chance on establishing tomahawk rights or enjoying use of the land until the sheriff finally ran them off, at which time better land might be opening farther west. Crawford began trying to drive off the squatters on Washington's Chartiers Creek land as early as 1773, but it was not until 1796 that Washington finally managed to evict them permanently. To prevent the same thing from happening to his lands on the Kanawha, he decided to have them settled himself, sending out an overseer and servants in March 1774 to clear and plant a few acres "nearest the middle." [10] When this party was turned back by Dunmore's War, he sent out another the following year, issuing instructions in close detail from his military quarters near Boston. Even landowners living on the frontier had trouble keeping track of such things. "As soon as a man's back is turned, another is on his land," Crawford complained in 1772. "The man that is strong and able

9. George Washington to Lord Botetourt, December 8, 1769, in Fitzpatrick, *Writings of Washington*, 2:530.
10. "Instructions for William Stephens," March 6, 1775, in Fitzpatrick, *Writings of Washington*, 3:269.

to make others afraid of him seems to have the best chance as times go now.'' [11]

Settlers also had the advantage of flexibility in locating their lands. Although the majority of ridges were ''hog backed,'' there were some hilltops suited to level or gently sloping fields. Many pioneers chose such locations; others favored upland glades. ''It seems very strange that any person should have settled there at that time when the whole country was almost vacant,'' wrote a son of William Haymond, who pioneered in the glades of Decker's Creek in 1771.[12] So it is strange to someone accustomed—as Washington was and as we are today—to judge the convenience of land in its relation to a transportation grid that generally follows large rivers. But the Indian trails followed the ridgetops, especially in the Allegheny Plateau. Consequently so did the pioneer roads. Travelers on these roads complained about the lack of water—as did the soldiers who traveled them in 1774 and during the Civil War—but this admitted inconvenience to man and horse greatly reduced the necessity for fords and bridges. Houses were not often built on top of a ridge owing to this same lack of water, but springs could usually be found not too far from the top. Thus a clearing made here close to the paths that linked the scattered individual holdings to each other and to the forts that provided shelter in time of Indian alarm might be convenient indeed for the man of modest ambition. Another sort of convenience attended those who settled in the glades. Crops grown here were not very productive until the wet lands were drained, but the natural meadows provided excellent pasture in addition to the fine hunting already noted. Comparing this with the bottomlands that Washington coveted—thickly forested and festooned with vines—a man who had to clear his own land might well prefer to rely on hunting and gathering for part of his harvest. Moreover, the initial settlement was not usually a permanent one. Haymond, for

11. William Crawford to George Washington, March 15, 1772, in Butterworth. *Washington-Crawford Letters,* p. 25.

12. William Haymond to Luther Haymond, February 18, 1842, Haymond Family Papers, West Virginia Collection, West Virginia University Library, Morgantown (hereafter cited as W VU).

example, later moved down from the glades to the Monongahela, eventually halting in Harrison County, where he became a surveyor and an influential man in his community.

The surveyors constituted the most important of the hybrid settler/speculator types to be found on the frontier. Indeed, they represent a type of middleman found at the heart of West Virginia's economy at every period of the state's history, providing services that linked the distribution of local resources with nonresident investors and public officials. Crawford, although he lived on land that eventually fell into Pennsylvania when the boundary was drawn, is a good example of the type. Born in eastern Virginia in 1722 and reared in an earlier frontier setting in Jefferson County, Crawford served as a scout in the French and Indian War and was promoted from the ranks to lieutenant, later to captain, thus qualifying like Washington for land warrants under the soldiers' bounty. When peace returned, he settled west of the mountains and became a surveyor for the Ohio Company, later a public surveyor, commissioned by both Virginia and Pennsylvania. This made him a man of considerable weight on the frontier and an ideal contact man for investors who needed advice and services in a distant and uncertain land market.

The deal that Washington offered Crawford in 1767 was representative of what became a familiar and mutually advantageous relationship. "Any person . . . who neglects the present opportunity of hunting out good lands, and in some measure marking and distinguishing them for his own, in order to keep others from settling them, will never regain it," Washington wrote. He proposed that Crawford search out desirable lands, while Washington took care of securing the titles and underwrote the cost of surveying and patenting. "You [Crawford] shall then have such a reasonable proportion of the whole as we may fix upon at our first meeting. . . ." [13] This was an arrangement that would be seen again and again in western Virginia. A similar deal probably existed between Andrew

13. George Washington to William Crawford, September 21, 1767, in Fitzpatrick, *Writings of Washington*, 2:469–470.

Lewis and John Stuart, who was one of the first settlers—and the first surveyor—in Greenbrier County, and a Lewis in-law to boot.

Surveyors swarmed over the mountains and down the Kanawha and Monongahela, south and west along the Ohio as far as modern Louisville in the years immediately preceding Dunmore's War. But settlers were not far behind them; some were already there. Thus it is impossible to say which group was more responsible for the war. Historians have usually blamed the "land grabbers." No fewer than fifty land prospectors appeared at Point Pleasant in the spring of 1774 in response to a call from the public surveyor of Fincastle County, which then embraced Kentucky and transmontane Virginia south of the Kanawha. Soon they were scattered down the Ohio as far west as the falls of the river at Louisville. Other parties inspected the bottoms along some of the lesser tributaries, including the Big Sandy and Little Kanawha.

The Shawnee, hearing in the clank of surveyors' chains the certain loss of their hunting grounds, determined to contest this advance. Although the Indians' first warnings were verbal, by the end of April both white and Indian blood had been spilled at three points—at least—on the river. The surveyors gradually banded together and made their way back through the mountains; meanwhile anxiety for their fate was a potent factor in recruiting Lewis's army on the southwestern frontier. In the northwest, Dunmore's deputy at Fort Pitt ordered Colonel Crawford out with 100 men to build Fort Fincastle (later Fort Henry) at the site of modern Wheeling, "where we shall wait the motions of the Indians, and shall act accordingly." [14]

Lord Dunmore, whose aggressive support of Virginian claims to the upper Ohio got him in trouble with authorities in both Philadelphia and London, shared the values of the speculators more than any of his predecessors and also expected to share in their rewards. Not surprisingly, he blamed the settlers for the war, describing them as "ungovernable" savages;

14. William Crawford to George Washington, May 8, 1774, in Butterworth, *Washington-Crawford Letters*, p. 49.

. . . impressed from their earliest infancy with Sentiments and habits, very different from those acquired by persons of a similar condition in England, they do not conceive that Government has any right to forbid their taking possession of a Vast tract of Country, either uninhabited, or which Serves only as a Shelter to a few Scattered Tribes of Indians. Nor can they be easily brought to entertain any belief of the permanent obligation of Treaties made with those people, whom they consider, as but little removed from the brute Creation.[15]

In support of his argument, Dunmore cited a particular atrocity already infamous on the frontier. It concerned the murder on April 30, 1774, at a place near the tip of modern West Virginia's Northern Panhandle, of ten Indians, including two women, all killed and scalped by whites. Several versions of the massacre circulated on the frontier, but they all emphasized the fact that the victims belonged to the household of a Mingo chieftain Tah-gah-jute, a baptized Indian who was known by his English name, Logan. Logan had always lived among the whites peacefully, supporting his family by killing deer and dressing and selling the skins. Now he took to the warpath, taking many scalps in four widely separated raids on the Virginia and Pennsylvania frontiers. Dunmore blamed a settler named Daniel Greathouse for the outrage. Logan blamed Michael Cresap, a Maryland soldier and land speculator who was in the habit of building cabins along the Ohio as a means of securing land. Cresap was indeed in the vicinity of the massacre as part of a surveying party, but the evidence suggested that he was almost certainly innocent of the charge. Logan's assertion points up the fact that from the Indian's standpoint it hardly mattered who menaced him. Speculator or settler, the result was the same.

The basic problem was again one of territory. Virginia authorities had purchased the release of Iroquois and Cherokee claims to the territory between the Ohio and the mountains in separate negotiations in 1768. But these powerful tribes, like

15. Lord Dunmore to the Earl of Dartmouth, December 24, 1774, in Thwaites and Kellogg, *Dunmore's War*, pp. 371, 376.

Washington, were nonresident claimants. It was the tribes resident in Ohio who hunted the region. "It seems that they say they have not been paid anything for their land—I mean the Shawanese [sic] and Delawares," Crawford explained to Washington at the beginning of the war.[16] But property as Crawford understood it was something quite different from what the Indian had in mind. When Christopher Gist, the Ohio Company's first surveyor, first contacted the Delawares for the company in 1752, he assured them that "You will have the same Privileges as the White People have, and to hunt You have Liberty every where so that You dont kill the White Peoples Cattle & Hogs." [17] The fact was, however, that none of the whites had any intention of sharing their property. The only sort of property they recognized was individual and exclusive, whether it was in use or not. Just as Washington wanted no squatters making use of his vacant land, the settlers wanted no Indians hunting in the woods around their farms. In the face of Indian warfare, settlers and speculators and all intermediate varieties closed ranks. Although the very poorest frontiersmen, the ones who did not plant but depended upon game to support their families, stayed home to pursue the fall hunt, the captains of Lewis's and Dunmore's armies had little difficulty in recruiting their troops and the supplies needed to sustain their long marches toward the Ohio. In the face of such singlemindedness, the Ohio tribesmen had the choice of fighting or surrendering their land peacefully, perhaps in exchange for the trifling payments that usually accompanied such transactions. They chose to fight. They fought well at Point Pleasant but, as we have seen, they lost the war.

The leaders of eighteenth-century Virginia expected an important city to grow up at Point Pleasant, perhaps the capital of Vandalia or some other jurisdiction in the west. Washington alluded to this hope in advertising his Kanawha lands in 1773.

16. William Crawford to George Washington, May 8, 1774, in Butterworth, *Washington-Crawford Letters*, p. 49.
17. "Christopher Gist's Journals," in Elizabeth Cometti and Festus P. Summers, eds., *The Thirty-Fifth State: A Documentary History of West Virginia* (Morgantown: West Virginia University Library, 1966), p. 31.

Indeed, tradition has it that he coveted the Point himself and only with reluctance yielded to the claims of Andrew Lewis, who took it as his share of Crawford's officers' survey and then gave it to the heirs of his brother, who was killed in the battle. At the time this seemed a valuable legacy indeed, because for a brief moment in history it seemed likely that some of the most traveled pathways of America's "new and rising Empire" would converge at this spot. But the moment passed, and no city grew up here—only a quiet, vaguely Southern courthouse and river town. To understand why things turned out this way requires a brief discussion of geography.

Imagine a map of eastern North America, showing its natural features, overlaid by a grid showing major transportation corridors as they existed, say, in 1776. Running diagonally along this grid in a roughly northeast/southwest direction were four longitudinal corridors. The first and most important ran along the Atlantic coast, connecting the colonial seaports via spurs in the tidal rivers; the second, along the fall line of those rivers,

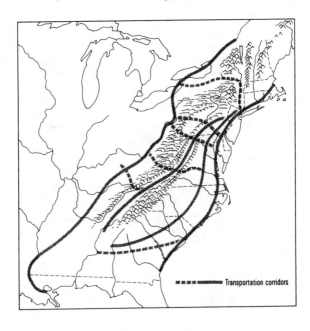

━ ━ ━ ━━━━ Transportation corridors

connecting towns like Augusta and Richmond with places like
Trenton and Paterson; the third, along the Great Appalachian
Valley from Pennsylvania to Alabama. At the northern end
these three corridors converged near the city of New York and
they nearly converged near Philadelphia and Baltimore, which
tells us something about the future importance of those cities as
compared with places in eastern Virginia where the corridors
are widely separated. The fourth longitudinal corridor ran west
of the Appalachian Mountains, along a line that today would
connect Montreal with New Orleans, via the St. Lawrence,
Lakes Ontario and Erie, the Ohio river between Pittsburgh and
Louisville, then the overland pathway through Nashville that
would later be known as the Natchez Trace.

Now sketch in the lateral bisecting lines of the grid. They
should run east and west at those points most convenient for
passing the obstacles—rapids and mountain ranges—that im-
pede communication by water between the interior and the
coast. Looked at strictly from the standpoint of the absence of
such barriers, the great interior rivers—Mississippi and St.
Lawrence—provide the smoothest thoroughfares into the continent's heart. These routes take travelers far from the Atlantic,
however. If distance were a factor, plus convenience to the
other longitudinal corridors, the gateway provided by the Hudson estuary and the Mohawk Valley would be clearly superior.
The route around the southern end of the mountains, passing
from Charleston, South Carolina, through Georgia to Alabama,
looks somewhat less convenient but, like the Hudson-Mohawk
route, it avoided climbing the Appalachians. From this standpoint, the least convenient east-west corridors were those that
ran through Pennsylvania, Virginia, and Maryland, connecting
the upper Ohio with the waters of Chesapeake Bay. None of the
tidal rivers of Chesapeake—Susquehanna, Potomac, and
James—breach the mountains as far as the Hudson. Their headwaters are swift-running mountain streams, separated from the
Ohio drainage by the parallel ridges of the Alleghenies and the
rugged gorges cut by the western rivers through the upper Allegheny Plateau. Judging strictly by natural assets, the Chesapeake region's backcountry might be expected to have been
Anglo-America's last eighteenth-century frontier.

Instead, this was where the Anglo-Americans first breached the Appalachians. Why? The answer begins to emerge if the map is overlaid with the shifting political boundaries of the last half of the century. What made Point Pleasant worth fighting for in the territorial sense of the matter and what also seemed to promise the spot an expansive future was this: The most attractive routes through the mountains were blocked in the eighteenth century. They were blocked by foreign powers, variously France, Britain, and Spain, and by the most powerful Indian nations, the Iroquois in the north, Cherokees, Creeks, and Choctaws in the south. It was man and not nature that made the Chesapeake-Ohio corridors the spearhead of advance into the interior. The Anglo-American frontier surged through the mountains here in spite of great natural obstacles precisely because of the region's border location. It was territory remote from the centers of foreign power on the St. Lawrence and Mississippi, claimed but not contested by the most powerful Indian tribes, unoccupied by any significant groups of Indians, and used for hunting chiefly by the Shawnees and smaller, fragmented tribes who had already been pushed out of their original hunting grounds in the east.

Thus the Virginian and Pennsylvanian breakthrough along the upper Ohio amounted to a wedge driven across the mountains into remote hinterlands of powerful enemies. The defeat of the French at Fort Duquesne in 1758 and of the Indians at Point Pleasant in 1774 secured the wedge at the time of greatest peril. Subsequent military and diplomatic victories expanded and consolidated it. The British ceded their claims to the eastern half of the Mississippi Valley in 1783; the French sold the western half twenty years later. Meanwhile Wayne defeated the Ohio tribes at Fallen Timbers in 1794; Jackson hammered the Creeks and Choctaws; Harrison won his victory at Tippecanoe. New York, North Carolina, and Georgia reduced what was left of the once-powerful eastern Indian nations and took the best part of their lands. The British finally surrendered the posts at Oswego, Niagra, and Detroit; soon afterwards Perry drove them from the Lakes as Jackson did from New Orleans. After two decades of harassment and pressure, Spain withdrew from the Floridas in

1819. By this time New York was hard at work digging its Erie Canal.

The point is this: The changes that followed the Revolution opened up more inviting pathways of empire than the rivers that flowed past Point Pleasant; the Revolution also made available millions of acres of land more attractive than the uplands drained by these rivers. It compounds the irony to realize that it was, in some degree, the battle fought here that made these changes possible. "Lord Dunmore's War," wrote Theodore Roosevelt in *The Winning of the West,* "was the opening act of the drama whereof the closing scene was played at Yorktown." Cornstalk's defeat gave the colonies a quiet frontier during the critical early phase of the Revolution. This same peace made possible the occupation of Kentucky and Tennessee and paved the way for the conquest of the Illinois country by George Rogers Clark. Point Pleasant, Roosevelt argued, "was the first in the chain of causes that gave us for our western frontier in 1783 the Mississippi and not the Alleghenies." [18] If one accepts this viewpoint, however, one must also concede that it was exactly this outcome that, more than anything else, cut away the geopolitical underpinnings of the Point's strategic location and left it to rely upon its unexceptional natural assets. Although the Ohio remained an important highway, gradually the paths of the Lakes and the Gulf and the Mississippi eclipsed it. By 1820 Point Pleasant and western Virginia in general lay far to the east of the cutting edge of American empire. One of the lessons of the place, therefore, is this: While western Virginia made important contributions to the national struggle for independence, ultimately the American Revolution had a far greater impact upon western Virginia than western Virginia had upon it.

In many respects what was true of western Virginia's position within the national transportation grid was also true of its position within the Chesapeake-Ohio sectors of that grid. By the time of the Revolution, four east-west corridors had been marked out through the mountains of this region, but only one

18. Theodore Roosevelt, *The Winning of the West,* 6 vols. (New York: G. P. Putnam's Sons, 1889), vol. 1, pt. 2, p. 34.

of these lay entirely within Virginia, and it was the most difficult route. This was the James-Kanawha corridor, the western terminus of which was Point Pleasant. The first English explorers who penetrated the mountains traveled over this route, moving west via the line of the Appomattox and Roanoke rivers through the Blue Ridge to New River, which they followed to the point where it crosses the present border of West Virginia before they turned back. "It was a pleasing tho' dreadful sight," Robert Fallam wrote in his journal in 1671, "to see mountains and Hills as if piled one upon another." [19] Later travelers tended to favor a more northerly circuit of this corridor, one that linked the two watersheds via the Jackson and Greenbrier, headwater streams whose tributaries rose on opposite sides of Allegheny Mountain near modern White Sulphur Springs. This pathway had pleasing and dreadful aspects of its own, although it was travelers at leisure who usually found it pleasant, while those on business errands were more likely to find it dreadful. The problem was not the dividing ridge of the Alleghenies, as it was at the Potomac headwaters; "the Allegheny . . . is but a small mountain here," noted John D. Sutton of Alexandria as he traveled west on land business in 1798. But on the other side of the Greenbrier Valley he found the muscular hulks of Sewell and Gauley mountains, the latter "the worst & steepest mountain I ever crossed." [20] Then the trail descended a stream called Rich Creek, which Sutton found he had to cross fifty-eight times in seven miles before reaching Gauley River a few miles above the point where it joins New River to form the Great Kanawha. Civil War soldiers and modern truck drivers echoed the complaints of the travelers on the James-Kanawha road, but the only alternative to crossing these mountains was the spectacular gorge of New River, a thousand-foot-deep trench winding through the mountains at the base of steep cliffs. The Indian Kiashuta told Washington of the impassability of this canyon in 1770, an opinion the general confirmed in 1784 by consulting white travelers who frequented the area. A group of Virginia officials led by Chief Justice John Marshall

---

19. "Journal of Robert Fallam," in Cometti and Summers, *The Thirty-Fifth State*, p. 8.
    20. Entries of November 1, 8, 1798, Diary of John D. Sutton, WVU.

navigated the canyon in 1812, searching for a canal route. They found it "awful and discouraging." [21] Washington's consultants advised him to look elsewhere for Virginia's highway to the west.

Of the three remaining routes, one lay entirely within Pennsylvania. This was the Forbes Road, constructed in 1758 in the course of the campaign against the French at Fort Duquesne; it connected Pittsburgh to a western branch of the Susquehanna, "an unfriendly water, much impeded . . . with rocks and rapids" in Washington's view, but one that nevertheless afforded convenient access to the west for both Baltimore and Philadelphia. [22] Far to the south, the Wilderness Road blazed by Daniel Boone led from the Valley through Cumberland Gap to Kentucky. The third (and in pioneer days the most important) route followed Braddock's Road connecting the Potomac and Monongahela watersheds. The settlement of the Virginia-Pennsylvania boundary dispute in 1779 gave Pittsburgh, the obvious and most desirable western terminus for this route, to Pennsylvania, along with control of the Monongahela and its two easternmost tributaries. These rivers thus became "subject to a power whose interest is opposed to the extension of their navigation, as it would be the inevitable means of withdrawing from Philadelphia all the trade of that part of its western territory." [23] Washington's judgment proved entirely correct. Pennsylvania authorities were never enthusiastic about transportation improvement that might draw trade down the Potomac, while the political separation of the northwestern Virginia hinterland from its natural metropolis at Pittsburgh proved to be a step toward the creation of West Virginia's tributary economy.

Almost as soon as Washington laid down command of the Continental army in 1783, he turned his attention to western matters, attempting to sort out the confused state of his land business and also promoting transportation development along the Potomac-Monongahela route. In September of the following

21. "Report of the Commissioners," in Cometti and Summers, *The Thirty-Fifth State*, p. 194.

22. George Washington to Benjamin Harrison, October 10, 1784, in Fitzpatrick, *Writings of Washington*, 27:473.

23. Entry of October 4, 1784, in Fitzpatrick, *Diaries of Washington*, 2:320.

year he crossed the mountains in person to look after both projects. But though he made careful efforts to do so, he could find
no practical all-Virginia alternatives to Braddock's Road. He
nevertheless returned convinced that the Potomac afforded
Virginia its best opportunity for attracting the trade of the west.
Frankly confessing his "interested" view of the matter as a
landholder at both ends of the corridor, he wrote a series of letters to Maryland and Virginia leaders, urging them to take action to develop the route and to do so soon, "for I *Know* the
Yorkers will delay no time to remove every obstacle in the way
of the other communication, so soon as the [British] Posts at
Oswego and Niagara are surrendered. . . ." [24] To Virginia he
proposed the extension of navigation along both of its rivers,
Potomac and James, along with explorations of possible connections between the latter stream and the Kanawha. Privately,
however, he confessed to Governor Benjamin Harrison a pessimis-
tic view of the results. The projects might fail for several reasons,
he wrote shortly after his return to Mount Vernon:

> The first and principal one is, the *unfortunate Jealousy,* which
> ever has and it is to be feared ever will prevail, lest one part of the
> State should obtain an advantage over the other part (as if the
> benefits of trade were not diffusive and beneficial to all); then
> follow a train of difficulties viz: that our people are already heavily
> taxed; that the advantages of this trade are remote [,] that the most
> *direct* rout [*sic*] for it is thro' *other* States, over whom we have no
> controul; that the routs over which we have controul are as distant
> as either of those which lead to Philadelphia, Albany or Montreal;
> That a sufficient spirit of commerce does not pervade the citizens of
> this commonwealth; that we are in fact doing for others, what they
> ought to do for themselves.[25]

It would be difficult to imagine a more complete catalogue of
the arguments used against Virginia's transportation develop-

24. George Washington to Thomas Jefferson, March 29, 1784, in Fitzpatrick, *Writing of Washington,* 27:373.
25. George Washington to Benjamin Harrison, October 10, 1784, in Fitzpatrick, *Writings of Washington,* 27:473-474.

ment during the half century following independence. The General Assembly, meeting in 1785, adopted Washington's plan as a more or less official blueprint for later development, created joint-stock companies to improve both the Potomac and the James, and made the general a present of shares in each one. But this brave start led to meager results, as Washington foresaw. Virginia's failure to develop adequate east-west transportation would play a momentous role in western Virginia's future.

It is important, finally, to notice some things that the Revolution did not do as far as western Virginia's future was concerned. For one thing, it did not end the manifold complications that grew out of speculation in wilderness land. Rather these complications were compounded in the guise of reform while the war was in progress. In 1779 the General Assembly quashed the lavish claims of corporate land speculators, although litigation deriving from the actions of some companies continued for years thereafter. The same legislation regularized procedures by which land could be obtained by rights of pre-emption and settlement. However the assembly also created a new soldiers' bounty, this one for Revolutionary veterans. Like the colonial bounties, this one rewarded officers with grants in the thousands of acres while privates got a couple of hundred; and again the soldiers' warrants passed quickly into the hands of speculators who, in the two decades following the establishment of peace in 1783, blanketed Kentucky and western Virginia with thousands of overlapping claims. In contrast to the careful selections of good agricultural lands that Washington, Crawford, and many earlier beneficiaries had made, the postwar speculators drew their boundaries in great polygons without much regard for, or knowledge of, the natural features of the land. Being well aware that a large part of their holdings would consist of ''waste''— untillable hillsides and ravines—and encouraged by a large supply of warrants, they made their grants as large as they could with correspondingly vague descriptions of boundaries. Thus when John D. Sutton came out in 1798 to inspect 7,000 acres in central West Virginia that his father had bought from a land jobber a few years earlier, he found that the tract lay in such remote and difficult country that it could not be reached by canoe. Accordingly, he traveled on horseback over the ridges between the Gauley and Elk river watersheds to the vicinity of the town that bears his name today. When he decided to continue northward and return to Alexandria via the Potomac, he found it was easier to scramble over the ridges on foot than on horseback. The land itself was disappointing. Except for a few "low ridges & glades," he found the uplands along the Elk "of little consequence." [26] Here and there were patches of bottomland along the river and larger creeks, none of them amounting to more than a few acres. Moreover, Sutton was unable to find the lines of any of the surveys that the speculators had run some years before. Despite these discouragements, he eventually returned in 1810 and settled the land himself.

Far more common were absentee owners who owned thousands of acres, even millions in a few cases, patented in their own right or perhaps with a minority share of ownership going to western residents who acted for these owners in the capacities in which Crawford had served Washington. Eastern politicians of the Jeffersonian persuasion who gained ascendance in Virginia during the 1790s and in the nation in 1800 (Albert Gallatin, DeWitt Clinton, John Beckley, Wilson Cary Nicholas, to name a few) claimed the most extravagant parcels of western land during this period, parcels that ranged in extent from 100,000 acres to 1,100,000. Prominent merchants in Baltimore, Philadelphia, and Richmond likewise secured large tracts. But as Otis K. Rice documents in *The Allegheny Frontier,* western merchants and public officials also benefited from the giveaway. Merchants operating at courthouse and crossroads settlements newly established in western Virginia bartered their goods for forest products (chiefly pelts and ginseng) harvested by backwoods customers, then shipped the products east and sometimes exchanged the proceeds for land warrants.

Local politicians were even more deeply involved. George Jackson, a lawyer and Jeffersonian leader of Clarksburg, led the

26. Entries of November 20–22, 1798, Diary of John D. Sutton, WVU.

fight in Virginia against postwar recognition of the Indiana and Vandalia corporate land claims; at the same time he accumulated some 60,000 acres in his Monongahela Valley constituency. His brother Edward, a surveyor and also a legislator, acquired 73,000 acres on his own and 52,000 in partnership with nonresident investors. Later generations of Jacksons as well as other dynasties enjoyed fortunes that were founded in the colonial or post-Revolutionary alienation of wilderness land.

One link between land speculation and politics was provided by the processes of locating, surveying, and patenting land, together with the massive volume of litigation that eventually grew out of uncertain titles and conflicting claims. Such matters all required local services in which local leaders like the Jackson brothers soon learned to specialize. Another link between land and politics concerned taxation. Since most of the postwar grants were like Sutton's land—hilly and mountainous country unattractive to farmers as long as better land farther west was easily available—and since settlement was further discouraged by the confusion in land titles, speculation in western Virginia land usually turned into long-term investment, whether the investors liked it or not. In these circumstances few owners were eager to pay taxes on their holdings. Consequently most holdings soon became subject to distraint and forfeiture procedures by which the land might be reclaimed by the state and sold for non-payment of taxes. Such procedures were well established in law, but they could be implemented or stayed, depending upon political arrangements and moods of the moment. Taxation and forfeiture thus became another staple of politics in the west and at Richmond. Virginia's failure to adopt a consistent policy for the taxation, or nontaxation, of wilderness land compounded an already confusing land-title situation and helped to make western Virginia a paradise for land lawyers.

Another thing that the Revolution failed to change was the Virginia constitution. Formal authority as in colonial times remained centered in the governor. He appointed sheriffs, prosecutors, judges at every level, and also the initial membership of each new county's governing body, the county court. The principal difference after 1776 was that the governor ceased to be the independent executive he had been in colonial times and became the creature of the General Assembly, which elected a new governor triennially and further circumscribed his power by means of a similarly chosen council. Apart from representatives in the lower house of Congress after 1789, members of the assembly were the only officials chosen by election in Virginia until 1851. Thus while power remained highly centralized in the formal sense, as a practical matter it was fragmented among oligarchies composed of local notables who dominated the county courts. Once chosen from among "the most discreet and honest inhabitants" of a new county, these magistrates (or justices of the peace, or squires, as they were often called, following the traditional English usage) formed a close corporation, such as had governed many colonial cities. This meant that surviving members chose the successor when one of their number died or retired. They also chose such minor local officials as clerks and constables; they nominated the man, usually one of themselves or a relative, whom the governor appointed as sheriff; the sheriff determined the time, place, and manner of holding elections, which chose the legislators, who chose the governor, who appointed the sheriff, and so on back to the local wellsprings of power. The system was further buttressed by the fact that suffrage was restricted to property owners, although the amount of property required was minimal. Moreover, there were usually few precincts, and voting was oral—viva voce. Traditionally the voter stepped up to a table set up by the sheriff in front of the courthouse, called out his name and his vote in a clear voice (presumably the timid did not bother to vote), then accepted the congratulations of the candidate or his representative, who was usually standing nearby ready to dispense a large amount of liquor. There was room for competition in this system, but it was obviously competition within severely circumscribed limits, and the fact that legislative apportionment favored the tidewater counties made it even more circumscribed from a western point of view. "An *elective despotism*," Thomas Jefferson complained, "was not the government we fought for." [27] Fought for or not, it was the government that Virginia retained notwithstanding the brilliant political assemblages that came together at Richmond during the Revolutionary years. The assembly repeatedly rejected Jefferson's proposals to democratize the system, until at length Jefferson forebore his assaults on the local oligarchies and concentrated on such things as education and disestablishmentarianism. Whether they liked the constitution or not, ambitious westerners were forced to adapt themselves to it and, as practical men are wont, they soon became adept in making it work for themselves as well as for tidewater planters. Along with land speculation, the oligarchical nature of Virginia institutions was a major formative influence in the political economy that emerged in western Virginia as the frontier era passed.

27. Thomas Jefferson, *Notes on the State of Virginia,* ed. by William Peden (Chapel Hill: University of North Carolina Press for the Institute of Early American History and Culture, 1955), p. 120.

2

Harpers Ferry

$\mathcal{E}$IGHTY-FIVE years and six days after the Battle of Point Pleasant, another West Virginia place on a point between rivers became part of American history. Like Point Pleasant, Harpers Ferry abounds with agreeable prospects, but there the resemblance ends. Where Point Pleasant spreads across a level bench beside broad and placid streams, Harpers Ferry climbs a hillside that echoes the sound of rushing water. Both the Potomac and the Shenandoah fall noisily across rapids here, one pounding through boulders and snags, the other rippling down across its bed in an elegant, trellised pattern that someone has named the Staircase. Together the turbulent streams have carved a beautiful forked gorge whose stem points south and east through the Blue Ridge to the plains of eastern Virginia and Maryland.

No one has described the site better than Thomas Jefferson. It was "one of the most stupendous scenes in nature," he wrote.

> You stand on a very high point of land. On your right comes up the Shenandoah, having ranged along the foot of the mountain an hundred miles to seek a vent. On your left approaches the Patowmac, in quest of a passage also. In the moment of their junction they rush together against the mountain, rend it asunder, and pass off to the sea.[1]

1. Jefferson, *Notes on Virginia,* p. 19.

The distant glimpse of blue horizon through the cleft in the ridge offered the perfect finishing touch, Jefferson added. Altogether, he found the scene worth a voyage across the Atlantic.

The town of Harpers Ferry grew up in the throat of the gorge, at the foot of the hill on which Jefferson stood. It developed as a transportation center, linking the east-west corridor that ran along the Potomac with the fertile intermontane valley that runs north and south along the west flank of the Blue Ridge. At first there was only the ferry, operated by Robert Harper, who secured title to his land from Lord Fairfax in 1747 and a ferry charter from the colony in 1761. Then came roads and flatboats and, in 1833, the Chesapeake & Ohio Canal, one of George Washington's pet projects, which had inched its way upriver from Georgetown along the Potomac's Maryland shore. One year later the Baltimore & Ohio Railroad reached the town, to be joined in 1836 by the Winchester & Potomac Railroad, which linked the rivers with the principal crossroads of the Shenandoah Valley farm country. Meanwhile flumes were dug along the rapids of each river, harnessing water power to drive factories that rose on the narrow margin of flat land at the base of the hill. Foremost among these was another Washington project, a United States arsenal and armory established in 1795, and Hall's rifle works, a privately owned armory that pioneered in the manufacture of breech-loading rifles. There were also cotton mills, flour mills, sawmills, and a carriage factory. Harpers Ferry's convenient location and ample supplies of energy made it a thriving town in the mid-nineteenth century, second only to Wheeling among the industrial and transportation centers of western Virginia. In short, it was everything Point Pleasant had failed to become in the decades following independence and the passing of the frontier.

In every age the place was celebrated for its beauty. Tradition has it that the scenery was what detained Robert Harper, a Philadelphian who had come to the Valley with no intention of settling. The subsequent century of human intervention in the landscape did not seem to spoil it. Nathaniel Hawthorne compared the picturesque spill of buildings and spires down the hillside to the cities of Tuscany. "But a beautiful landscape is a luxury,"

Hawthorne added when he viewed the town as a ruin in 1862.[2] Harpers Ferry's most celebrated visitors did not come to admire the scenery. John Brown and the Civil War soldiers who marched through the town in Brown's footsteps came with their eyes set against the charms of the landscape and their hearts steeled to work of destruction. By the time they had finished with Harpers Ferry, the landscape remained but the century's accumulation of man-made works was a rubble of charred brick and orphaned piers.

Brown carried his war against slavery into Virginia on the moonless Sunday night of October 16, 1859. Leading eighteen men and a wagon full of guns, pikes, and faggots, he crossed into Harpers Ferry from Maryland. The clatter of his little army on the planks of the Potomac bridge was apparently lost in the tumult of the rapids, for no one stepped out of the night to challenge his conquest until it was nearly complete. Spreading across the lower streets of the town, the raiders seized the Shenandoah bridge, Hall's rifle works, and the federal arsenal, together with a number of prisoners, whom they shut up in a fire-engine house in the arsenal yard. Then they barricaded the B & O bridge across the Potomac and cut the telegraph wires. In less than two hours Brown had captured one of Virginia's most strategic crossroads and a major storehouse of U.S. government arms. Only then did things begin to go wrong.

First, Brown and his men stopped an express train from Wheeling, then foolishly allowed it to pass through their barricade into Maryland, where the trainmen spread the alarm, destroying the surprise that had made initial success possible. Within hours militiamen assembled in all of the surrounding counties, and U.S. Marines were en route from Washington, commanded, as fate would have it, by two Virginia-born cavalrymen, Colonel Robert E. Lee and Lieutenant J. E. B. Stuart. Another twist of fate occurred when Brown's men claimed their first victim. He was a free black man named Heyward Shepherd or Shepherd Heyward—he was one of sev-

---

2. "Harpers Ferry in Wartime, 1862," in Cometti and Summers, *The Thirty-Fifth State,* p. 413.

eral participants, black and white, who bore those curious reversible names so beloved of Virginia gentility, and no one was sure which way his name went. All we know is that he worked at the railroad station, where he wandered unsuspectingly across the raiders' path and was shot as he hastily sought to retreat. Another victim Fontaine Beckham, the mayor of the town, was killed on the afternoon of October 17. Five slaves belonging to the mayor were freed by his will; these turned out to be the only slaves set free by the raid.

Meanwhile, piecemeal skirmishing killed some of the raiders. Dangerfield Newby, a black man who had joined up with Brown in hopes of freeing his wife, still held a slave in Virginia, died trying to escape across the Shenandoah, while townsmen, enraged by the death of Mayor Beckham, shot William Thompson, a white raider who had fallen into their hands. Two of Brown's own sons lay wounded and moaning at his feet in the gloom of the engine house, where the surviving raiders with their prisoners retreated as their plans went awry. Yet still the survivors held out through a long, rainy Monday. Thanks to two saloons that did a thriving business throughout the affair, the militiamen, railroad workers, and factory hands who crowded into the town got too drunk to be purposeful. Thus it was left to Lee and his soldiers to put an end to the bloodshed, which they did in the first light of Tuesday morning, some thirty-six hours after the raiders entered the town. Young Stuart delivered a note to the door of the engine house, demanding surrender. When Brown refused the terms, Stuart leapt dramatically aside, flattened against the wall, and signaled a charge that quickly overran the defenders. One marine was killed in the final assault, bringing to sixteen the total number of dead.

John Brown was clubbed unconscious in the final assault on his "fort." When he woke up, he found himself surrounded by angry, excited, curious men. Why had he done this? they asked. Who had helped him? Was he a madman or a fool? The questions continued for weeks while Brown, forming his answers with assurance and dignity, talked with reporters, with his captors at Harpers Ferry, with his judges at Charles Town, where in the Jefferson County courthouse he and six of his followers were tried for murder and treason against the Commonwealth of Virginia. The trial itself was a speedy observance of what one prosecutor called "the judicial decencies." At its conclusion, Brown delivered one of the great courtroom orations in American history. If he had acted as he did in behalf of the rich, the powerful, the intelligent, or the wellborn, then "it would have been all right, and every man in this Court would have deemed it an act worthy of reward rather than punishment." Instead he had acted in behalf of God's "despised poor" and he had no apology to make.

> Now, if it is deemed necessary that I should forfeit my life for the furtherance of the ends of justice, and mingle my blood further with the blood of my children and with the blood of millions in this slave country whose rights are disregarded by wicked, cruel, and unjust enactments, I say let it be done.[3]

John Brown's eloquence flowed out of the beautiful valley where he was hanged to an unseen but eager audience on both sides of the Potomac, inspiring northerners, horrifying southerners, fascinating them all. And as his words renewed the battle that his rifles and pikes and bad strategy had lost at Harpers Ferry, he seemed to relax from the stern demands of his mission and to notice at last what most visitors to this valley usually saw right away. "This *is* a beautiful country," he remarked as he was led to the gallows on a mild day in December. "I never had the pleasure of seeing it before." [4]

Most histories of West Virginia treat the Harpers Ferry raid as they might treat the fall of a meteorite: The event requires notice but it seems to stand apart from the state's main lines of development. This is because Harpers Ferry's relationship to West Virginia's history has several dimensions. John Brown's raid contributed greatly to the coming of civil war to the United States, and without that war the state of West Virginia would probably never have been created. Moreover, the local reaction

3. Quoted in Stephen B. Oates, *To Purge This Land With Blood: A Biography of John Brown* (New York: Harper & Row, 1970), p. 327.
4. Quoted in Oates, *To Purge This Land with Blood,* p. 351.

to the raid tended to drive Virginians together, not apart, and so made West Virginia's separation all the more painful when it finally came about. The town of Harpers Ferry—an industrial town set in an agricultural valley—was itself a crossroads between a West Virginian future and a Virginian past. Finally, there is no more important symbol for black people in West Virginia than this town and the men and events that made it famous. For all of these reasons, Harpers Ferry is a good place to begin an exploration of West Virginia history between the Revolution and the Civil War.

A long-established West Virginia tradition holds that western Virginia had produced by 1861 a society so radically different from eastern Virginia that a division of the state was inevitable. According to this tradition, the Civil War was not the cause of West Virginia statehood; it was only the catalyst. Separation from Virginia would have happened sometime, somehow, in any event. The argument is supported by the persistence of sectional conflict between east and west through most of the antebellum period, conflict that was punctuated by frequent threats of "dismemberment"—the West Virginia term for what Virginians usually call a "partition." Newspapers kept readers across the country well informed on the conflict; the distinguished debates at the constitutional conventions of 1829–1830 and 1850–1851 were especially well broadcast. Historians on both sides of the present state border have since painstakingly documented Virginia sectionalism. Indeed Charles Henry Ambler's *Sectionalism in Virginia from 1776 to 1861* (1910) became something of a minor classic in the nation's historical literature, since Ambler found in Virginia an unusually complete justification of Turnerian ideas about the influence of geography upon society. Western Virginia was hilly; eastern Virginia was flat; the rivers in each section flowed in opposite directions. From these basic differences, other more complex ones grew until bold men, obeying the dictates of nature, split the Old Dominion asunder during the ultimate sectional crisis of 1861–1863.

Documents captured with John Brown at Harpers Ferry make it clear that he was aware of differences between eastern and western Virginia and that he hoped to exploit Virginia sectionalism in pursuing his abolition crusade. He expected nothing less than to make transmontane Virginia the base for a new Southern state government, an Appalachian commonwealth based upon free labor, a project that Brown expected would win support from the local white population as well as from escaped slaves. Like so many of Brown's hopes, this expectation proved false, but the notion was not necessarily a foolish one. After all, a free Appalachian commonwealth did emerge in the mountains of western Virginia less than four years after Brown's death. Was he simply the wrong catalyst? Or did the all-but-unanimous white hostility evoked in western Virginia by the raid mean that the underlying unity of Virginia was stronger than the rhetoric of sectionalism had led Brown to believe?

There is no simple answer to these questions. Like most arguments that see the hand of destiny behind a given course of events, the assertion that West Virginia's separation from Virginia was inevitable would be difficult to disprove, but it is not a very useful theory. Most events seem inevitable after the fact. If we place the conflict between eastern and western Virginia in comparative perspective, West Virginia's creation does not seem inevitable at all. Sectionalism was the stuff of state and local politics in nineteenth-century America; it still is, in many places. The conflict in Virginia was no worse than the conflict between eastern and western Tennessee or upstate and downstate Illinois or northern and southern California. What distinguishes Virginia from these states is that the Civil War threw a military line across the state. The line remained relatively stationary for more than two years, cordoning off the most dissatisfied section of the state, the northwestern corner, from the rest of the Old Dominion. If this had happened elsewhere, other states might have divided, but it happened only in Virginia and only Virginia split.

Another problem with the traditional view of statehood is that it does not look beneath the surface of sectional politics to illuminate the ties that held Virginia together during the eighty-odd years that West Virginia was a part of the state. These ties are important because they shaped the future of West Virginia once its separate identity was established. They also explain why the separation was so traumatic and incomplete. West Virginia history after 1863 was shaped by continuities as well as discontinuities with Virginia and it is important to understand this in interpreting the antebellum past.

An idea of the ties that bound antebellum Virginia to West Virginia may be gained by examining the biography of a man who happened to be watching with solemn detachment as John Brown climbed the steps of his scaffold in December 1859. The man's name was Thomas Jackson. Dozens of relatives in northwestern Virginia knew him as Tom, an orphan who, at the age of two, had lost his father and at seven, had lost his mother. Later, as a cadet at the United States Military Academy, he added his father's name, Jonathan, to his own and thereafter styled himself Thomas J. Jackson. The Virginia Military Institute cadets whose ranks he arranged around Brown's scaffold in 1859 called him the Major or, beyond his hearing, Old Jack. Within two years after the hanging, Virginia and then the world would know him by a more romantic sobriquet: "Stonewall."

As a soldier and as a man, Stonewall Jackson has always fascinated biographers. His experience with tragedy—an orphaned youth, the loss of his first wife and an infant daughter, his own bizarre death after being shot by a Confederate sentry in May 1863—lends a human dimension to his military achievements. Some writers have dubbed Jackson "the Confederate Cromwell," but if he were to be compared to anyone, it might well be John Brown. If Jackson's convictions were more moderate and conventional than Brown's, they were no less definite. Both men held intense and personal religious beliefs and an exalted concept of duty. Both confronted the world from behind thick beards and penetrating eyes, and the world stared back, deciding that each was a courageous and able man, useful though perhaps a bit odd. It goes without saying that Jackson was the better soldier. Although he, too, was unable to hold Harpers Ferry when he took command of Virginia troops there in 1861, he had the good sense not to get trapped as Brown had. A year later Jackson's forces surrounded and recaptured the town, forcing the Union garrison to surrender in the largest single Confederate catch of prisoners during the Civil War, proving once more that Brown had made a poor choice of a stronghold.

Stonewall Jackson is the most prominent American produced by the region that is now West Virginia, and so here we are less interested in his character as a man or a soldier than in what his life can tell us about the society that produced him. Jackson was born in western Virginia—in Clarksburg in 1824; he grew up there, chiefly at Jackson's Mill on the West Fork of the Monongahela near Weston; and he always considered the region his home, even though he lived in many other places after he embarked on a military career. Modern West Virginians feel an understandable pride in so eminent and interesting a native son and have honored his memory in many ways. There is only one problem. As Jackson's widow explained with emphasis, the general "died, as he was born, a Virginian." [5] He disapproved of the division of Virginia and several times during the early months of the war asked to be ordered into the northwest to drive out the unionists who were creating the new state. "I feel deeply for my own section of the State," he explained, but the state he referred to was Virginia.[6] Most biographers, if they take more than passing notice of Jackson's background, slide over the problem by trying to fit Stonewall into some sort of "typical mountaineer" mold, creating a personage who may be identified with West Virginia not by virtue of his conscious choices and acts, but as a social creature who represents in his character, if not in his behavior, the salient features of the society that made him. Thus Frank Vandiver in *Mighty Stonewall* presents Jackson as one bereft "of the traditional pose of fame. He was a mountain man [with] the blunt honesty, the firmness, and the self-reliance of a frontiersman from the remote western parts of Virginia." [7] Such an attitude completely misses the point about Jackson's antecedents and what they can tell us about the western Virginia society of his day.

5. Mary Anna Jackson, *Memoirs of Stonewall Jackson by his Widow* (Louisville: The Prentice Press, 1895), p. 14.

6. Thomas J. Jackson to Jonathan M. Bennett, June 24, 1861, in Thomas J. Arnold, *Early Life and Letters of General Thomas J. Jackson* (Richmond: The Dietz Press, edn. 1957), p. 334.

7. Frank Vandiver, *Mighty Stonewall* (New York: McGraw-Hill, 1957), p. 2.

Someone who did understand the character of Stonewall Jackson's antecedents was Francis Asbury, the frontier apostle of Methodism, who visited western Virginia several times in the course of his career. In July 1788, while Asbury was struggling through the rugged mountains and "devious lonely wilds" across which his holy errand directed him, he met two women who were also bound for a religious meeting at Clarksburg. One of the women was Mary Hadden Jackson, the grandmother of Stonewall. At Clarksburg the party lodged with Mary's brother-in-law Colonel George Jackson, a hero of frontier warfare and a companion-in-arms to George Rogers Clark, for whom the wilderness village was named. We have already noted how George Jackson and his brother Edward (Mary's husband and Stonewall's grandfather) were accumulating thousands of acres of wilderness land, both in their own right and in partnership with nonresident investors for whom they served as the local agents. Bishop Asbury noticed this, too, and he made in his diary some shrewd observations about the future of western Virginia and the roles that families like the Jacksons would play in it. "This country will require much work to make it tolerable," the bishop noted. From the appearance or manners of the pioneer Jacksons, or from the quality and comfort of their beds—a standard by which Bishop Asbury set great store—there was little to identify them with the aristocratic eastern Virginia ancestors of, say, Stonewall's military commander Robert E. Lee. And yet a connection was already discernible to someone with Asbury's experienced eye:

> The great landholders who are industrious will soon show the effects of the aristocracy of wealth, by lording it over their poorer neighbors, and by securing to themselves all the offices of profit or honour. On the one hand savage warfare teaches them to be cruel; and on the other, the preaching of [rival churches] poisons them with error in doctrine: good moralists they are not, and good Christians they cannot be, unless they are better taught.[8]

Asbury did what he could to make the Jacksons good Christians and, if Stonewall is any example, he and the divines who

8. Elmer T. Clark, J. Manning Potts, and Jacob S. Payton, eds., *The Journal and Letters of Francis Asbury*, 3 vols. (Nashville: Abingdon Press, 1958), 1:576–577.

followed were most successful. The family already had a great
deal of land. Whether or not this led them to "lord it over their
poorer neighbors," they certainly got more than their share of
the offices. Apart from his service as surveyor in Randolph and
Harrison counties, Edward Jackson's political career reached no
higher than the legislature. But George Jackson, after service in
the legislature and in the Virginia Convention of 1788, went on
to three terms in Congress, where he was succeeded by his son,
John George, who served six terms. When John G. Jackson
moved from Congress to a federal judgeship in 1819, his
brother Edward B. succeeded to the family congressional seat.
Meanwhile Jonathan Jackson (Stonewall's father, Edward and
Mary's son) won admission to the Harrison County bar at the
age of twenty in 1810 and shortly thereafter embarked on his career in public office, starting near the top with a major federal
appointment—the collectorship of internal revenue for the district of western Virginia. The appointment was made by a president of the United States, James Madison, into whose family one
of Jackson's cousins had married. Power then, as now, flowed
from the center, and this was especially true of Virginia.

The complete catalogue of Jackson family officeholding
would cover federal, state, and local officials; Democrats,
Whigs, and Republicans; Virginia and West Virginia; before
and after the Civil War. The scions of George Jackson won the
most important jobs and honors, but Stonewall's branch of the
family did well enough. The lands of Edward Jackson the surveyor, divided among a numerous progeny, did not provide a
legacy as handsome as the bequests of Andrew Lewis or of
George Washington, but they were superior to the lands of less
fortunate and less influential families. The farm at Jackson's
Mill, where Stonewall grew up in the home of a bachelor uncle,
consisted of handsome bottomlands and low hills embraced by a
wide bend in the West Fork River—hardly the typical western
Virginia farm of its day. The mill itself, which still stands as a
favorite Stonewall shrine, represented an important piece of
capital equipment in an emerging agricultural society, one that
nearly always distinguished its owners from the average run of
their neighbors.

Jonathan Jackson's premature death in 1826 ended a promising career and introduced an element of tragedy that would follow his son for the rest of his days. Admirers of Stonewall Jackson have been too eager, however, to make his struggle against these tragedies a social struggle instead of a personal one. Some accounts even have the young Stonewall walking barefoot to Washington in search of his future career. In truth, the social and political influence of an extended family helped to cushion the shocks that young Stonewall faced and protected him against the hardships that would probably have confronted a more typical western Virginia orphan. His mother's marriage to a ne'er-do-well lawyer in 1831 was promptly followed by the stepfather's appointment to a clerkship in the newly formed county of Fayette. Stonewall himself held a local office in Lewis County at the age of seventeen. Even his appointment to West Point owed something to family influence. As his widow remarked of the future general's departure for the Hudson in 1842 "his friends had done for him all they could," which was a lot.[9] And they could do more. Following graduation, political friends of the Jacksons intervened to hasten the young soldier's advance up the army's promotion ladder; their influence was probably decisive in his selection from a distinguished field of candidates for the V.M.I. professorship that he held from 1851 until 1861. Stonewall himself appreciated the value of his "connections," and during the summer of 1861, when the Confederate command structure was still fluid, he relied upon Jonathan Bennett, a Weston politician who was both a relative and a high-ranking Virginia official, for information and influence, including support for his promotion to brigadier-general. Jackson's military genius was his own and so were his admirable personal qualities, but without his friends the world might never have had the benefit of these attributes. Indeed Stonewall's own ambition drew strength not only from his conception of duty but also from a desire to embellish further what he called the "ancient reputation" of his clan.[10]

The Jacksons were not the only political clan to emerge from

9. Mary Anna Jackson, *Memoirs of Stonewall Jackson*, pp. 32–33.

10. Thomas J. Jackson to Laura Jackson Arnold, April 2, 1851, in Arnold, *Life and Letters of Jackson*, pp. 171–172.

the western Virginia frontier. A similar path was followed by the descendants of other pioneers who, like George and Edward Jackson, had parlayed their service in conquering and parceling out the land into legacies of wilderness real estate. The transition from buckskin to broadcloth, from soldier and surveyor to lawyer, legislator, and judge, rarely took more than two generations. The sons of Zackquill Morgan, the founder of Morgantown, for example, served in the legislature and succeeded the younger Jacksons in Congress. Thomas Haymond of Fairmont, the son and successor of a public surveyor, was also a lawyer. He went on to a judgeship and then, in the 1830s, to Congress; three of his lawyer descendants succeeded him on the circuit bench, extending the family's claim on the post into the twentieth century. And what was typical of these Monongahela Valley families was even more typical of families whose fortunes had been built upon lands in the more desirable agricultural districts. Among the foremost leaders of the later antebellum period, Charles James Faulkner of Martinsburg married close to the center of established wealth and standing in the Shenandoah Valley, as did Samuel Price of Lewisburg, whose Greenbrier Valley croplands originated with the pioneer surveyor Colonel John Stuart. In the southwest, George W. Summers of Charleston inherited rich Kanawha bottomlands that his father, a planter from eastern Virginia, had purchased from one of Washington's associates. An exhaustive list would produce many other western hybrids of classic Virginia types. The point is that the Jacksons and families like them represent a phenomenon that is vital to our understanding of western Virginia history. Adapting the institutions of the Old Dominion to the circumstances of their highland frontier, the leading pioneers and their descendants created nothing less than a resident western version of the traditional Virginia oligarchy. It was this same oligarchy that bore the brunt of sectional battles with eastern Virginia, which may help to explain why the meaning of those battles has misled so many historians, not to mention John Brown.

The emergence of a social and political elite in western Virginia is partly explained by the character of Virginia's institutions, to which ambitious westerners readily adapted, no matter how ill-suited those institutions may have been to the region to start with. The centralized and undemocratic political structure tended to make influence cumulative and hereditary. Appointive local offices became sinecures for impecunious relatives (Stonewall Jackson's stepfather, for example) or training posts for the promising young (Stonewall himself). Even after state and local offices became elective in 1851, the practice of oral voting preserved habits of political deference to local notables, while lawyers retained the prerogatives of bench and bar. Lawyers were also helped by the rugged terrain and a settlement pattern that scattered homes and farms in narrow ribbons along the networks of the streams. The itinerant nature of the legal profession after judicial circuits were instituted in 1809 had many advantages. It gave the lawyers superior access to information about the value and availability of wilderness land and also allowed them to provide political linkages between and within the dispersed western settlements. Based in the larger courthouse towns, such as Clarksburg, Weston, Parkersburg, Charleston, and Lewisburg, and traveling the judicial circuits that spread out from them, the circuit riders connected the backwoods districts with one another and with the metropolitan centers of influence at Richmond, Baltimore, and Washington. The leading men competed with one another for judgeships and for seats in the legislature and in Congress, a competition that further augmented their influence at both the local and state levels.

The elite of western Virginia thus constituted a governing class, in the sense that it sought and won governmental power to protect and advance its interests, to provide for its posterity, and to admit outsiders only on appropriate terms. What we are talking about here is a system within which there was plenty of room for disagreement between political parties or individuals, along with all the other fascinating variants and peculiarities that we expect to find in real political life. To be sure, western Virginia's system produced a more open and less polished oligarchy than the older one in the east, and it had many attractive features. If the land-alienation system allowed large tracts to be held for speculation, other holdings originally large were eventually parceled out among numerous children. Oral voting and the large and difficult distances between polling places preserved the hegemony of local notables, even after offices became elective in 1851. This did not mean that ordinary people were wholly without leverage; the predominantly oral means of communication meant that the transmission of political information was a two-way process. Unlike citizens in later periods who were on the receiving end of mass-communications media, listeners at the court-day hustings and political entertainments could talk back.

Once we recognize the existence of antebellum western Virginia's governing class, we should no longer insist that Virginia sectionalism was a struggle between mountain democrats and plantation oligarchs, as West Virginia traditions maintain. It is true that western spokesmen nearly always pressed for liberalized representation and taxation policies and they loved to prick their eastern opponents with shafts forged from the democratic principles of Jefferson and other Revolutionary Virginians. But these efforts also represented an attempt by the western elite to expand its local autonomy and to widen its influence in state affairs. The constitutional reforms of 1830 and 1851 both moved Virginia closer to political democracy, yet neither change disturbed the basis of the elite's hegemony at home, while both enlarged the west's representation in statewide political balances.

In this regard it is noteworthy that the reform of 1830 was followed by legislation that declared forfeit and liable to entry all previous land grants on which owners failed to pay taxes within a brief grace period. A related change transferred the point of condemnation and sale of these lands from Richmond to the circuit courts of the counties wherein they lay. This meant that the western leaders were no longer confined to acting primarily as middlemen—clearing titles, collecting rents, or making sales for nonresident owners. They were able to use the new laws to get more of the land for themselves. "Good souls, how uproarious you would all be if an abolitionist was to steal a darky from one of your citizens," a bitter Maryland speculator complained to a western Virginia lawyer in 1856, "but you

have no compunction of conscience about taking lands owned
by citizens of another state [in accordance with] laws framed by
your own management . . . you have not only the bar interested in your favor, but the judges on the bench are interested in
the speculation of forfeited lands.'' If the old owners defended
their titles, he added, ''you are not only in a fair way to get all
our lands in Virginia, but in addition you will get all the spare
cash we can raise in the way of lawyers fees & costs.'' [11]

In other words, western leaders used political power to gain
the dominant access to their region's premier resource—its un-
developed wilderness land. This achievement naturally reinforced their interest in acquiring better transportation facilities,
which would make the land more valuable. Seen from this
angle, Virginia sectionalism—like state politics elsewhere during this age of ''transportation revolution''—involved many of
the same forces that later appeared in the ages of cities and
streetcars or of suburbs and superhighways. The land developer
who can get the government to run a road or canal or railroad or
sewer line or whatever past his land is a happy man in any century. Indeed, one of the key issues of antebellum-Virginia reform was analogous to the suburban cry of the 1960s: ''One
man, one vote.'' White manhood suffrage, coupled with the
''white basis'' of legislative apportionment that counted the
total white population but eliminated eastern Virginia's large
population of slaves, would have given the counties west of the
Blue Ridge control of the legislature after 1840, and with it,
control of the treasury. Eastern Virginia conservatives realized
this and feared that their slaves would be the principal form of
property taxed to build western railroads and roads. Consequently, at the convention of 1850–1851, the east refused to
give in on the apportionment issue, and the subsequent crisis
brought the most serious wave yet of western threats of dismemberment. If the white basis could not be obtained, David Goff, a
Randolph County land lawyer, wrote to a western member of
the convention, then western delegates should try for peaceful

11. George Smith to David Goff, January 23, 1856, David Goff Papers, WVU, box
1, folder 2.

dismemberment; if that was refused, "then for a revolutionary war . . . I would prefer to be killed in battle fighting for my country than to live in bondage. . . ." [12]

To point out that the conflict involved something less than the loftiest principles is not to indict the western leaders' sincerity. The reforms they sought were in keeping with the democratic spirit of the age and were universally popular among their constituents. As in other eras, the twin thrusts of democracy and development were complimentary, not opposed. They were also powerful. Had there been no concession, Goff may well have gotten his "revolutionary war."

But there was concession. The last antebellum decade was one of sectional reconciliation in Virginia, not conflict. The crisis of 1851 ended in compromise, with the west getting everything it asked for except the white basis of apportionment. Here a formula was adopted that gave the east a slight edge in the legislature but promised the white basis by 1865 at the latest. The reforms were followed by another spurt in the west's influence in Richmond, a revitalization of the state-sponsored transportation program, and the growth of conciliatory attitudes among easterners who wished to promote internal unity in Virginia in response to the deepening national crisis. Not all western Virginians were satisfied by these concessions, and of those who were not, two groups—the economic leaders of the Wheeling area and a minority of western Whigs who found themselves isolated by the political regroupings of the 1850s—provided key cadres of the West Virginia separatist movement. Among the established leaders of the time, however, the malcontents were far outnumbered by those who had flourished as Virginians and who expected, in 1859, to flourish even more in the future.

Thus in 1861 when David Goff, along with many western Virginia leaders more prominent than he, appeared in arms as they had often threatened to do, they took up weapons as Stonewall Jackson did, to defend Virginia, not to dismember it. If

12. David Goff to Gideon Camden, March 8, 1851, Gideon Draper Camden Papers, WVU (A & M 1199), box 2, folder 4.

there were no other proof of the overemphasis that West Virginians have placed on Virginia sectionalism, it should be sufficient to point out that most of the leaders who fought those sectional battles also fought the creation of West Virginia, either as Confederates or as Union supporters who refused to go along with the division of the state. In other words, sectionalism did not march hand in hand with separatism. If the old leaders tended to oppose West Virginia's creation, however, they also survived it, a fact that would have momentous consequences for the new state once the separation was made.

Stonewall Jackson began his defense of Virginia at Harpers Ferry, where he took command of the militia assembled there on April 29, 1861. The small federal garrison had already blown up the arsenal and evacuated the town. When Stonewall pulled his men back toward Martinsburg six weeks later, he had the bridges blown up, along with some of the factories. This left the lower part of the town in ruins, but it added a clutch of military shrines in the neighborhood to compliment those that commemorated John Brown's raid.

Many of the tourists who visit Harpers Ferry today are unaware that the place is in West Virginia. The town is altogether too charming and quaint to meet their expectations of what West Virginia should be. Besides, the neighboring Shenandoah Valley countryside has too many Confederate monuments, too many fine old houses set in groves of fine old trees to be anywhere else but Virginia. A somewhat related notion is one held by many of the people who inhabit, or who would like to inhabit, these same houses. They think of West Virginia's eastern border counties in general, and Jefferson and Berkeley in particular, as conquered provinces, a sort of Virginia irridenta taken without cause or justice from the Old Dominion and pining ever since to be returned. "Perhaps in another hundred years it will have ceased to matter," sighed Julia Davis over the fate of these counties in *The Shenandoah* in 1945.[13]

Both of these notions are misleading. Harpers Ferry is very

13. Julia Davis, *The Shenandoah* (New York: Rinehart & Co., 1945), p. 291.

much a West Virginia place if seen with an eye for historic detail. It is true that the town lacks the litter of industrial debris that disfigures most other West Virginia communities, but this is like comparing a person who died in the bloom of youth with someone who went through the normal process of aging. Harpers Ferry was an industrial town cut down in its prime, first by the Civil War, then by devastating floods that followed soon after. Beneath the manicured ruin that tourists visit today lie the bones of an industrial community that might easily have served as a model for the numerous railroad towns and coal camps that later spread across West Virginia. Like Grafton or Mullens or many other such places, Harpers Ferry occupies an ungenerous spot for a townsite. The narrow strips of flat land along the rivers were given over to factories, shops, and the railroad, forcing residential streets and housing to perch upon slopes too steep for convenience. Appropriately, too, there were "company houses" at Harpers Ferry and a more spacious hilltop home for the armory superintendents, a layout repeated in hundreds of West Virginia coal camps later on. The large number of immigrant workers to be found at Harpers Ferry was another harbinger of West Virginia's industrial future.

The Ferry was not the only enclave of industrialism in the Shenandoah region. Nearby Martinsburg was in some respects even more of a crossroads between a Virginian past and a West Virginian future. Founded in 1778 and named for a relative of Lord Fairfax, Martinsburg was a courthouse and market town of a familiar type in the Valley until the B & O Railroad arrived in 1842. The railroad increased the town's commercial possibilities and made it a center for the manufacture of flour and woolens. The B & O's repair shops were also located here and provided the town's major payroll. The marching and countermarching of armies during four years of Valley campaigns destroyed many of these beginnings, but in contrast to Harpers Ferry, Martinsburg's industrial foundations were relaid and expanded after the war. It was here that B & O workers began the nationwide 1877 railroad strike and here, too, that authorities employed state and federal troops against the strikers, providing another premonitory sounding of what, in time, would be a familiar West Virginia theme.

Most parts of western Virginia in 1859 were like the Shenandoah region, a true borderland between the North and the South. The South Branch and Greenbrier valleys shared the Great Valley's peculiar mix of Pennsylvanian agriculture and Virginian style. Another version of the same mix was to be found along the Monongahela, where small farmers, herdsmen, and iron-mongers flourished under the leadership of landed families like the Jacksons and Haymonds. In the southwestern districts along the Kanawha and Ohio, pioneer industrialists extracted salt, timber, and cannel coal for sale in Ohio and other midwestern markets, yet tobacco plantations set down in the bottomlands gave Kanawha County western Virginia's second largest concentration of slaves in 1860 (Jefferson County was first) along with other social features of a definite Virginian cast. Here and there were islands of New England influence, such as the antislavery colony of Ceredo on the Ohio River near present-day Huntington. Irate Wayne County neighbors all but destroyed the colony in the reaction that followed John Brown's raid, however, and its leaders fled northward to Wheeling. Notwithstanding a persistent legend to the contrary, there was no "Yankee peninsula" extending southward through the western Virginia mountains into the slaveowners' sea.

There was, however, a Virginia peninsula thrusting northward into the heartland of Yankeedom. This was the Panhandle, an anomalous sliver of Virginia territory wedged between the Ohio River and the Pennsylvania border as it was definitively drawn in 1779. Here the threat to secede from Virginia was more than a ploy of sectional politics. It was an idea that had been discussed seriously and even plotted for more than a generation. Here, too, antislavery ideas had rooted more deeply than anywhere else in Virginia, and though moderates dominated the political scene here during the 1850s, the antislavery men reaped a good harvest once the day of moderation had passed. Prodded by Archibald Campbell, publisher of the *Wheeling Intelligencer* and founder, in 1860, of a Virginia branch of the Republican party, and Chester D. Hubbard, a New England–born iron manufacturer, Panhandle leaders made their district the citadel of Virginia Unionism and the cradle of West Virginia statehood.

Ever since Colonel Crawford came out to raise the stockade of Fort Henry in 1774, Wheeling had been the Panhandle's capital. Seated upon a narrow bench between the Ohio and the steep bordering hills, the town found room to expand along the margins of Wheeling Creek, which cut through the hills to the river just south of the original townsite. Later the city spilled out onto a large, flat island in front of it. By 1860, it had grown to a city of 16,000—but its modest size concealed two facts that Wheeling spokesmen were always ready to emphasize: It was the largest in a string of growing and increasingly integrated industrial towns extending along both sides of the river from Steubenville, Ohio, to Moundsville; and it was Virginia's second-largest city in terms of white population, surpassed only by Richmond. It might be added that Wheeling dwarfed the other cities of transmontane Virginia. Staunton and Winchester in the Valley were each around 4,000 in population in 1860. Martinsburg, the second largest town in what is now West Virginia, had 3,400; Parkersburg and Harpers Ferry, including its hilltop suburbs, were both around 2,500.

Although Wheeling was neither a large nor an elegant city in 1860, most visitors found it impressive. It had a full array of well-built commercial and residential structures. It had a banking system that flourished in spite of the archaic banking laws of Virginia. Local capital had built a feeder railroad extending into Pennsylvania, a bridge spanning the Ohio, and wharves along the riverfront. The local iron and glass industries drew upon Pennsylvania, Maryland, and New England supplies of capital and entrepreneurship as well as upon local supplies. More than five thousand German, Irish, and other immigrants augmented the labor supply, while easily accessible coal promised an abundant, if somewhat smoky, industrial future in the new age of steam and steel.

Despite its success, Wheeling's history had been full of disappointment. The city had only two locational assets to speak of. One was a pioneer trail that provided a more direct connection between the Ohio and Braddock's Road than the river route via Pittsburgh. The other was the head of low-water steamboat navigation on the Ohio. The National Road, whose western terminus Wheeling secured in 1818 after much haggling with rival settlements, improved upon the first asset. A celebrated suspension bridge augmented the second. Completed in 1849, the bridge aroused a storm of protest and legal harassment from Pittsburgh boatmen, who claimed that the bridge made Wheeling the head of high-water travel upstream. The Supreme Court sided with Pittsburgh, Congress with Wheeling, but nature tipped the balance against the city when a storm destroyed the bridge in 1852. By this time also New York and Pennsylvania railroad and canal systems had reduced the commercial importance of the National Road.

During Wheeling's brief glory as a major transportation center in the 1820s, its leaders conceived the hope of challenging Pittsburgh's supremacy in the trade and industry of the upper Ohio Valley. Pennsylvanians may have snorted with contempt at this ambition, but it might not have been wholly beyond reach had Wheeling leaders been able to make up for their slow start and meager natural assets with political capital. Virginia presidents and congressional votes had helped bring Wheeling the National Road, but as the Era of Good Feelings closed, eastern Virginia representatives at both Richmond and Washington began to vote down transportation expenditures. Consequently, Wheeling's boosters tended to blame eastern Virginia, not for what it did so much as for what it failed to do in their city's behalf. This was not quite a fair grievance. It is true that the General Assembly made the James-Kanawha corridor Virginia's "leading line" of internal improvements, but from the standpoint of the state at large, the "leading line" policy made as much sense as Pennsylvania's concentration on a central "main line." Moreover, this Richmond-oriented policy actually did Wheeling a very good turn, since it kept the Baltimore & Ohio Railroad from building over its preferred route to the Ohio via the Shenandoah, Greenbrier, and Kanawha valleys. When Pennsylvania denied the road's bid to build to Pittsburgh, Wheeling became the B & O's western terminus by default. But there was even disappointment in this result. Although the B & O did finally reach Wheeling in 1852, it decided to bridge the Ohio at Benwood, a few miles south. Moreover, the pattern of midwestern railroad development led the B & O southern branch, which it had built from Grafton to Parkersburg in 1857 and then on to Cincinnati and St. Louis, to eclipse the main, or Wheeling, line. Thus while Wheeling had ample railroad connections by 1860, it was by no means a railroad center; indeed, it sat somewhat forlornly in the midst of a collection of spurs. The economic decline of the late 1850s, which hit Wheeling and northwestern Virginia harder than other parts of the commonwealth, increased the Panhandle's sense of frustration and grievance against Virginia just as the nation's sectional crisis grew more acute.

Despite its disappointing contribution to Wheeling's development, the B & O Railroad had a decisive impact on the future of western Virginia. The railroad's completion gave definitive form to the Potomac-Monongahela corridor that Washington had scouted in 1784. It also gave definite, if somewhat irregular, form to the West Virginia border drawn in 1863. The two panhandles—the existing northern one and the eastern one created when the Potomac counties were included in West Virginia—give the state the most unusual borders to be found in the Union, save perhaps those of Alaska. But if we imagine the two extensions to be arms rather than handles, each arm grasping an important crossroads on a vital corridor of trade, then the irregular boundaries begin to make sense. In 1859 Wheeling, along with other northwestern communities, sent a troop of armed volunteers eastward over the B & O to stand guard in Jefferson County lest John Brown escape the noose that Virginia arranged for him. But two years later, when John Brown's soul began to march in the tramp of the Federal armies, Wheeling men cashed in upon the grievances they had nursed against the Old Dominion. When they left Virginia, they made sure that Harpers Ferry at the opposite end of their lifeline came with them, whether the Ferry's neighborhood gentry liked it or not.

Few of the 25,000 black people who found themselves living in West Virginia after the Civil War are likely to have wept for the loss of the Old Dominion. What was Virginia irridenta for some of their former masters became a haven of freedom for ex-slaves. Some blacks served as spies or couriers for Union troops operating in the Shenandoah region; others simply followed the soldiers northward to freedom. More than one Valley white family was shocked by the departure of "faithful old family retainers" who left at the first good opportunity. Julia Davis tells the story of a husband and wife who belonged to Miss Davis's grandmother; they took off once looking for Yankee protection at Harpers Ferry but became lost and had to return. On the next opportunity, they took off again. This time they appropriated a horse and carriage from their mistress—and they made it. Farther south, a Union soldier noticed a 75-year-old black woman accompanying the army as it retreated across Gauley Mountain after the Lynchburg Raid of 1864. Over terrain so rugged and barren of food that it reduced war-hardened men to tears of frustration, she was "striding along on foot with wonderful endurance and zeal . . . walking for freedom." [14] After the war the family of Booker T. Washington followed a similar path, moving from southwest Virginia to Malden on the Kanawha River near Charleston. There young Washington went to work for the saltmakers and began the educational adventure that took him up from slavery to fame as the nation's most influential black leader at the end of the century.

West Virginia's provision of a haven of freedom for blacks cannot be credited to the men who created the state during the war. When the state makers were forced to confront the issue of slavery, they grew very uncomfortable. There were a few abolitionists, notably Gordon Battelle, a Methodist preacher of Wheeling, along with less prominent voices raised chiefly in the centers of New England influence. More common were men like Archibald Campbell or Francis H. Pierpont who, without being particularly concerned about the welfare of Negroes, were antislavery because of the institution's economic and political impact upon white society. Some leaders were sensitive to the moral implications of slavery, but the majority preferred to treat the matter as a question of property rights. "I most heartily

14. Cecil D. Eby, Jr., *A Virginia Yankee in the Civil War: The Diaries of David Hunter Strother* (Chapel Hill: University of North Carolina Press, 1961), p. 275.

agree with you," wrote a Morgantown legislator to his fellow townsman Senator Waitman T. Willey, "that we should entirely ignore the whole subject in our constitution." [15] Congress would not let them ignore it, however. When congressional Republicans forced the state to add a slavery emancipation clause to its constitution as a condition of admission to the Union, Willey and a majority of statehood leaders went along. But a minority led by Senator John S. Carlile went over into opposition at this point, preferring no new state at all to accepting the congressional terms.

White West Virginians manifested a similar indifference to the memory of Harpers Ferry and John Brown in the post–Civil War era. In 1893 someone disassembled the engine-house "fort" and carried it off to the Chicago World's Fair, not as part of the state's exhibit but as a private sideshow. It was expected to make money but drew only a handful of customers. Later the "fort" was returned to Harpers Ferry and re-erected on top of the hill on the grounds of Storer College. This institution opened its doors as one of the country's first Negro colleges in 1866 and thus served as something of a memorial to Brown and the raid, but Storer's primary support came from out-of-state philanthropists and the tuition of its students. A more typical expression of traditional local white attitudes toward the raid is the memorial that the United Daughters of the Confederacy erected near the B & O station at Harpers Ferry in 1931. It is dedicated to Heyward Shepherd and proclaims that unknown and innocent man to have been an exemplar of the South's idea of a "good Negro."

It was primarily due to the efforts of black men that Harpers Ferry became a national shrine. In 1881 Frederick Douglass, the leading black spokesman of the Civil War era, came there to speak in praise of Brown and of the black raiders who fought and died beside him with courage and dignity. An even more moving tribute was offered by the twentieth-century leader W. E. B. DuBois in 1906, when he selected Harpers Ferry as

15. Henry Dering to Waitman T. Willey, February 5, 1862, Waitman T. Willey Papers, WVU, box 1, folder 4.

the site for the first public meeting of the "Niagara Movement," the black-led civil-rights organization that, in a few
years, would give birth to the National Association for the Advancement of Colored People. After a preliminary survey in
which he found that his own reputation for radicalism caused
concern among local black leaders, DuBois returned to Harpers
Ferry in August. There he led the Niagara group on a barefoot
pilgrimage at dawn to the engine house. "And here on the scene
of John Brown's martyrdom," as DuBois told the story, "We
reconsecrated ourselves, our honor, our property, to the final
emancipation of the race which John Brown died to make
free." [16]

16. W. E. B. DuBois, *The Autobiography of W. E. B. DuBois,* (New York: International Publishers, 1968), p. 251.

3

Droop Mountain

ROOP MOUNTAIN is a flat-topped, steep-sided ridge that cuts across the Greenbrier Valley like the crossbar of a lopsided letter H. The western leg of the H, which actually runs northeast-southwest in line with the general trend of ridges and streams in eastern West Virginia, is formed by the massive knobs of a range formally known as the Yew Mountains but more commonly known by the names of individual peaks and streams. The eastern leg is formed by Allegheny Mountain and its subordinate ridges, which march off into the sunrise like well-tended rows in a gigantic garden. Here the ridge-and-valley landform of the central Appalachians is easily discernible, with the parallel ridges divided by narrow but fertile valleys and pierced by water gaps that connect the valleys with one another and the streams that carved them with Greenbrier River. The river itself flows south through a canyonlike bed below Droop, but elsewhere it meanders beside rich bottoms such as the one occupied by modern Marlinton. Here Jacob Marlin and Stephen Sewell came hunting in 1749 and established what is generally believed to have been the first habitation by white men in trans-Allegheny Virginia. A favorite story among West Virginians tells how the two men quarreled on a point of religion; Sewell moved out of their shelter into a nearby hollow tree and then in the spring wandered off alone into the wilderness until the Indians found and killed him on the mountain that bears his name.

It is not places like Marlin's Bottom or Sewell Mountain that provide the Greenbrier Valley's most distinctive features, however. It is two handsome intermontane basins that occupy the interstices of the H. The pioneers called these basins "levels." The Little Levels of Pocahontas County lies below Droop Mountain's sharply rising northeast front, while the Great Levels of Greenbrier County spreads out south and southwest of the mountain. Throughout the nineteenth century these basins were known for the excellence of their gently rolling pastures and fields and for the charming contrast that these features presented against the surrounding backdrop of mountains. Thus while the neatly interconnecting valleys east of Greenbrier River and the river itself have afforded thoroughfares in most periods of history, the main road through the Greenbrier Valley has always run between the two Levels, climbing directly over the top of Droop. The flat top of the mountain added to its appeal as a thoroughfare—or as a battlefield.

As Civil War battles go, the battle of Droop Mountain was not very impressive. It was not even the largest or most important battle fought in West Virginia. The Confederate capture of Harpers Ferry during the Antietam campaign of 1862 involved larger numbers of men, while the summer skirmishes of 1861 that secured northwestern Virginia for the Union were more consequential. Droop Mountain was an important battle because it was a turning point. It grew out of the interrelated political and military strategies that gave West Virginia its present borders, and it broke a stalemate that had existed between the two armies since the first year of the war. In a sense, then, Droop Mountain was West Virginia's Gettysburg.

Few people doubted before 1861 that if Virginia succumbed to the lure of secession and if secession led to war, then western Virginia would become a battlefield. But when this actually happened, it came about in ways that no one could have predicted. The winter and spring of 1861 were seasons of tense expectancy for most western Virginians. Even after the fall of Fort Sumter and President Lincoln's call for troops had shattered the hope for peace, a new period of uncertainty settled over

Virginia. The Richmond Convention, which had gathered in February to chart Virginia's course in the crisis, approved an ordinance of secession on April 17, 1861, by a vote of 88 to 55. The ordinance required ratification by the voters, however, and this was not scheduled until the regular spring elections on May 23. Both unionists and secessionists began acting as though the issue were settled. State authorities at Richmond called the militia to state service and co-operated with Confederates and local secessionists in seizing control of the Harpers Ferry arsenal and the Norfolk navy yard. Meanwhile western Virginia unionists gathered at Clarksburg on April 22 and at Wheeling on May 13, where they set in motion the process that led to the separation of West Virginia from Virginia two years later. At the same time, Union volunteers began drilling at Wheeling, Wellsburg, and other Panhandle locations. But all of these steps were reversible, at least in theory, if the voters failed to ratify the secession ordinance. Hoping for the best, the Lincoln administration held in check the Federal forces then gathering along Virginia's borders. The idea was to take no action before the spring elections that might create a reaction in favor of secession.

Then on May 23 Virginia voters ratified the secession ordinance, and events began to move swiftly. Ohio troops commanded by Major-General George B. McClellan crossed the river at Wheeling and Parkersburg on May 27. On the same day the Panhandle men—now the First (West) Virginia Volunteer Infantry under the command of Colonel Benjamin F. Kelley of Wheeling—started east over the Baltimore & Ohio Railroad toward Grafton, a key railroad junction where Confederates had started to gather. The Rebels evacuated Grafton on May 31. Three days later, Kelley's troops, augmented by the Ohioans and an Indiana regiment, caught up with the Confederates at Philippi and defeated them in what is usually regarded as—apart from Fort Sumter—the first full-scale engagement of the Civil War. There followed a month of additional skirmishing culminating on July 11 at Rich Mountain in Randolph County. There the Federals slogged through mud and rain to a decisive victory that gave the Union control of the Monongahela Valley and its railroads for the duration of the war.

Invasion proceeded at a more leisurely pace in the Kanawha Valley. Although McClellan had originally expected the Kanawha route to carry the main Union thrust into western Virginia, the race to keep the B & O out of Rebel hands diverted attention northward. Consequently, it was not until July that the Kanawha invasion got under way. By this time a large Confederate force commanded by a former Virginia governor with a brigadier-general's rank, Henry A. Wise, had occupied the valley, but Wise offered only token resistance. Led by another politician-general Jacob D. Cox of Ohio, the Yankees occupied Point Pleasant on July 11 and slowly pushed eastward toward Charleston, which they reached on July 25. Although Wise had equal numbers of men and enjoyed the advantage of terrain superbly adapted to defensive strategy, the best he could manage was a series of panicky retreats. Consequently, Cox pushed on up the Kanawha River to Gauley Bridge, which he reached on July 29. Here the riverside highway turned up across the mountains to avoid the impassable defile of New River Gorge. Wise kept retreating until he reached the Greenbrier Valley, halting only after he had placed the bulwarks of Gauley and Sewell mountains between his forces and Cox's men.

Confederates enjoyed better success east of the Alleghenies during the first weeks of the war. Stonewall Jackson, then a colonel, assumed command of the troops gathered at Harpers Ferry on April 29 and remained there until the middle of June. In the meantime, he worked to shape his army into an effective fighting force—one that included many soldiers from West Virginia's Potomac counties—and he also managed to capture or destroy a large amount of the B & O's rolling stock. When Jackson (by this time a brigadier-general) evacuated Harpers Ferry and Martinsburg in June, he left the line of the B & O entirely in Union hands, but the line was by no means a secure one. The Union's inability to penetrate the Valley much beyond Winchester, and the ability of Jackson and his successors to push the Federals back across the Potomac from time to time, left the railroad subject to frequent harassment. Moreover, the adjacent parallel valleys of the upper Potomac region proved well adapted to Confederate raids on the B & O. Consequently, many of the Union soldiers recruited in West Virginia found themselves guarding the railroad. It was not very adventurous duty. But since the B & O offered the most efficient connection between Washington and the western theaters of the war, the railroad guards performed a vital service for the Union cause.

The summer skirmishes of 1861 established the Union and Confederate lines as they existed in West Virginia until the battle of Droop Mountain two years later. The Federal forces held the line of the B & O and generally managed to keep the railroad running despite persistent Confederate raids. They also controlled the Kanawha Valley, along with a series of outposts—Guyandotte, Barboursville, Hurricane, Fayetteville, and Raleigh Court House (modern Beckley)—that protected the Kanawha line against disruption from the south. Gauley Bridge on the Kanawha and Beverly in the northwest became the principal forward bases.

The Confederacy retained control of the Greenbrier Valley and of the New River and Bluestone regions immediately south of it. On the west these bases were separated from the Union bases by a wall of mountains extending from Flat Top in the south to Sewell and the Yew Mountains in the center to Cheat Mountain in the north. Union pickets were usually stationed on top of these mountains, where they enjoyed a commanding view of the Confederate valleys to the east. On the other hand, Confederates in Huntersville, Lewisburg, or Princeton could rest secure in the knowledge that Federal movements east of the mountain wall involved fragile supply lines stretched over unfriendly terrain. The Confederate hold on the upper Potomac region was much less secure than along the Greenbrier, but Hardy and Pendleton counties generally remained in Rebel hands through the war. Romney, the principal crossroads town of the South Branch Valley, suffered a different fate. Because its location made it an ideal jumping-off point for raiders in both armies, Romney became the most volatile post in all of West Virginia, changing hands more than fifty times in the course of the war.

In August 1861, Robert E. Lee came out in person to western Virginia to try to recoup Confederate losses in the Kanawha and northwestern campaigns. But despite Lee's superior organization, he could not overcome the problems of overextended supply lines, bad weather, and rugged terrain. The result was a further round of Confederate defeats in early September on Cheat Mountain above Beverly and at Carnifex Ferry on the Gauley River near Gauley Bridge. These engagements confirmed the results of the summer fighting. Notwithstanding the durability of the lines laid down in 1861, they were established in almost a festive atmosphere. The summer weather was generally fine, and many of the Ohio invaders could scarcely contain their delight in West Virginia's scenic terrain. Especially was this true of officers like Colonel Rutherford B. Hayes, who viewed the scenery from horseback rather than while trudging over the hills on foot. Clarksburg was "a pleasant village," Hayes reported upon his arrival in July. But Weston was lovelier, Buckhannon lovelier still, Beverly the nicest of all. "You will think me insane," Hayes wrote to his wife, "writing so often and always with this same story: Delighted with scenery and pleasant excitement." [1] Along the Kanawha, too, the summer of 1861 brought out "the very romance of campaigning," according to General Cox. The Union forces moved upriver on flag-bedecked steamboats. Bands played, Union citizens shouted encouragement, to which the troops responded with husky cheers. The retreating enemy stirred up just enough rumors and excitement "to double the vividness of every sensation. The landscape seemed more beautiful, the sunshine more bright, and the exhilaration of out-door life more joyous than any we had ever known." [2]

A Charleston lady who mourned the Confederate retreat might speak of "the saddest summer of our lives," [3] but the Rebels who established themselves in the Greenbrier Valley did

1. Rutherford B. Hayes to Lucy Hayes, July 27, August 26, 1861, in Charles R. Williams, ed., *Diary and Letters of Rutherford Birchard Hayes*, 5 vols. (Columbus: The Ohio State Archaeological and Historical Society, 1922), 4:47, 79.

2. Jacob D. Cox, *Military Reminiscences of the Civil War*, 2 vols. (New York: Charles Scribners' Sons, 1900), 1:64–65.

3. Sally Carr to Annie McFarland, August 22, 1861, in Virginia Fulknier, ed., *Dear Annie, A Collection of Letters, 1860–1886* (Parsons, W. Va.: McClain Printing Co., 1969), p. 13.

not lack consolations. General Wise made his headquarters at White Sulphur Springs, an elaborate and famous watering place that had long been popular with the leaders of Southern society. Here the Southern nationalists had come every summer during the 1850s to harangue vacationing planters and statesmen about their dream of secession. Now that the dream had become a reality, Wise's "legion" took its ease in what an envious Union general later described as "comfortable, even elegant quarters." [4] In other parts of the Greenbrier region Rebels feasted on fresh cream and wild strawberries and wrote home *their* praises of the enchanting scenery. "The views are magnificent, the valleys so beautiful, the scenery so peaceful," wrote General Lee from Huntersville in August. "What a glorious world Almighty God has given us. How thankless and ungrateful we are, and how we labor to mar his gifts." [5]

Eventually the soldiers had to confront their most persistent enemies—boredom and bad weather—while the generals learned some of the less enchanting features of mountain warfare. As Lee prepared his Cheat Mountain campaign, it rained almost constantly, reducing his eager volunteers to "the most forlorn and wretched set of human beings that ever existed in this world." [6] The rains continued throughout the fall, causing more sickness and death in western Virginia, according to one Confederate authority, than the Rebels had suffered on the Bull Run battlefield in July. The extent of Rebel discomfort, if not its precise nature, was revealed by the surgeons of a Tennessee regiment stationed at Huntersville, who requisitioned some ninety quarts of whiskey "for medical purposes" in a single week of November 1861. [7]

On the other side of Cheat Mountain things were not much

4. U. S. War Department, *The War of the Rebellion: The Official Records of the Union and Confederate Armies*, 71 vols. (Washington: U. S. Government Printing Office, 1890), 1st ser., vol. 29, pt. 1, p. 927. (Hereafter cited as *Official Records.*)

5. Quoted in Jack Zinn, *Robert E. Lee's Cheat Mountain Campaign* (Parsons, W. Va.: McClain Printing Co., 1974), p. 69.

6. Zinn, *Lee's Cheat Mountain Campaign,* p. 152.

7. Vouchers signed by John S. Fletcher and W. L. Nichols, McNeel Family Papers, WVU, box 1, folder 5.

better. "There is nobody lives here and it is very lonesome," wrote a western Virginia soldier from Camp Elkwater, a Union outpost on Cheat. "I have not saw but one woman since we came here and she is about sixty years old. . . . And the sun dont show itsself [*sic*] more than once a week for it rains or snows about seven or eight days out of a week and the ballance of the time it is cloudy." [8] The weather in the Kanawha region was less predictable but no less a problem. While the skies were sunnier, the mountain rains drove the Kanawha River to record heights and played havoc with Union supply lines. The floods were followed by an Indian summer that lingered past Christmas. The warm days and cold nights charmed Hayes and other admirers of the scenery, but the alternate freezing and thawing further damaged the roads, to say nothing of the "streets" of the soldiers' campgrounds. Then came a winter and spring full of cold rain and snow, disrupting planned advances on both sides of the mountains. "We are still on this Mountain and are very near froze," wrote an Ohio soldier from Flat Top in June 1862. [9] In place of the accommodating Tennessee surgeons, the Union soldiers had to put up with the good Colonel Hayes, whose diary entry for April 8, 1862, tells of a poignant occurrence at Camp Raleigh: "Rained all day. At night heard a noise; found the sutler was selling whiskey; ordered two hundred bottles poured out." [10]

The West Virginia weather did more than provide excuses for men to get drunk. Combined with the rugged terrain, it helped to create a military stalemate that persisted through the first two years of the war. The reason had to do with logistics. Hayes described the problem at Fayetteville, some twenty miles south of Gauley Bridge.

All our supplies come from the head of navigation on the Kanawha over a road remarkable for the beauty and sublimity of its scenery,

8. William ――― to Dear Sister, March 10, 1862, Civil War Collection, WVU (A & M 1021).

9. William Ludwig to George Ludwig, June 11, 1862, William E. Brooks Collection, WVU (A & M 485), box 2.

10. Williams, *Diary and Letters of Hayes,* 4:216.

the depth of its mud, and the dizzy precipices which bound it on either side. On yesterday one of our bread waggons with driver and four horses missed the road four or six inches and landed . . . in the top of a tree ninety feet high after a fall of about seventy feet. The miracle is that the driver is here to explained [sic] that one of his leaders hawed when he ought to have geed.[11]

Flood, ice, or low water could further disrupt this communication, pushing the steamboat landing farther west in the direction of Charleston. The Federal supply depot on the railroad at Clarksburg was stationary, but it was more remote from Beverly and its satellite camps than the steamboats were from Gauley Bridge. The lack of locally produced supplies compounded the problem. The Tygarts Valley farmland around Beverly produced some food and forage, but elsewhere in the mountains farms were sparse and unproductive; moreover, during the war, they were often abandoned. "Our living is hard, the grub I mean, and likely not to improve," Hayes reported from Camp Raleigh in March 1862. By this time, the two armies had picked the highlands clean of their skimpy offerings, leaving only "A few eggs once in a great while." [12] Otherwise everything had to be hauled in by wagons: ammunition, tents, medical supplies, food for the men and the horses.

After 1861 the Union's supply problems were further compounded by "bushwhackers"—Confederate irregulars who operated in the western Virginia backcountry. Those guerillas who operated in the Potomac counties, such as McNeill's Rangers in the South Branch Valley, were generally detached units of the regular Confederate army. But in other parts of West Virginia, particularly in the interior counties that surrounded the Union's Kanawha line, bushwhackers organized with no official mandate other than the governor of Virginia's commission to resist invasion by the best means available, to be "soldiers when they had a chance to do us a mischief," as Cox explained it, "and citizens when they were in danger of capture

11. Williams, *Diary and Letters of Hayes,* 4:216.
12. Rutherford B. Hayes to Lucy Hayes, March 22, 1862, in Williams, *Diary and Letters of Hayes,* 4:216.

and punishment.'' [13] Thus early in 1862 there appeared in
Logan County an outfit that called itself "the Black Striped
Company," comprising some sixty to seventy men but which
operated in much smaller bands to harass Union soldiers and citizens in the backwoods districts along the Coal, Mud, and
Guyandot rivers. North of the Kanawha in Roane and Calhoun
counties, the "Moccasins" operated as irregulars in 1862; later
many of the members went east and formed a regular company
of the 19th Virginia Cavalry (Confederate). A smaller and
nameless band appeared in the wild Birch Mountain country of
Braxton, Nicholas, and Webster counties, while other Confederate guerillas operated in the wilderness that lay astride the Cheat
and Potomac watersheds in the northeast. Hayes's Ohio regiment, which, in the fall of 1861, passed a month or longer
without being shot at by anyone, found itself increasingly beset
by bushwhackers in the winter of 1862, when the guerillas appeared in the Flat Top region in bands as large as fifty men.

The bushwhackers provided the most controversial element of
the fighting in West Virginia. Union authorities and citizens
universally condemned the guerillas as horse thieves and murderers. Since the unionists were in a position to press these
charges in the courts after 1865, few former bushwhackers
stepped forward voluntarily to defend themselves, preferring
"silk to hemp, for a necktie," as one man put it. [14] It is certainly true that the guerillas stole horses; whether this or other
types of booty were used in support of the Confederate war effort is impossible to prove. There were also murders and kid-
nappings, including some of the atrocious ones that are usually
encountered in a guerilla war. One Union courier bushwhacked
in the spring of 1862 was disemboweled and beheaded, his
bloody head stuffed into the cavity in his trunk. Another victim
was found stripped naked and tied to a tree, his body riddled
with bullets.

Such instances served to redouble the conviction of Union

13. Cox, *Military Reminiscences,* 1:421.
14. Samuel Young to Isaac McNeel, February 26, 1866, McNeel Family Papers,
WVU, box 1, folder 6.

authorities—that guerillas so overstepped the bounds of "civilized" warfare that draconian measures to combat them were both justified and necessary. The "search and destroy" tactics that have traditionally characterized the United States' Indian and imperial wars, and which were finally adopted by General Philip C. Sheridan in his march up the Valley in late 1864, first began to be seen in southern West Virginia in the winter of 1862. On Hayes's initiative, his command at Raleigh began patrolling the Flat Top region "to ascertain the hiding places of the bushwhackers and when found . . . all houses and property in the neighborhood which can be destroyed by fire will be burned, and all men who can be identified as of the party will be killed, whether found in arms or not." [15] "We do not take prisoners if we can help it," reported one of Hayes's Ohioans a few months later.[16] If prisoners were taken, they were usually sent in chains to prisons in Columbus or Wheeling. Summary executions were not unheard of, however. Usually a small group of soldiers escorted the prisoner into the woods where, it was said, he "fell off a log." The body of one such victim, killed in Monroe County in 1864, was later strung up by the roadside, with a note pinned to the chest warning other guerillas of a similar fate.

It should be noted that the Confederates faced the same problems that beset the Yankees in West Virginia. So long as the Rebels remained on the defensive behind the Flat Top–Sewell–Cheat Mountain line, they enjoyed the advantages of interior lines of communication and the harvest of the highland valleys' fine pastures and farms. If they moved west in significant numbers, however, their supply lines also began to ravel as they stretched over the mountain roads. Confederate marches also encountered occasional Union bushwhackers, particularly when their raids took them into the Union heartland north of the B & O. Armed Union citizens in the Flat Top area, in the Dry

15. Rutherford B. Hayes to Jacob D. Cox, March 14, 1862, in Williams, *Diary and Letters of Hayes,* 4:208.
16. William Ludwig to George Ludwig, July 29, 1862, Brooks Collection, WVU, box 2.

Fork district of Randolph County, and in the Shenandoah Mountains of Morgan County were among those who helped Federal soldiers round up Rebel guerillas operating nearby. The Confederates also had another sort of "irregular" to deal with—slaves who watched silently and shrewdly while awaiting their opportunities. Colonel David Strother used black servants as couriers and spies while stationed with Union forces at Martinsburg. In the south, Hayes was regularly visited at Camp Raleigh by refugee blacks who supplied useful intelligence about the Confederates' Greenbrier Valley and southwestern Virginia strongholds.

Bad weather and worse roads, uncertain communications, rugged terrain, and the presence of resistance and subversion in the rear of both armies: these conditions conspired to make the Civil War in West Virginia "an affair of outposts" after 1861. And yet the military planners were not content to leave it that way for two reasons, one political, the other geographic. The Lincoln administration found West Virginia a convenient place to install certain generals whose political influence was too great to pass over, but whose military talents were too limited to trust in a more important theater of war. These included John C. Frémont, the declining "Pathfinder" (commanding at Wheeling from March to June 1862), Robert Schenck, an Ohio politico (fall 1862–spring 1863), and Franz Sigel, popular with German-American voters (spring 1864). Sigel was followed by General David Hunter, a professional soldier who was popular in West Virginia because he was a native of Martinsburg. Although Hunter achieved some success with his raid down the Valley to Lynchburg, he is best remembered for burning the houses of prominent Confederate citizens beginning with some of his Rebel relatives near Charles Town. The organizational requirements of this procession of generals caused West Virginia to be attached first to a Mountain Department created for Frémont, then to the Department of Ohio, then to a Middle Department headquartered in Baltimore, then to a Department of West Virginia that survived from mid-1863 until it was merged into Sheridan's Army of the Shenandoah in August 1864.

Changes in command were usually followed by an effort to

end what General Cox bluntly described as West Virginia's "insignificance as a theatre of war." [17] McClellan launched his national career via his West Virginia campaign of 1861, and his successors were understandably tempted to do likewise. But glory was not the only temptation. Another inducement to break out of the 1861 stalemate was West Virginia's location with respect to the transportation corridors upon which both armies relied. Of the four corridors that made up antebellum western Virginia's transportation grid, the Union controlled two from the early months of the war. These were the Ohio River on the west and the B & O Railroad on the north. The Confederates controlled the Valley corridor on the east, beginning at a fluctuating point between Winchester and Martinsburg. This corridor, like the northern one, now included railroads: the Virginia Central, running from Richmond across the Blue Ridge to Staunton and then southwest to Covington, a point about twenty miles east of White Sulphur Springs; and the Virginia & Tennessee, running across southwest Virginia connecting Lynchburg and Richmond with east Tennessee. The Kanawha-James corridor was, as always, the central link of this grid, but here control was divided, as we have seen, with the Union taking the Kanawha Valley, the Rebels, the Greenbrier and Jackson watersheds, leaving a mountainous no-man's-land in between.

In Cox's view, both armies should have accepted this division of western Virginia as permanent and concentrated their energies in other theaters of the war. Instead, they persisted in trying to break out of the stalemate. From the first days of the war, General McClellan dreamed of making the Kanawha corridor a base of operations against the Tennessee Railroad ("the jugular vein of Rebeldom," as Hayes described it). [18] His successors inherited this scheme, frequently adding embellishments of their own. "It was easy," Cox recalled, "sitting at one's office table, to sweep the hand over a few inches of chart showing next to nothing of the topography, and to say, 'We will march

17. Cox, *Military Reminiscences*, 1:445.
18. Rutherford B. Hayes to Lucy Hayes, January 12, 1862, in Williams, *Diary and Letters of Hayes*, 4:184.

from here to here'; but when the march was undertaken, the natural obstacles began to assert themselves, and one general after
another had to find apologies for failing to accomplish what
ought never to have been undertaken.'' Eventually, he added,
the planners learned to accept their dependence upon the rivers
and railroads for moving large bodies of troops; "but they
seemed to learn it only as the merest civilian could learn it, by
the experience of repeated failures of plans based on long lines
of communication over forest-clad mountains, dependent upon
wagons to carry everything for man and beast." [19] Confederates, it may be added, were no freer from these delusions where
West Virginia was concerned, except, of course, they wished to
march in the other direction, using the eastern valleys to launch
raids against the B & O while dreaming of a Confederate Kanawha Valley pointed at Ohio's heart.

It was thus against a background of protracted stalemate,
punctuated by ambitious but unsuccessful raids, that the Union
forces launched their expedition against Lewisburg in November
1863, the one that became the Droop Mountain campaign. The
planner of the campaign was General Benjamin F. Kelley, the
hero of Philippi, a stalwart if colorless commander who endured
the procession of political generals through West Virginia with
the same imperturbable patience with which he had borne a terrible wound suffered in the first battle of the war. After his return to active duty, Kelley had charge of the railroad guard
along the B & O and, during the intervals between the political
generals, took over command of the entire West Virginia theater. The fall of 1863 was one of those intervals. Schenck had
gone, Sigel had not arrived, and Kelley was on his own in command of the West Virginia Department. Appropriately, too,
most of the Rebels that Kelley planned to "capture or drive
away" from Lewisburg were also western Virginians, now
made West Virginians by an act of a Congress they no longer
recognized. These included General John S. Echols, a resident
of Monroe County, and his cavalry commander William L.
Jackson of Parkersburg, Stonewall's cousin and a former judge.

19. Cox, *Military Reminiscences,* 1:145.

Kelley's plan of campaign was a simple one. Since his cavalry at Beverly, commanded by General William W. Averell, had exhausted the Tygarts Valley's natural forage, Kelley decided to have it move to the railroad by a roundabout route, striking south through the Greenbrier Valley to Lewisburg, then north to the B & O via the Jackson and South Branch valleys. Another column would advance from Charleston on the west. Each column would contain infantry, cavalry, and artillery units, for a total of about 4,000 men. Together they would form pincers closing on Lewisburg and the force of about 2,000 Confederates in Echols's command. This military result would be attended by a political one. The new state of West Virginia had been established in June; a victory at Lewisburg would assert its sovereignty in the last important Confederate stronghold within the new borders. There was no notion of permanent occupation at this time, but Averell was given the option, if conditions were right, of leading a cavalry raid farther south to the Tennessee Railroad.

Blockaded roads and raw troops unused to marching in the mountains delayed the advance from Charleston, but for Averell the plan worked like clockwork. His column crossed Cheat Mountain to Bartow at the head of the Greenbrier country on November 1, then moved south in leisurely fashion down the back valleys to Huntersville, which it reached on November 4. Here Averell divided his force, sending a detachment after Rebel cavalry camped at Marlin's Bottom on Greenbrier River, but continuing south with the main body of troops down the back valley of Beaver Creek, then west over Beaver Lick Mountain, across the river, and up onto the Little Levels above Hillsboro, where the reunited Union command camped the night of November 5. He had deliberately delayed to give the other column more time to close the southern half of the pincers. But the swiftness with which Echols moved up to dig in on top of Droop Mountain, and Averell's exposed position under the mountain brow, permitted delay no longer and so on the following day, a Friday, Averell attacked. His march had been made in the last days of Indian summer, and the absence of commentary about the weather on November 6 in reports of the battle suggests that if the skies were not clear, at least it was not raining.

On top of Droop Mountain the Confederates had fortified a defensive position already made formidable by nature. The Union soldiers had to approach over an open expanse of cultivated fields which, near the base of the mountain, crumpled into "low rolling hills and . . . bewildering ravines" where men could crouch in relative safety among the fresh-fallen leaves.[20] In the face of such an objective Averell mounted an attack of textbook simplicity. Under cover of an artillery demonstration against the Confederate right, he dispatched a column of dismounted troopers and infantry that ascended the mountain by an obscure and circuitous route west of Hillsboro that for some inexplicable reason the Rebels had neglected to guard. When in the early afternoon this column burst upon the startled Confederates from the thickets behind them, Averell sent the rest of the command charging straight up the mountain. The steep angle of ascent made for a difficult charge, but it gave the Federals some protection from Rebel volleys that whistled by just over their heads. There was an hour's fierce fighting at a "bloody angle" near the top of the mountain. Then the outflanked Confederate lines bent back on themselves and crumbled. By five o'clock the defeated Rebels were scrambling down the south side of the mountain and streaming toward Lewisburg, which they passed through that night without bothering to pack up their camp. The second Union column arrived early the next morning, but the trap closed too late. By this time the defeated army was well south of Greenbrier River in Monroe County. Although Echols and other commanders tried to put as good a face as they could on the debacle, General John D. Imboden, who hurried up to Covington to block Averell's path toward the Virginia Central, spoke scornfully of the "panic-stricken refugees" from Echols's command.[21] Although the bulk of the Confederacy's Greenbrier army escaped capture, it was never afterwards able to resist Yankee incursions into the valley. Averell's victory thus shat-

20. *Official Records*, 1st ser., vol. 29, pt. 1, p. 505.
21. *Official Records*, 1st ser., vol. 29, pt. 1, p. 548.

tered the military stalemate that had prevailed in West Virginia since the early months of the war.

Imboden's presence and the season's first snowstorm dissuaded Averell from striking south to the Tennessee Railroad, but as soon as his men and horses were resupplied and rested, he led them out again on December 8. While an infantry rear guard occupied Lewisburg with little trouble, Averell struck south through the Greenbrier region toward Salem, Virginia, where on December 16 his troops hit the Tennessee Railroad a destructive blow and burned three large supply depots. Then he scurried back through the mountains, adroitly slipping from one back valley to another to the bewilderment of an encircling Confederate pursuit. General Jubal A. Early, Stonewall Jackson's successor in the Valley command, came to Covington to close the trap. He formally demanded Averell's surrender on December 20, but the Yankees had already slipped past him. "Early was late," Averell chortled in his report.[22] The raiders crossed Allegheny Mountain near Huntersville on December 21 and marched into Beverly on Christmas Day.

The Federals repeated the success of this "Salem raid" on a grander scale the following spring, moving under General George E. Crook in a wide arc from Charleston via Princeton and Wytheville to Lewisburg. There the bluecoats took their ease amid the lush Greenbrier pastures as Rebels had once done, while wagons lumbered over the mountains from Gauley Bridge with more food and supplies. Crook left Lewisburg on June 1 and moved east to Staunton along the route of the Virginia Central Railroad, which his men destroyed and placarded with taunting reminders of Confederate raids on the B & O. At Staunton the column joined General Hunter, leading the Valley Division of the West Virginia Department, and marched with Hunter's forces on to Lexington and Lynchburg. When Hunter ordered the Virginia Military Institute burned as a cradle of secession ideals and Confederate officers, many West Virginians in his command found it a richly symbolic moment, although few of them shared Hunter's zeal for putting things to the torch. David Strother had a bronze statue of Washington re-

---

22. *Official Records*, 1st ser., vol. 29, pt. 1, p. 925.

moved from the V.M.I. grounds and packed off to Wheeling "as a trophy for West Virginia. . . . I felt indignant," Strother explained, "that this effigy should be left to adorn a country whose inhabitants were striving to destroy a government which he founded." [23]

To be sure, all the problems that had hampered the Union forces in West Virginia before the Droop Mountain campaign did not vanish overnight. The Union forces still encountered guerillas, bad roads, and bad weather. The difficulty of hauling over muddy mountain roads induced Crook's column to abandon its wagons midway in its march, which sent it half-starving into the Greenbrier Valley in May. Since Hunter also exhausted his supplies, his withdrawal from Lynchburg via Lewisburg to Charleston came very near to turning into a rout because of hunger. Strother supped on hardtack, two onions, and "a stiff nightcap of applejack" while resting near Lewisburg during Hunter's retreat.[24] But two days later, on June 27, a great supply train met the hungry soldiers near Hawks Nest, the spectacular overlook on Gauley Mountain above New River Gorge. While the men feasted, the officers lounged and sipped wine, talking over the possibility of repeating the Lynchburg raid in the fall.

As it turned out, "the great skedaddle" from Lynchburg to Charleston in June 1864 was the last major action of the war in West Virginia. Most of the remaining engagements were raids by small detachments of hungry Confederates looking for food and supplies. One such raid sought another prize, however: two Yankee generals, Kelley and Crook, who were spirited out of Cumberland by some sixty of McNeill's Rangers on a wintry night in February 1865. Crook sportingly called this "the most brilliant exploit of the war," but that is all it was—an exploit.[25] Its brilliance shone with the light of individual daring, not the fading gleam of Confederate hopes.

There were many West Virginia units that served in places

---

23. Eby, *A Virginia Yankee*, pp. 256–257.

24. Eby, *A Virginia Yankee*, p. 274.

25. Quoted in Virgil C. Jones, *Gray Ghosts and Rebel Raiders*, (New York: Henry Holt & Company, 1956), p. 361.

like Vicksburg, Gettysburg, or Atlanta, but for the Union soldiers who had stayed close to home, the last months of the war brought the heaviest fighting. Merged as West Virginia divisions into Sheridan's Army of the Shenandoah, they took part in the great duels with Early's troops in the Valley in the fall of 1864. Then, as resistance in the Valley melted away during the winter, the West Virginians moved into the trenches around Richmond and Petersburg. As it happened, many West Virginia Confederates were in the lines opposite them; "thus we stand virtuly [sic] the father against the son and the son against the father," wrote a sentimental Wood County soldier from the Petersburg front.[26] However fratricidal these last fights may have been, they were assuredly deadly. As General Grant mounted his final assault on April 1, artillery rumbled the whole night long. "This night I shall never forget," a Union soldier wrote in his diary. "The earth trembled. . . ."[27] Across the lines, J. J. Stuart, a Confederate infantryman, was mortally wounded that night. "Poor fellow," wrote a Barbour County buddy, James Hall, "he had his retiring papers, and would have left the Regiment in a few days."[28] The next day the 12th West Virginia led the charge against one of the powerful Petersburg forts, winning an eagle for its regimental flag but at a terrible cost in killed and wounded. That night the Confederates began their evacuation of Richmond. Not far away William L. Wilson, a Rebel cavalryman from Jefferson County, drifted "in a crowd of stragglers" trying to find and rejoin his command. On April 5 he found it merged with some other troopers into a surviving remnant of the famous Laurel Brigade. The next two days brought almost constant skirmishing as the troopers sought to protect the plodding infantry and wagon trains from Grant's pursuing army. Then on Saturday, April 8, Wilson bedded down with his command near Appomattox Court House.

26. Lemuel Prettyman to Charles W. Athey, January 9, 1865, Athey Family Papers, WVU.

27. Michael A. Ayers, Diary, April 1, 1865, WVU (A & M 325).

28. Ruth W. Dayton, ed., The Diary of a Confederate Soldier, James E. Hall. ([Philippi, W. Va.], 1961), p. 132.

"There is an air of repose and security about Camp tonight which I can not understand," he wrote in his diary. "Are we safe at last? My thoughts turn homewards and I find myself repeating Joan of Arc's farewell to her loved mountains. When will I ever see the blue mountains and green fields of Jefferson again?" [29]

In point of fact, Wilson and most other West Virginia Confederates got home to the mountains sooner than most of their Union counterparts. They were allowed to start home immediately after Lee's surrender, while the victorious Federals had to hang around mopping up and waiting for the formality of discharge. The homecoming of thousands of former Confederates posed a new challenge for the authorities of West Virginia, a political challenge. Up until this point, the new state of West Virginia was indeed "the child of the storm," a product of military conquest. The state makers had worked in safety behind the military cordon thrown up across the mountains in 1861. The Droop Mountain victory extended that conquest to the new state's borders at the end of 1863. The triumph of Union arms assured West Virginia's permanence. It remained to be seen whether the men who made the state could keep control of it by peaceful means.

The creation of West Virginia was one of the few unambiguous results of the Civil War, but the process of state-making was anything but uncomplicated. When the Richmond Convention voted its secession ordinance in April 1861, several of the northwestern unionist delegates led by John S. Carlile of Clarksburg reassembled in the latter city a few days later to denounce the secessionists and to call for a division of the state. This Clarksburg Convention summoned the First Wheeling Convention (May 13–15, 1861), which organized to defeat ratification of the secession ordinance but provided, in the event of its passage, for still another convention, the Second Wheeling Convention, which assembled in that city on June 11. Conservative

29. Festus P. Summers, ed., *A Borderland Confederate: His Diary and Letters* (Pittsburgh: University of Pittsburgh Press, 1962), pp. 95–104.

unionists such as Waitman T. Willey of Morgantown and
Francis H. Pierpont of Fairmont dissuaded this convention from
proceeding directly to the formation of a new state. Instead it
created a "Loyal" or "Restored" Virginia government with
Pierpont as governor, Willey and Carlile as United States senators, and the unionist rump of the Virginia General Assembly as
a legislature. Wheeling became the capital.

The Pierpont government provided the sanction that the U. S.
Constitution required from "Virginia" for the erection of a new
state within its borders. The Wheeling legislature passed a dis-
memberment ordinance and held a plebiscite on the question in
October. A final convention sat at Wheeling from November
1861 through February 1862 to write a constitution for West
Virginia. It assembled again in February 1863 to adopt a
slavery-emancipation clause (the Willey Amendment) that
Congress required as a condition of admission to the Union.
Then a slate of West Virginia officials was chosen, headed by
Senators Willey and Peter G. Van Winkle of Parkersburg and
Governor Arthur Boreman, also of Parkersburg. Throughout
these preparations Congress and the Lincoln administration debated the matter, and only after much heated discussion did the
two branches of government give the separatist movement a
stamp of approval. At last, on June 20, 1863, everything was
ready for West Virginia to pin its star to the national flag.

Apart from the step of dismemberment itself, three issues
generated most of the controversy associated with the new
state's formation. First, the state makers confronted the question
of "a natural and proper boundary" for the new state. Whenever dismemberment had been discussed in the past, the Blue
Ridge was usually assumed to be the point of division. There
were some separatists who still insisted on the Blue Ridge as
"The true division line of Virginia," [30] but the majority wished
to avoid the Valley and Southwest Virginia's large number of
Rebels and slaves. Deprived of this traditional border, the

30. Charles H. Ambler, Frances H. Atwood, and William B. Mathews, eds., *Debates and Proceedings of the First Constitutional Convention of West Virginia*, 3 vols. (Huntington: Gentry Brothers, 1939), 3:411.

state makers searched at length for some principle of separation that would allow them to take the territory they wanted and leave the rest behind. Various formulae were put forward, but eventually it came down to questions of power and expediency. Drawing upon the laws of nations and the experience of the United States in its westward expansion, James H. Brown, a Kanawha County delegate in the constitutional convention, explained that "wherever a territory becomes essential to the prosperity and safety of a State, it may purchase it if it can, and if it cannot, it may take it." [31] In the case of present southern and eastern West Virginia, the territory was taken, but only after considerable debate. Original proposals for a new state had centered on the unionist strongholds of northwestern Virginia, roughly comprising the Ohio and Kanawha river counties and most of the Monongahela Valley. The dismemberment ordinance of October 1861 added the interior counties drained by the Elk, Gauley, Coal, Guyandot, and Big Sandy rivers, making a total of thirty-nine counties in all. The constitutional convention decided to take eleven more, comprising the present tier of eastern border counties running from McDowell in the south to Jefferson in the northeast. This last step was the most controversial. McDowell, Mercer, and the three Greenbrier counties were included mainly to round out the southeastern border in a manner that suited the Kanawha delegates. The step was justified, Brown explained, if only one Union man groaning under the Confederate heel in these counties desired it.

Expediency was even more nakedly at work in the inclusion of the Potomac counties, although here, too, a unionist minority lived whose real or threatened oppression might be summoned to justify the act. The B & O railroad was the real reason for creating this "eastern panhandle." "Sir, we must have our lines of communication," exclaimed Van Winkle, who in private life was president of the Northwestern Virginia Railroad, a B & O subsidiary. It was of "the utmost—the almost indispensable—importance to the proposed new State" to remove every mile of B & O track from the reach of Virginia. Otherwise, if

31. Ambler et al., *Constitutional Debates and Proceedings*, 1:218.

experience with Richmond governments were any guide, they might visit the B & O with "all sorts of crippling legislation, all sorts of restriction" and so put a crimp in northern West Virginia's lifeline of trade. These considerations, Van Winkle added, more than counterbalanced the inexpedient aspects of annexing this territory, such as its comparatively large black population.[32]

We have already noted the leading state makers' predisposition to dodge the slavery issue, but the question would not down. The constitution, as completed in 1862, left existing slave property undisturbed, but prohibited the settlement of any additional Negroes, *slave or free*, within the new state's limits. Radical Republicans in Congress were disappointed by this provision, to put it mildly. They forced instead the adoption of the Willey Amendment, a scheme for gradual slave emancipation, which was duly adopted by plebiscite in March 1863. The majority of statehood leaders went along with this scheme, although some, like Van Winkle, expressed deep reservations. A minority refused to go along, however. Raising the cry of "congressional dictation," Senator Carlile first sought to sabotage the free-state West Virginia bill in Congress and then to defeat the Willey Amendment at home. Historians have variously portrayed Carlile as the Judas, Talleyrand, or misunderstood-man-of-principle of the state-making process, but whatever his motives, his objection to statehood on congressional terms struck a responsive chord in West Virginia in 1862. Many agreed with a Clarksburg unionist who "look[ed] upon secession and abolition as twin brothers." [33] For many people, this attitude expressed distaste for the ascendant Republican Party, which had polled less than 2,000 votes in West Virginia during the 1860 election, most of these in the Northern Panhandle; it also expressed distaste for the centralizing tendencies displayed by the Lincoln administration's conduct of the war. But this attitude also re-

32. Ambler et al, *Constitutional Debates and Proceedings*, 1:451–455.

33. Quoted in Richard O. Curry, *A House Divided: Statehood Politics and the Copperhead Movement in West Virginia* (Pittsburgh: University of Pittsburgh Press, 1964), p. 109.

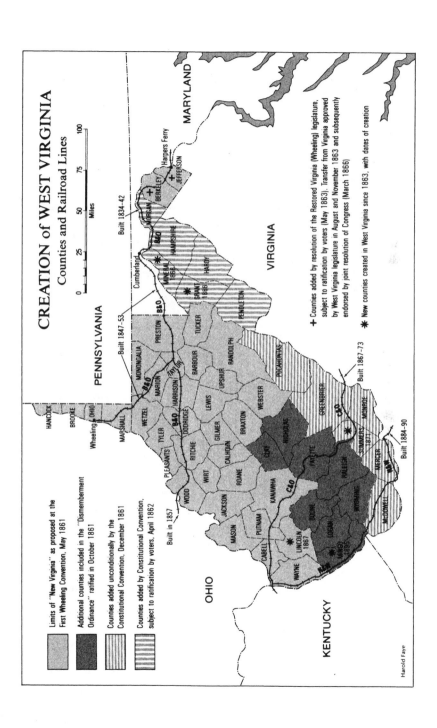

CREATION of WEST VIRGINIA
Counties and Railroad Lines

Limits of "New Virginia" as proposed at the First Wheeling Convention, May 1861

Additional counties included in the "Dismemberment Ordinance" ratified in October 1861

Counties added unconditionally by the Constitutional Convention, December 1861

Counties added by Constitutional Convention, subject to ratification by voters, April 1862

+ Counties added by resolution of the Restored Virginia (Wheeling) legislature, subject to ratification by voters (May 1863). Transfer from Virginia approved by West Virginia legislature in August and November 1863 and subsequently endorsed by joint resolution of Congress (March 1866)

✻ New counties created in West Virginia since 1863, with dates of creation

PENNSYLVANIA

MARYLAND

OHIO

VIRGINIA

KENTUCKY

Built 1834–42

Built 1847–53

Built in 1857

Built 1867–73

Built 1884–90

Harold Faye

vealed, avowedly or by implication, a racist view of blacks and their aspirations for freedom. A strain of violent negrophobia would surface again in West Virginia politics before the statehood era was through.

Another set of questions concerned whether West Virginia should closely resemble the Old Dominion or whether it should discard Virginia institutions in favor of other models. At the First Wheeling Convention, Carlile denounced "the Court House cliques" of antebellum times and laid at their door Virginia's descent to secession and ruin.[34] During the constitutional convention, reformers and conservatives debated Virginia and New England models of government, the latter as it was filtered through the experience of nearby Ohio. As on the battlefields, Ohio won many of the constitutional scuffles. Despite the best efforts of Brown and his fellow Charleston lawyer Benjamin Smith to oppose such "Yankeefied" innovations, the convention mandated universal free education, replaced the county courts with the township form of local government, established the secret ballot in place of oral voting, and buttressed these changes with frequent elections and short terms for most offices. The Kanawhans also lost out on a key economic issue. The new constitution prohibited West Virginia from subsidizing, as Virginia had done, railroads or other "improvement" corporations, a move that Brown and Smith understandably saw as a slap by the B & O hinterland at the economic ambitions of their part of the state. By threatening to withdraw the Kanawha region from the new state, they won a compromise by which counties and municipalities were allowed to vote transportation subsidies. A more recognizable Virginian feature of the new constitution was the land-title provision, where the Kanawha lawyers beat back the threat of reform.

In the end, all of these controversies were subsumed in the controversial nature of statehood itself. The makers of West Virginia invoked the ideals of popular sovereignty at every turn in the road, and yet they prosecuted their efforts amid circum-

34. Proceedings of the First Wheeling Convention in Virgil A. Lewis, ed., *How West Virginia was Made* (Charleston: News-Mail Printers, 1909), p. 37.

stances that made it all but impossible for citizens to exercise the prerogatives of democratic choice. The voters of West Virginia were called to the polls repeatedly, to vote on the secession ordinance, the dismemberment ordinance, the new constitution, the Willey Amendment, in addition to elections held for representatives at Wheeling and Washington and for the nonpartisan slate of West Virginia officials that took office in 1863. And there were other ways of registering choices for men of the right age, fitness, and temper: by putting on a blue or a gray uniform or by taking up the bushwhacker's gun. Any one of these choices could express in some way a citizen's support or lack of support for the separatist movement.

Unfortunately, a rugged hill country in time of civil war was not the place to appeal to the calm and deliberative processes of the democratic ideal. The secession referendum, for example, took place before the shooting started, but the Virginia practice of oral voting invited intimidation, and it was widespread in both secessionist and Union strongholds. Historians used to claim a unionist margin in West Virginia of better than ten to one. But Richard O. Curry's revisionist study, *A House Divided,* challenges the old figures. More than a third of the voters in present West Virginia approved of secession, Curry argues; it seems reasonable to assume that these voters were opposed, or at best indifferent, to a division of Virginia.[35] As for the later referenda, wartime conditions made a mockery of democratic forms in most places south of the Northern Panhandle. Such counties as Harrison and Kanawha returned absurdly large thousand-to-one counts in favor of dismemberment and the Willey Amendment. By way of contrast, Raleigh, Braxton, and Hardy, among others, returned handfuls of votes cast under the protection of soldiers, and often *by* soldiers, in a precinct or two held open only by force of arms. Apart from small numbers of voters who balloted in precincts scattered along the line of the B & O, the eastern border counties took no part in the plebiscites that decided their fates.

Confederates naturally boycotted all steps in the state-making

35. Curry, *A House Divided,* pp. 6–8, 141–147.

process, and so we should probably count them opposed—if we could count them at all. There are no reliable musters of bush-whackers, while regular Confederate soldiers were usually merged into regiments with other Virginians with no distinctions of east or west. On the Union side, soldiers from Ohio and Pennsylvania often enlisted in West Virginia regiments, while the subsequent availability of pension and other benefits to Union veterans encouraged some natives to exaggerate their commitment to the Union cause in later records. Thus we should look askance at the traditional figures that give the Union a three- or four-to-one edge in West Virginia troop enrollments.

After spending nearly a month at Weston in the summer of 1861, Rutherford B. Hayes wrote home to Ohio that "The Secessionists in this region are the wealthy and educated, who do nothing openly, and the vagabonds, criminals, and ignorant barbarians of the country; while the Union men are the middle classes—the law-and-order, well-behaved folks." [36] Theodore Lang, whose *Loyal West Virginia from 1861 to 1865* was one of the first formal histories of the statehood era, offered a similar analysis, and was especially anxious to emphasize that "the improvident mountaineers" had contributed little "to the advancement and elevation of the State." [37] This social analysis—the rich and poor for secession, the middle classes for the Union and West Virginia—may be accepted only with numerous reservations. It is true that the social elite in nearly all parts of West Virginia became Rebels or Confederate sympathizers. Even in Wheeling, where the leaders of the city's commercial and industrial establishment were staunchly pro-Union, the young bloods of the town, the sons of lawyers and judges, of Zanes and other "first families," slipped off to fight for the Confederacy. They took the rector of the city's most fashionable Episcopal church with them and told the tailor who made their matching gray uniforms that the outfits were for use in a wedding. Here and in

---

36. Rutherford B. Hayes to Samuel Birchard, August 17, 1861, in Williams, *Diary and Letters of Hayes,* 4:68.

37. Theodore Lang, *Loyal West Virginia from 1861 to 1865* (Baltimore: Deutsch Publishing, 1895), p. 8.

other West Virginia cities, it was not uncommon for fathers to remain at home, "remaining neutral to save their hides and property," in Charles Ambler's contemptuous phrase,[38] while the sons went off to fight for Virginia. As for the mountaineers, provident or improvident, a great many surely became Rebel soldiers or bushwhackers, but there is abundant evidence of poor men who stood for the Union at great personal risk. In the backwoods reaches of Randolph County, for example, small farmers, organized into an "Independant Company of Scouts," did perilous battle with bushwhackers in the late years of the war. In the Kanawha region General Cox reported finding "little farms in secluded nooks," full of staunch Union supporters. Cox wrote of the Union men of the Flat Top region:

They worked their farms but every man had his rifle hung upon his chimney-piece, and by day or by night was ready to shoulder it and thread his way by paths known only to the natives, to bring us news of open movement or of secret plots among the Secessionists.[39]

Another feature of backwoods Unionism was the role played by preachers of the Methodist, Baptist, and other evangelical sects. Russell G. French, a preacher of Mercer County, served Hayes's troops as a guide in the Flat Top region and was desperately wounded in an encounter with bushwhackers at Camp Creek in 1862, whereupon Hayes got him an appointment as chaplain. In politics there is evidence that preachers, who were also itinerants and enjoyed wide contacts in the backwoods districts, competed with lawyers for the allegiance of citizens in some interior counties during the late antebellum years and the secession crisis. No fewer than twelve ministers or licensed lay exhorters sat in the constitutional convention, where they generally pressed for democratic reforms and spoke for constituents in such interior counties as Fayette, Boone, Wyoming, Upshur, and McDowell.

As for the "middle-class, law-and-order, well-behaved

---

38. Ambler, "Introduction" in *Constitutional Debates and Proceedings,* 1:16.
39. Cox, *Military Reminiscences,* 1:221.

folks,'' they seem to have gone with the prevailing authority, as law-and-order people usually do. Behind the Confederate lines in the Greenbrier and Potomac counties, ordinary townsfolk and farmers made just as good Rebels as they made Union men north and west of the military lines. Lang is almost certainly correct in asserting that such people provided the backbone of the West Virginia movement, especially in the more advanced commercial farming districts and in the rising towns along the Ohio River and the B & O. Here the old western-Virginia style of leadership gave way to a time of new men. A newspaperman who visited the first court held in Cabell County after West Virginia's admission in 1863 noted that ''The youthful appearance of the judge, the clerk, and the members of the bar is in remarkable contrast with the old officers and members of the bar constituting the Cabell circuit court of former times. . . .'' The men who had dominated Cabell law and politics ''for more than thirty years'' were gone, he added: dead, retired, or ''somewhere in Dixie.'' [40] They would be back, as we shall see. But in the meantime, West Virginia politics experienced an infusion of new blood at every level. While lawyers had dominated politics before the war, and would in the future provide over half the membership of the constitutional convention of 1872, they provided less than a third of the 1862 convention's membership and only six of the 75 members of the first legislature. In their places sat farmers, merchants, a banker or two, but also preachers, teachers, carpenters, tanners, and others who were not seen in high places in West Virginia before or since. Most of the new men were obscure ones, backbenchers even in statehood politics. After 1871 many of them moved away. Others simply disappeared back into the mass of ordinary citizens whence they had come. Conservative lawyers like Willey, Van Winkle, and Brown, although greatly outnumbered, dominated the statehood proceedings and must ultimately be given most of the credit for its successes—and failures. Still one cannot help wondering what sort of place West Virginia might have become had the democratic ferment represented

40. Quoted in *Hardesty's West Virginia Counties,* 8 vols. (1883; reprinted Richwood, W. Va.: Jim Comstock, 1973), 6:96.

by these new forces in politics had a chance to develop under more favorable conditions.

Unfortunately, the makers of West Virginia were trapped in paradoxical circumstances. However democratic the substance and promise of their movement may have been, their opportunities occurred amid conditions that forced them to proceed in arbitrary, undemocratic ways. Neither ballots nor bullets can tell us precisely how many of the people included in the new state actually wanted to be there. This is doubly unfortunate, because the fathers of West Virginia ultimately grounded the sanction of their work in the doctrines of majority rule and due process of law. Driven by circumstances and by that peculiar Anglo-American form of legal radicalism that strains to mold precedents to fit unprecedented schemes, the state makers clothed their work in transparent legalisms that fooled nobody but their friends. "Virginia" gave its permission for West Virginia to form, but everyone knew that the "real" Virginia had done no such thing, and so West Virginia's right to existence appeared to rest on a sham. The founders recited the long history of Virginia sectionalism, while admitting among themselves that most of the leaders and half the territory that had fought the sectional battles wanted to stick with Virginia. For the benefit of Congress and posterity, they described mountains of Alpine proportions and intricately traced the courses of rivers to justify Virginia's partition, but the boundary they drew coursed diagonally across the tops of mountain ranges and followed the watershed between eastern and western rivers for only 75 miles out of nearly 400 miles of border with Virginia.

The state makers can hardly be blamed for their procedures. The subterfuge was forced upon them by the same circumstances that gave them their opportunity. Who knows how a straightforward revolutionary approach may have fared among the constitutional theorists of Lincoln's Washington? Had the Confederacy established its independence, its legitimacy would have rested upon the force of arms, as did that of the American Republic founded in 1776. But circumstances led defenders of the Union during the Civil War to pose as conservatives—as guardians of law and established procedures. West Virginia had

---

to be presented as something other than what it was: the only successful example of secession in American history. Unionist leaders could hardly admit this in the midst of the Civil War, and so they resorted to legal pretenses that served them well enough at the time but which, after the emergency passed and the state-making process was examined at leisure, could be made to seem expedient, unprincipled, cheap. And so from the state makers' predicament, we may date two unfortunate traditions that surfaced again and again in West Virginia's public life. One of these was an official cynicism, a propensity to ignore the spirit of democratic institutions so long as the form was observed. The other was an apologetic posture, a defensiveness that made West Virginians overly eager for friendly national attention and for outsiders' approval but overly sensitive to bad publicity and criticism, whether it came from within or without. Feasting on the sour grapes of postwar reconstruction, Virginia stuck the first needle under West Virginia's collective skin late in 1865 when the General Assembly, meeting in Richmond, repealed all of the sanctioning legislation upon which West Virginia statehood was based, notwithstanding the fact that Governor Pierpont had brought his "Loyal Virginia" government from Wheeling via Alexandria to Richmond and was installed there as governor of Virginia by force of the victorious Union army. Congress and the federal courts ignored this gesture, but West Virginia did not. The needle has been there ever since.

To understand what happened in West Virginia after the Civil War, it is important to recognize that each step that brought the state closer to its place in the Union had also created an angry minority. There were, first of all, those secessionists and "conditional unionists" who followed Virginia into the Confederacy in the spring of 1861, a group that included moral supporters of the rebellion as well as its fighting men. Secondly, there was a small group of unionists who resisted the division of Virginia from the very beginning. Another unionist bloc that defected over the slavery issue in 1862 merged with the antistatehood men to create a Union Conservative, or Copperhead, movement, which, the first time its strength was tested at the polls, won nearly a third of West Virginia voters under restrictive conditions in the presidential election of 1864. While the majority of new-state advocates followed Willey and Boreman into the Republican party, some West Virginians balked at this step, and others defected later in response to the development of the national GOP's racial and reconstruction policies. By the end of the war it was clear that the state makers faced a potential hostile majority inside their own state.

The trend was made all the more ominous by the fact that many of the dissident leaders outranked the state makers in experience and prestige. As Governor Pierpont stated in his inaugural address at Wheeling in 1861:

> The leading politicians of Virginia, both in the East and the West, embarked on the scheme of secession . . . the Governor, Lieut.-Governor and all the state officials, and four out of five of the Judges of the Court of Appeals, all the Judges of the Circuit Courts except one, and, as far as I am advised, nearly all the prosecuting attorneys and sheriffs. . . .[41]

Of the most prominent West Virginia Confederates, former congressman Albert G. Jenkins had been killed in battle, while a few, such as David Goff of Beverly, dreamed of somehow restoring the state to Virginia. But the most eminent returning Rebels, led by Charles James Faulkner, publicly embraced the new state. These included Gideon Camden, the richest and most eminent of the former judges; Jonathan Bennett and Samuel Price, both former officials of the Confederate Virginia government; and Allen Caperton, recently a Virginia senator in the Confederate congress. While none of these men had any personal enthusiasm for West Virginia, neither were they willing to turn away from the postwar opportunity of becoming bigger fishes in a smaller pond.

Since there had been no prominent Republicans outside of Wheeling in 1861, President Lincoln had initially searched the ruins of Virginia Whiggery for allies. He came up with several

41. Speech of June 17, 1861, in Lewis, *How West Virginia was Made*, p. 164.

who later declined to support the division of Virginia. Foremost among these was George W. Summers, the Charleston Whig eminence who worked tirelessly to promote peace during the 1861 crisis but then retired from public life and withheld his blessing from both sides of the conflict. It was not that he opposed a new state in western Virginia, he later explained, but he felt that state-making as it proceeded in 1861 was unconstitutional and illegal and so he could not personally take part in it. George W. Thompson of Wheeling, the solitary unionist circuit-court judge referred to in Pierpont's speech, was equally fastidious and resigned from the bench rather than take an oath of loyalty to Pierpont's government. Other antistatehood unionists took a more active role. The John J. Jacksons of Parkersburg, father and son of the same name and the same distinguished and wealthy patrimony, attended the First Wheeling Convention, but withdrew once the process moved from one of preserving the Union to building a new state. The son then accepted an appointment from Lincoln as judge of the western (West) Virginia federal district court, from which post he would eventually strike the Republican state makers a telling blow. The father helped to organize the Union Conservative movement.

The controversy over slavery and the Willey Amendment brought another batch of eminent unionists into opposition. Besides Carlile, these included Sherrard Clemens of Wheeling, a former congressman, and Daniel Lamb, also of Wheeling, a banker and lawyer who compiled the state's first legal code. Benjamin Smith, member of the constitutional convention and another Lincoln appointee to federal office, also became a Union Conservative and ran as that party's first candidate for governor in 1866. Senator Van Winkle, already wavering as a result of the slavery issue, hung on to become the Republicans' most prominent postwar defector when he voted against the impeachment of Andrew Johnson in 1868.

As if all this were not enough, the remaining state makers were divided among themselves over how to deal with the opposition. Anticipating that the return of former Confederates after the war would swell the Union Conservative ranks till they gained a majority, the legislature in 1865 began constructing elaborate safeguards. By law and by constitutional amendment, it became illegal for former Confederates to vote or hold office, and a wider net was cast to separate Rebels and nonbelligerent Rebel sympathizers from the body politic and also from the ranks of teachers, lawyers, jurors, and suitors. This was done by voter-registration procedures and a series of loyalty oaths, or "test oaths," the administration of which was tightly controlled from Wheeling in order to insulate it against local majorities in the southern and eastern counties. The dilemma that these measures expressed was not unlike the problem that national Republican leaders faced in dealing with the defeated South. Their goals were democratic and egalitarian, but they believed that circumstances obliged them to proceed in undemocratic ways. Arbitrary procedures further alienated their marginal supporters and increased the temptation to define "loyalty" so as to exclude everyone but faithful Republicans. Sporadic incidents of violence complicated the problem in West Virginia, although not to the extent that was true of other parts of the South. Unionists attacked returning Confederate soldiers in the Clarksburg-Fairmont area; there was a race riot at Charles Town; Virginia loyalists attacked West Virginia authorities at Princeton; while an occasional bushwhacker surfaced in the interior counties. Small detachments of Federal soldiers helped the Wheeling government to keep the situation under control.

Soldiers could not stem the growing number of Conservative ballots, however, and so, late in 1869, a group of "Let Ups" or "Liberal Republicans" formulated a constitutional amendment designed to change the Republicans' course by adopting more liberal policies. Called the Flick Amendment from the name of one of the sponsors, the measure extended the vote to former Confederates and also, by omitting the word "white" from the qualifications for voting, it enacted Negro suffrage as well. The racial angle became a strictly symbolic one after the Fifteenth Amendment to the U.S. Constitution became effective in March 1870, but the issue nonetheless continued to arouse strong emotion in West Virginia. The Let Ups hoped that the effect of their actions would be to broaden the Republican party's appeal to moderate voters. Instead it further divided their party while the opposition found elsewhere the chance it needed to drive the state makers from office.

The Democratic party that came to power in West Virginia in 1871 was itself no model of unity. In fact it could not agree upon a name; Conservative, Conservative-Democratic, and Independent were all used at one time or another until Democrat came back into general use after 1872. The party was divided along several lines: between former secessionists and separatists, Union men and Confederates, ex-Whigs and lifelong Democrats, established leaders and ambitious new ones; cutting across all these divisions was another between men who looked to the future and those who brooded about the past. The party could not even unite in response to the Flick Amendment. A majority favored supporting it as a means of restoring ex-Confederates to their rights. "I confess its odour is not savory," wrote Samuel Price; "It strikes the word 'white' from the constitution and enfranchises all citizens. Our prejudices stand in our way but I think we should consult our judgments rather than our prejudices." [42] But a minority of "bitter enders" declined to accept this gift horse from Republicans; *"by voluntary state action,* [the amendment] *recognized the validity of the 15th amendment,"* one irreconcilable explained with emphasis.[43] As it turned out, it was this same Fifteenth Amendment, not the Flick Amendment, that gave the Democrats their chance. In March 1870 Congress enacted laws empowering federal district courts to intervene in local registration procedures to protect the rights of Negro voters. Judge Jackson used these provisions in West Virginia to intervene in behalf of ex-Confederate voters. Not all registrars complied with his rulings, and those who refused were later sustained by higher courts. But the tactic worked long enough in enough counties to give the Democrats a slight edge in the fall elections. They took over the legislature and the governor's chair, passed the Flick Amendment, ger-

42. Samuel Price to Gideon Camden, March 27, 1871, G. D. Camden Papers, WVU, box 10.

43. John J. Davis to "Dear Sir," July 12, 1872, John J. Davis Papers, WVU (A & M 1385), box 1.

rymandered the state, and then set about to write a new state constitution, "a thing most devoutly to be prayed for" in the words of Samuel Price.

James H. Brown of Charleston, himself soon to be retired as presiding judge of the state supreme court, provided an epitaph for the statehood era in consoling Senator Willey on the occasion of Willey's defeat for re-election to the Senate in March 1871. "There is at least consolation in the reflection that *something* has been accomplished when we contemplate the Union saved—a new state founded—peace restored—universal liberty proclaimed—the rights of man recognized & guaranteed & the land of Washington & Lincoln, of ourselves & our sires no longer trodden by the foot of a slave—" Brown might have added other achievements to the list. Inheriting only an insane asylum and a few law books from the Old Dominion, the state makers had founded most of West Virginia's modern institutions, including the educational system from the university to the public schools. Instead, Brown concluded with only a modest valedictory: "May those who follow after complete whatever has been left undone." [44]

Apart from the ironic circumstance that West Virginia was "redeemed" from the very men who had made it, its fate did not differ greatly from that of other Southern and Border states that were "redeemed" from Republican governments during these years. "Bitter enders" and other unreconstructed types dominated the speech making at Charleston when the second constitutional convention opened there in January 1872. But moderates such as Price and Faulkner dominated the inner workings of the body. "Although its general deliberations did little credit to modern ideas," wrote a Republican observer of the 1872 convention, "the products of its labors were not fraught with the same baneful consequences that its daily proceedings seemed to have indicated." [45] "The men who desire a

44. James H. Brown to Waitman T. Willey, March 7, 1871, Willey Papers, WVU, box 3.
45. *New York Times*, August 15, 1872.

change," explained one member, "cannot always agree among themselves, and hence a very great contrarity of opinion prevails." The result was less a spirit of moderation than of mutual exhaustion.[46] The finished product itself was essentially an updated version of the Virginia constitution of 1851. It replaced townships and boards of supervisors with the traditional county court, reduced the numbers and lengthened the terms of state and local officials, reorganized the judiciary, and replaced the secret ballot with a unique provision that gave voters a choice of sealed, signed, or oral ballots. The moderates successfully channeled demands for racial restrictions on voting and officeholding away from the constitution itself into the form of an amendment that later failed of ratification at the polls. The land-title provisions, written as usual by a select committee of land lawyers, escaped debate entirely but later encouraged critics of the new constitution to describe it as "the Lawyers' Constitution," "a contrivance gotten up to make litigation the principal business in West Virginia—to the great impoverishment of suitors and the enrichment of the swarms of one-horse political lawyers that now feed upon the body politic. . . ." [47] While there is no evidence that this was the intended result, it is true that the constitution entailed further confusion in land and tax policies and facilitated, under the supervision of "distinguished land attorneys," the eventual transfer of titles from small owners to mining and lumber corporations in later years. In spite of this and other imperfections, the voters accepted the new constitution in a referendum held the following summer. Subject to later amendments, it is still in effect.

The "redeemers" who wrote the new constitution failed thereafter to act as a cohesive force in West Virginia politics. They divided among themselves on the economic issues that surged to the fore in the 1870s and 1880s. They also competed among themselves for offices and honors, as the older men among them had done in the heyday of antebellum politics. Nevertheless, while the redeemers were unable to dominate the

46. Samuel Woods to Isabella Woods, February 2, 1872, Samuel Woods Collection, WVU (A & M 1445).
47. *New York Times*, September 7, October 4, 12, 1872, July 25, October 4, 1876.

Democratic party themselves, they could prevent anyone else from dominating it, and they often benefited as compromise leaders chosen in the wake of the many factional outbreaks that marked the Democrats' quarter century of rule. The "Confederate counties" along the Virginia border provided the backbone of Democratic electoral majorities, and so the Greenbrier and Potomac regions produced a disproportionate share of West Virginia's leaders, with governors from Romney, Lewisburg, and Charles Town; senators from Lewisburg, Martinsburg, and Union. Price, Faulkner, and Caperton shone brightest among the older men; Representative William L. Wilson and Senator Charles James Faulkner, Jr., were pre-eminent among the younger leaders. Indeed, Wilson, the former Confederate cavalryman who sat by a campfire in 1865, puzzling about his future, was embarked twenty years later upon a congressional career that no West Virginian has matched in distinction. There are many other examples that link the post-Reconstruction era with the antebellum and Confederate past.

Clearly the state makers had bitten off more of the Old Dominion than a middle-class, unionist commonwealth was able to digest. One reason for this element of continuity in leadership is that there was much social and economic continuity between postwar and antebellum times, especially in the eastern and southern counties. Writing in 1876, a Wheeling correspondent of a New York Republican newspaper explained the GOP's enfeebled condition in West Virginia in revealing terms. "It is exceedingly difficult to reach the voting masses of the state," he wrote.

> Thousands of the people live in remote and almost inaccessible mountain districts, where they have but few means of communicating with the outside world. Many of them are unable to read, and they are Democrats because they don't know any better. Of course among this class of people public speaking is the only kind of campaign work which accomplishes anything . . .[48]

Republicans, he went on to say, were hampered by a lack of funds and of "home speakers." Country lawyers, plying the

48. *New York Times*, October 8, 1876.

paths of backwoods politics in traditional ways, speaking at the court-day festivities, greeting clients and constituents by name, inquiring about their crops and their families and in other ways adding to their sense of importance and breaking the tedium of rural existence: these were the sort of "home speakers" the interior counties listened to. In the wealthier sections along the Greenbrier and South Branch and Shenandoah, politics had begun to assume a more modern aspect, but here in the absence of more compelling persuasions, men continued to vote as they had shot and to look for leaders who fit old Virginia ideals of statesmanship. In the second congressional district, Representative Wilson won the votes of railroadmen and coal miners and achieved a national reputation by virtue of his mastery of the complex tariff issue, but he frankly admitted that he was at his best and most comfortable haranguing a Confederate reunion somewhere in the South Branch Valley. These were the voters that sustained Wilson and others like him in office. As long as they could stand together and outweigh the divided constituencies of northern and western West Virginia, then West Virginia was firmly attached to the Solid South.

But things *were* changing after 1865 and especially after 1880. As industrialism advanced southward and eastward through West Virginia along the expanding network of railroads, new types of communities began to appear and with them new political balances, new ways of appealing to voters, new types of leaders. In most places the transition took place gradually, peacefully. But in the most primitive part of West Virginia, in the southern interior counties along the Kentucky and Virginia borders, the economic and political transitions were sudden and drastic. In these places, change produced a new flare of violence known to lore and legend as "mountain feuds." Properly understood, these occurrences illuminate other paths of continuity in West Virginia history, paths that not only lead backward to a Virginian past, but which also point to the industrial future and to the place we know today as Appalachia.

4

Tug Fork

*S*OUTH and west of the Kanawha River, extending 150 miles or so in the direction of Tennessee, are found the most deeply dissected portions of the plateau that stretches west of the Appalachian mountain ranges. It takes a powerfully trusting schoolchild to believe, as the experts instruct us to do, that this region was once nearly flat. But the experts are right, and this fact is important, for it was the plateau's geological history as the alternating bottom and marshlands of ancient inland seas that gave it its characteristic subsurface structure of layered shale, sandstone, and bituminous coal.

After the plateau rose a final time from the sea, running water went to work on it. The water carved the surface into hog-backed ridges and narrow ravines, exposing the layers of coal here and there and sometimes leaving sandstone formations to stand like craggy turrets above the rocky beds of the streams. In contrast to the trellislike pattern of ridges and valleys in eastern West Virginia, the plateau drainage is dendritic, or treelike. There is no distinct directional trend to the flow of the waters except for the trunks of the drainage systems. The larger rivers, Big Sandy and Guyandot, flow north by northwest and, near their confluence with the Ohio, intercept the line of an ancient river (Teays River) that flowed west from a point near Charleston across the Midwest to an arm of the Gulf of Mexico in modern Illinois. The glaciers dammed this ancient river and buried its valley except for two portions, one in what is now southern Ohio, along the Scioto River where the Shawnee tribesmen later built their towns, and the other in what is now West Virginia, where the pioneers found a natural depression in the midst of the plateau and named it Teays Valley after the first settler. The Ice Age converted Teays River into a lake and then into a silt-filled valley that today channels trade between the modern cities of Charleston and Huntington. Along the Monongahela the glacial blockade also created a prehistoric lake that acted to gentle the slopes of the plateau terrain. No such mediating forces intervened in the plateau south of Teays Valley, however. Here the tributary waters ate their way into the earth without hindrance, twisting and turning in every direction, performing powerful feats of erosion but creating only the narrowest of flood plains where there are any at all. There was no ponding of headwaters to create glades, no carving of riverside benches such as the one that attracted settlers to Wheeling, no stairstepping of waters to create falls that might excite the attention of tourists. There was only the monotonous conjunction of steep hillsides, rocky streams, and unbroken forests. Today the only suggestion of flatness found in this region is in the work of men who strip away the jagged hillsides to expose the layers of coal.

Almost twenty years before the battle of Point Pleasant, during the French and Indian War, Andrew Lewis commanded another army of frontiersmen that tried to cross this region from southwest Virginia to get at the Shawnee towns in Ohio. The effort failed miserably. The hills were too steep, the paths too bewildering, the streams too rocky and swift to follow. Game was scarce, horses faltered, soldiers starved and plotted against the officers. Finally the mutinous men forced Lewis to abandon the expedition and fled in disorder back to the settlements. This was the first of many ugly incidents that have happened when men asked more of this harsh land than they had a right to expect from it.

In 1792 someone drew a political line through this region and gave half of it to Kentucky. Seventy years later the makers of West Virginia drew another line, taking the Coal River and Guyandot valleys plus three of the counties drained by Big

Sandy, leaving two other Big Sandy counties behind in Virginia. The state makers were tempted to take these, too, but decided against it in order to avoid a third panhandle curving around Kentucky the way the Eastern Panhandle curves around Maryland. And so the region came to be divided politically. The Kentucky and Virginia part came gradually to be known as the Cumberland Plateau or simply as the Cumberlands, after a mountain range and river that border the region on the south. West Virginia's share is sometimes called this, but it is more commonly grouped with the hills north of the Kanawha as part of the Allegheny Plateau. The names Kentucky and West Virginia, Cumberland and Allegheny, were, of course, man-made conventions. They could disguise, but not change, the natural integrity of the region. The Big Sandy River and its east fork, called the Tug Fork—supposedly after the leather thongs or tugs that starving soldiers boiled and tried to eat here in colonial times—provide a clear separation on maps. But nature made these streams narrow and easily forded through most of their length, and so they became the region's natural thorough-fare. People distributed themselves in the hollows along both sides of the Tug Fork without paying much attention to the invisible boundary. It was just such people who suddenly made this obscure region famous in the last decades of the nineteenth century. Hatfield was the name of a family that lived on both sides of the river, and McCoy was the name of a family that lived mainly in Kentucky. The Hatfields and McCoys drew another invisible line along the Tug Fork, making it a boundary in a legendary family feud.

Taken out of its social context, the Hatfield-McCoy feud still makes a rousing good story—there are violence and humor and sex enough—but certain features of the conflict are harder to explain, such as when it started, why it stopped, and why it attracted so much attention. There were not only powerful emotions and personalities involved in the feuds; there were also powerful social forces. It is no coincidence that the feud broke out at the turning point from preindustrial to industrial society in this part of West Virginia. The wider ramifications of the feud reached back to the Civil War when, according to tradition, hostility rose between Confederate Hatfields and unionist McCoys. Much later, members of both families were involved in the labor violence that drew national attention again to the Tug Fork Valley during the twentieth century. The central events of the feud took place during the 1880s, however, and these were the years of critical change in West Virginia, especially in the southern part of the state. The changes of this decade were political and economic in character. Both types of changes affected the course of the feud.

Appropriately enough, the feud broke out on an election day. The election practices of old Virginia survived throughout the interior for a generation after the Civil War, and they flourished on both sides of the Tug Fork. Campaigning and voting were social as well as political occasions, and though the formal "treating" of Washington's day had passed, there was still plenty of whiskey available at the polls, which meant that there were also plenty of fights. The particular election in question took place on the Kentucky side of the valley on August 7, 1882. Two earlier incidents had intensified ill feelings between Hatfields and McCoys. One involved the disputed ownership of a razorback hog of the type that backwoodsmen still ran loose, frontier-style, in the forest. The other involved Rose Anne McCoy and Johnson Hatfield and the birth, in 1881, of an illegitimate child to the couple. Lovers of feud lore have had a field day with young "Johnse" and Rose Anne, but the sexual angle seems to have been less important to the two families than the hog. A Kentucky jury had awarded ownership of the contested animal to the Hatfield claimant, but the McCoys were unsatisfied. When one of the trial's key witnesses, a Hatfield relative, was found shot to death some time later, the Hatfields accused two sons of Randolph "Rand'l" McCoy, the clan's leader. A jury acquitted them, but the affair still rankled when men from both families encountered one another at the hustings in 1882. The first part of the balloting passed off peacefully, but during the afternoon, after the men had had a chance to nap and were now hitting the whiskey jugs in earnest, Tolbert McCoy, another of Randolph's sons, let the "corn" get the best of him.

"I'm hell on earth!" he shouted in the direction of Ellison Hatfield, a large and powerful man of forty who had been in the thick of the hog dispute. "What?" answered Ellison. "I'm hell on earth," Tolbert repeated. "You're a damn shit hog," said Ellison.[1] With this unforgettable exchange, the two men fell grappling to the ground, Ellison's shirt already bloody from the work of Tolbert's knife. Two more McCoys sprang to the aid of their brother, stabbing Hatfield repeatedly, but the larger man held his own until one of the brothers ended the struggle with a single bullet in Hatfield's back. Ellison was not dead, but he was grievously wounded. While some of his friends made plans to pursue the fleeing McCoys, others helped to carry Ellison across to the West Virginia side of the Tug Fork, where, in a cabin near the mouth of Mate Creek, he lingered near death for two days. Meanwhile Hatfield's three older brothers—Valentine ("Wall"), Anderson ("Anse"), and Elias—captured his assailants and brought them over to West Virginia, lodged them in an abandoned schoolhouse, and informed them that their fate depended upon the outcome of Ellison's struggle for life. Ellison Hatfield died on August 9, 1882. At dusk on the same day, the three McCoy brothers were taken across the river into Kentucky, tied to some bushes, and shot.

No one ever proved Anse Hatfield's personal involvement in this execution or in any subsequent killing, but the commanding presence of this tall, black-bearded veteran of fifty and his patriarchal status at the head of a large and vigorous clan made him the central figure in the publicity that later attached to these events. Fame was not yet in the offing, however. The first round of killings attracted little attention outside of the Tug Fork region. The feud simmered with only one serious outburst during the middle 1880s. A grand jury in Pike County, Kentucky, returned some twenty indictments against Anse and his clansmen for the McCoy brothers' deaths, but no effort was made to

---

1. Virgil C. Jones, *The Hatfields and the McCoys* (Chapel Hill: University of North Carolina Press, 1948), p. 42.

enforce them until the summer of 1887. Then the appearance of a McCoy relative in the prosecutor's office at Pikeville and a new governor at the Kentucky state capital led to a request to West Virginia for the Hatfields' extradition and the offering of rewards for their capture.

West Virginia officials turned down the Kentucky requests, but a Pike County deputy Frank Phillips acted on his own authority and began slipping over the Tug Fork and spiriting various Hatfield clansmen back across the river to the Pike County jail. A West Virginia posse, formed in Logan County to resist these incursions, staged a shoot-out with Phillips's men on January 19, 1888, an event that attracted nationwide attention, since it involved something of an official confrontation between the two states. Meanwhile, the Hatfields themselves made a retaliatory raid into Kentucky. On the cold and moonlit night of January 1, 1888, eight men surrounded the cabin of Randolph McCoy in Kentucky and set fire to it when McCoy refused to surrender. McCoy escaped during the ensuing battle, but one son and one daughter were killed, and his wife was seriously injured. Two weeks later, one of the raiders, Jim Vance, Anse Hatfield's brother-in-law, was dead in West Virginia at the hands of Phillips's posse. Another of Phillips's captives, Ellison Mounts, reportedly the illegitimate son of Ellison Hatfield, was later tried and hanged by Pike County for his part in the New Year's Night raid.

The sensational newspaper coverage that these events inspired all over the country failed to notice that these were the last killings associated with the Hatfield-McCoy feud. The Tug Fork Valley remained a violent region; indeed it grew more so. A number of subsequent murders in the area involved members of one clan or the other, but none of these actually grew out of the feud. A number of Hatfields, headed by Wall, went to prison in Kentucky, notwithstanding the questionable means of their capture. Phillips's raids and West Virginia's counterdemand for his extradition led to a number of judicial clashes between the two states, but neither ordered its militia to the border as newspapers excitedly anticipated in 1888. The legal battles kept the feud in the limelight and, though respectable West Virginians hotly resented the publicity at the time, it helped make the feud a permanent part of their folklore. It also helped to make the southern highlander a stock figure in American popular culture, reinforcing the picturesque image of the stalwart mountaineer, but also helping to create the negative stereotype of the hillbilly, with his period costume of slouch hat and jeans, a full beard, a rifle, a whiskey jug, and a demeanor that one of the Hatfield chroniclers of 1888 neatly characterized as dull when sober, dangerous when drunk.

The way the feud actually ended provided a rather undramatic conclusion for so entertaining a conflict. Writers searching for a more compelling denouement have sometimes turned to the romantic entanglements of Johnse Hatfield, changing his affair with Rose Anne McCoy into a "Romeo and Juliet" story. As it actually happened, however, Johnse's love life was much too complicated for a Hollywood ending. He never married Rose Anne and indeed dropped her fairly quickly in favor of her cousin Nancy McCoy. Nancy became the first of Johnse's four wives, but she in turn dropped him in 1888 and went to live with Frank Phillips, the avenging Kentuckian. Another favorite device is to end tales of the feud with some sort of personal confrontation between Anse Hatfield and Rand'l McCoy, though the two men never actually met in the course of the conflict. The most recent version of the story, a television play broadcast early in 1975, shows the two men engaged in a blazing, Western-style gun battle, after which they are swept by a wave of pacifist feeling that also has ecological overtones, since they decide to give up hunting as well as shooting rival clansmen. It is safe to predict that even less plausible versions will appear as long as the feud remains a favorite part of American lore.

The irony of the Hatfield-McCoy feud is that it dramatized the traditional life of backwoods West Virginia at precisely that time in history when the mountaineer's way of life was beginning to disappear. It was giving way before the forces of modernization, forces that may be difficult for tellers of feud tales to dramatize in an amusing way, but which were nevertheless powerful. The economic and political changes of this period are worth a detailed examination, for they help to explain the abrupt and undramatic ending of the feud and, more importantly, they created the new industrial society to which the Hatfields and other backwoodsmen were forced to adapt.

The notion that mountain people are somehow different is an old one in western culture, but when we try to pin down what the differences are, they usually turn out to be nothing more than survivals of older cultural, social, and economic conditions that had once prevailed in the lowlands as well as in the hills. So it was in the Appalachian regions of the southeastern United States. The conditions that attracted so much notice in southwestern West Virginia during the 1880s were essentially survivals of the late-eighteenth-century frontier of settlement. A century earlier the same conditions had prevailed in all western Virginia localities. On the frontier, as in the mountains, life was often crude and violent, and the predilection for drinking and brawling reported by chroniclers of the feuds had been described and condemned long before by Bishop Asbury and by most other travelers who followed the backwoods trails. As the era of settlement passed, the older communities matured along conventional lines and came to resemble lowland places of the same age and extent, but the frontier lingered on in the backwoods. A northern missionary based in Fairmont and Lewisburg during the 1840s found nothing picturesque or depraved to report about life in these villages. But venturing out among "the poor people of the mountains," he found "was like a translation from sunlight into darkness—from a high civilization into one of ignorance and superstition." Most of the backwoodsmen he encountered were generous and appealing folk, but there were also the "savage-looking men . . . all intoxicated" and draped in weapons that travelers were still encountering along the Tug Fork a generation later.[2]

The economic aspects of mountain life provided other examples of frontier survivals. Subsistence farming and the graz-

2. *Five Years in the Alleghenies* (New York: American Tract Society, 1863), pp. 51–58, 69, 116–117.

ing of hogs in the forest remained the principal forms of agriculture. Diet consisted of corn and other nonperishable vegetables, supplemented by fruits and fresh greens in the summer. The forest provided an indispensable harvest in the form of game meats for the table, of ramps (wild leeks), sassafras, berries, nuts, and other supplements to a protein-rich diet, and in the form of skins and herbs, especially ginseng, that could be exchanged for cash or, more commonly, bartered for sugar, coffee, nails, metal utensils, and fabric. At Logan Court House and other interior trading centers, the exchange of finished goods for such items as skins, herbs, wild honey, and beeswax remained as lively in the 1880s as it had been at Wheeling one hundred years earlier.

If a mountain farmer produced any other market commodity, it was probably whiskey. Just as in frontier times, whiskey was a vastly more efficient way of storing and marketing corn than handling the grain itself. Monongahela Whiskey was famous in America long before the frontier reached Bourbon County, Kentucky, and when the federal government started taxing it during the 1790s, the result was a violent protest, called the "Whisky Rebellion." Although nearby western Pennsylvania harbored the most determined of the whiskey rebels of 1794, the Wheeling and Morgantown areas both had their share. Another drive to assert federal supremacy in the area of whiskey taxation began during the late 1870s and probably had more than a little to do with the outbreak of the feuds. Civil War tax legislation had restored a stiff excise tax on distillery products, but it was not until a decade later that enforcement of the excise made much of an impact in the mountain regions of the South. Appropriately it was the administration of Rutherford B. Hayes, that upright Ohio veteran whose wife introduced lemonade in place of champagne at the White House, that organized the first great drives against Appalachian "moonshiners." The most spectacular of the raids was a co-ordinated series of actions involving some two hundred revenue agents operating in states from West Virginia to Georgia early in 1880. Such activities unquestionably had a disruptive effect in the mountain strongholds of moonshining. The "revenuers" introduced a system of espio-

nage into the backwoods, bribing neighbors to inform on dis-
tillers and dispatching spies throughout the region disguised as
peddlers, cattle and timber merchants, and land prospectors.
They also staged ambushes and shoot-outs with the " 'shiners"
in all of the mountain states and, in general, behaved in ways
that probably were as instrumental as the Civil War in intensify-
ing violent behavior and suspicious attitudes among the mountaineers. It is worth noting that Johnse Hatfield's first scrape
with the law came on a moonshining charge in Kentucky and
that his betrayer was none other than Tolbert McCoy. In the fall
of 1889, revenuers escorted Anse Hatfield, Johnse's father, to
Charleston where, in the federal court of Judge Jackson, he
stood trial for moonshining. Anse was acquitted, as was his
brother Elias the following year, but this display of federal
power probably had something to do with the winding down of
the feud.

Another traditional avocation that came under pressure during
these years was pothunting, which was nothing more than the
ancestral practice of a man shouldering his gun, calling his
dogs, and going out into the woods to stock the family larder
with game. West Virginia adopted its first modern fish-and-
game laws in 1887, and though these were poorly enforced for
many years thereafter, backwoods hunters suffered from the
same conditions that had called the new laws into being: the
depletion of game and fish stocks caused by overhunting, the
pollution of streams, and the destruction of forests. Some game
birds were threatened with extinction by 1890, and deer, rab-
bits, and squirrels were noticeably scarcer. "This is the best
poor man's county on the globe," an exuberant Logan man was
quoted as saying in 1894. "You can 'coon hunt all winter and
fish all summer." [3] But in fact it was becoming harder each
year to rely on this traditional bounty of the mountain frontier.

The drives to bring whiskey making and hunting and fishing
under control were only two of a general concentration of pres-

3. Quoted in Edwin A. Cubby, "The Transformation of the Tug and Guyandot
Valleys: Economic Development and Social Change in West Virginia, 1888–1921" (unpublished Ph.D. dissertation, Syracuse University, 1962), p. 64.

sures that bore in upon backwoods society during the late nineteenth century. If some of the pressures were hostile, others
were benign, such as the work of schoolteachers and preachers
who came into the highlands in increasing numbers during this
era. Benign or hostile, however, the effect of the pressure was
the same. Mountaineers had to abandon traditional ways of living and working and adopt new ways.

If a mountain man could no longer depend upon trade in
whiskey or pelts, other ways to earn cash were becoming available. He could cut and sell the timber on his hillsides, as Anse
Hatfield and his sons did on their lands in the Beech Creek area
of the Tug Fork during the 1870s and early 1880s, or he could
sell to someone else the right to this harvest. By 1900 much of
the commercial timber of southwestern West Virginia had
passed into the hands of nonresident owners; the extent ranged
from forty percent in McDowell County to seventy-five percent
in Wyoming, but the McDowell figure was exceptionally low
since much of the land in that county had already been sold as
coal land before the timber buyers appeared. Ownership of the
trees did not always mean ownership of the surface or of the
minerals lying under it. These could be sold separately. After
Anse and his family retreated across the ridge to the Guyandot
section of Logan County to be safer from the raiders and reward
seekers that harassed them from Kentucky, he is supposed to
have sold some of his Tug Fork land outright and "the mineral"
on other acreage to raise money to buy ammunition and guns to
stock his new stronghold in the Island Creek district. Later some
of the younger Hatfields hired out in gangs to work for the
timber cutters; others went to work for the railroads and coal
companies and in the new towns that were established to serve
the new industries. Mountain women also found new ways to
get and spend money. They could earn cash by selling eggs,
milk, and vegetables in the lumber and coal camps, and they
could spend it in stores there or in such service towns as Logan
and Williamson.

The spread of a cash economy introduced significant changes
in a society where, as on the frontier, money had been a scarce
and valuable item. These changes were generally welcome.

"The entire community was elated at the coming of the saw mills," wrote the labor organizer Fred Mooney of his youth in the rugged Davis Creek section of Kanawha County. " 'There will be plenty of work,' was the general expression." And if the elation later turned to "bitterness and chagrin," as Mooney wrote in reference to his district's reaction to the devastation caused by timber cutting and the low wages paid by the mills, there was usually quite a long interval between the welcome extended to "progress" and the disillusionment that often came in its wake.[4] This interval served to cushion the shock of the changes but it also helped to make them permanent. Once men were accustomed to working for wages and their household economies shifted from barter to cash, there was no going back. The enforced self-sufficiency that had ruled their lives since frontier times gave way to tastes and habits that only the new stores could satisfy, and these could not be sustained by the un-supplemented income of a hill-country farm. If the wages played out or became lower or less dependable than they had been at the start, the young men and women of the backwoods had no choice but to follow the job market as best they could. The frontier had lived on in West Virginia's interior for more than a century, but it had been irreversibly set on the road to extinction by 1900. A great nostalgia for some of its habits and customs welled up in subsequent years, but there was no returning to the old ways, no matter how unpalatable the new industrial frontier might turn out to be.

Some of the greatest and most far-reaching changes of this era had to do with the land itself. Small proprietors found it very tempting to sell land during this period; the backcountry swarmed with small-time promoters and lawyers who collected titles and options to land that they would then try to sell to local or metropolitan capitalists. If small owners sold land as a matter of choice, they preserved the cleared slopes and the little patches of bottomland where their crops grew and sold the steep

4. Fred Mooney, *Struggle in the Coal Fields: The Autobiography of Fred Mooney*, edited by J. William Hess (Morgantown: West Virginia University Library, 1967), pp. 5–6.

hillsides. Concurring with George Washington's judgment of a century earlier, the mountaineers thought the slopes useless except for the hardwoods that clung to their stony soils. The Cincinnati lumber firm of Cole & Crane acquired thousands of acres in the Guyandot watershed from backwoods owners who insisted that the timber buyers take the land with the trees. Later, when the value of the coal underlying the land became apparent, Cole & Crane gradually phased out its lumber business and reorganized into a real estate trust that still earns income from coal and natural gas leases. Another big landholder in this region was Stuart Wood of Philadelphia, who got his start peddling sewing machines in the backwoods districts and taking land in lieu of cash payments. The tradition that nearly every rural West Virginia family seems to have about some ancestor who exhanged his land or its resources for a pittance has an abundant basis in fact.

However, a great many small landowners in West Virginia sold their mineral rights for little or no money because they had to, not because they wanted to. The reason lies in the tangled condition of land titles. West Virginia's land policies were more intelligible and consistent than Virginia's had been, but even though most small proprietors enjoyed a secure title by 1890, proving that title could be an expensive and time-consuming proposition. The overlapping claims and hazy surveys of earlier days meant that an arguable claim could be raised against almost every acre in West Virginia, especially in those interior districts subject to the extravagant grants of the late eighteenth century. Virginia and West Virginia laws forfeiting these grants for nonpayment of taxes had piled thick upon the law books since the 1830s, but claims based on these grants were still worth raising after the timber and mineral value of West Virginia land became apparent. Since the claimants were nearly always nonresidents, the suits they initiated could be transferred to the federal district court. Not only did a federal trial render the suits safe from the prejudices of local communities, but Judge Jackson—who remained the only federal judge in West Virginia from 1861 to 1902—was noted for his tender concern for the rights of nonresident landowners.

The most celebrated suit of this period was brought by Henry C. King, a New Yorker whose claim descended from a 1795 grant of 500,000 acres to Robert Morris of Philadelphia, a grant that embraced most of Logan and Mingo counties and parts of McDowell and Wyoming. From 1893 until 1910, King's litigation occupied state and federal courts, finally reaching the U.S. Supreme Court. All the courts ruled against King in favor of the thousands of proprietors whose titles derived from the forfeiture of Morris's grant. However, King won title to those portions of the Morris tract that, through faulty surveys or other oversights, had been left outside the boundaries of later proprietors, and though much of this was wasteland that no one wanted, some of it held valuable timber and minerals. Moreover, King had acquired thousands of acres during the course of the suit from owners who preferred selling to fighting. Even if the current occupant's title was finally upheld by the courts, as was usually the case, there were lawyers to pay and years of litigation that was complicated and, as far as most people were concerned, mysterious and frightening. Predictably, some mountaineers took down their rifles and fired warning shots across the paths of the new breed of surveyors who appeared in the mountains in the 1880s and 1890s, creating incidents that were often reported by metropolitan newspapers as new repercussions of feuding.

As with the Shawnee a century earlier, however, violent resistance did not save the land. Anse Hatfield and his brother Elias, along with other proprietors who had faith enough in their titles to wait out the lawsuits, lived to enjoy a comfortable old age on the money from coal leases. The average small owner lacked the resources and the patience to wait out the suits, however, and so he was easily tempted by offers of cash or, more commonly, of deals that involved the surrender of his mineral rights. The Philadelphia firm of Low & Aspinwall, claimants to thousands of acres in Wayne, Mingo, and other southwestern counties on the basis of another eighteenth-century grant, dispatched agents throughout the region who offered to exchange quitclaims on the surface of the land for the proprietor's quitclaim on the mineral rights. Most small owners accepted such deals with relief. Metropolitan claimants and their local agents repeated these tactics throughout West Virginia's mineral regions, and the courts invariably upheld their titles. The tragedy was compounded by future developments. Not only did the owners who signed away or sold their mineral rights at this time deprive themselves or their descendants of the minerals' value, the "broadform deeds" that they signed gave the mineral owners rights of access to the minerals by any and all means necessary to their extraction. In 1890 this meant a drift mine opening in a hillside and room for a railroad spur and a tipple, or, in the case of oil or natural gas, a drilling platform that could be hauled into place by horses and wagons. Sixty years later these same deeds allowed modern drilling equipment to do serious damage to agricultural land, while strip-mining altered the contours of mountain slopes and threatened the valleys below.

The forces that transformed life in late-nineteenth-century West Virginia naturally reached far beyond the experience of any one family or region. "Boom" and "development" were everywhere the watchwords. In fact they had been watchwords in such places as Wheeling and Charleston for nearly a generation before the boom actually got under way. Many of West Virginia's founders had been full of the economic disappointments of antebellum times and had hoped that freedom from Virginia was itself a sufficient guarantee of a prosperous future. J. H. Diss Debar, an Alsatian-born land speculator and quasi-official promoter of development during the statehood era, proclaimed to the world in 1870 that West Virginia was bound to be rich. "That such a country . . . so full of the varied treasures of the forest and the mine . . . should lack inhabitants, or the hum of industry, or the show of wealth is an absurdity in the present and an impossibility in the future," Debar exclaimed.[5] To give visual representation to this faith, Debar designed the official state seal to be a talisman of development. A miner and a farmer display their tools on the front, under a banner bearing

5. J. H. Diss Debar, *The West Virginia Handbook and Immigrant's Guide* (Parkersburg, W. Va.: Gibbens Bros., 1870), p. 11.

the motto *Montani semper liberi* (Mountaineers [are] always free), while the obverse features the B & O's Cheat River viaduct portrayed against the backdrop of a mountain sunrise. It is not beside the point to mention here that Debar ended his career in prison, after having been convicted in New York of operating a confidence game.

The actual performance of the state's economy during the first decades after statehood produced further disappointments. The most notable achievement of the early years was the completion of the Chesapeake & Ohio Railroad in 1873. The new road extended westward from the old Virginia Central, which it incorporated, to the Ohio via the Greenbrier River, New River Canyon, the Kanawha, and Teays Valley. Where the C & O struck the Ohio, Collis P. Huntington, the California magnate who had financed the railroad's completion, laid out a new city in 1871, created a land company to sell lots and promote settlement, and named it in honor of himself. At Charleston, however, the railroad failed to set off a long-anticipated "Kanawha boom." The national economic depression that began in 1873, and a remote management interested more in transcontinental railroad strategy than in developing the C & O's local traffic retarded growth in the Kanawha region. As the town of Charleston languished, the state capital returned to Wheeling in 1875 and stayed there until a referendum sent it back to Charleston ten years later.

Notwithstanding the C & O's completion, railroad construction in West Virginia did not keep pace with the national rate of expansion during the 1870s, while the 1880 census showed stagnation in other areas. "When the war ended, it was confidently expected that West Virginia would advance in population and wealth more rapidly than any other state. But she has not done so," wrote the West Virginia Tax Commission of 1884. The commission could not agree as to the cause of the lag, but it already knew by heart a promotional litany that West Virginia boosters have recited since the days of Debar.

Situated near the capital of the United States, within the very heart of the population and wealth of this country, with a good climate, richer in minerals than the same area anywhere else, with all her timber and all her coal then untouched, she offered to enterprise and to capital by far the most inviting field on this continent . . . considering our great and peculiar advantages, this State has not progressed one half as much as she ought to have done.[6]

During the 1880s, however, the boom finally arrived, thanks to a number of factors. One was a return of prosperity in the nation and particularly in the burgeoning cities of the East and Midwest, where a construction and urban utilities boom called for the delivery of immense amounts of lumber and coal to markets within easy range of West Virginia producers. Originally it was thought that the coal could be combined with iron ore deposits found in the mountains along the Virginia-West Virginia border to form the basis of a new steel-producing region; the ore turned out to be of a disappointingly low grade, but the coal found a market anyway as the nation's urban-industrial complex expanded. Another stimulus was the appearance of a new trunk-line railroad extending from Chesapeake Bay to the Ohio, called the Norfolk & Western Railway, and the replacement of older B & O and C & O managements by officials determined to increase the coal traffic over these lines. There were also technological breakthroughs in the lumber industry: The band sawmill and the geared locomotive both appeared in West Virginia around 1880. Band mills tripled and even quadrupled the capacity of the older circular mills, while the new locomotive made possible the hauling of logs in quantity over inexpensive tramways and so greatly increased the potential range of logging operations in mountainous regions. Finally, there is some evidence of a postwar "baby boom" in the Appalachian states, which brought to maturity in the mid-1880s a new generation of workers whose numbers greatly exceeded the capacity of the available agricultural land in the highlands and who, therefore, were eager to find work in the new industries that pressed upward into the hills. Native workers were augmented by European immigrant labor and by blacks who moved

6. West Virginia Tax Commission, *Preliminary Report* (Wheeling: C. H. Taney, 1884), p. 4.

north from Virginia and North Carolina. Native whites still constituted ninety-three percent of the population in 1890, but this figure would decline to eighty-three percent by 1910.

The lumber industry led the advancing boom in districts close to the major rivers or along streams, such as the Greenbrier, Cheat, Elk, Gauley, and Guyandot, where logs could be felled and rafted out to the railheads during spring floods. But the most spectacular changes came about as coal, lumbering, and railroads expanded in concert. The sudden and drastic transformation of the valleys flanking Flat Top Mountain in the extreme southern part of the state was due to the interrelated efforts of Virginia promoters, Pennsylvania investors, and black and immigrant workers who came to supplement the native white work force. The greatest achievement of this team was the Norfolk & Western, created from a heterogeneous collection of Virginia railroads, including the Tennessee Railroad of Civil War fame. Reorganized under the leadership of Philadelphia investors during the early 1880s, the N & W pointed itself away from Tennessee, built northward toward the Ohio, and began to specialize in coal traffic generated by operators who leased their land from another Philadelphia syndicate, the Flat Top Land Association, owners of a 600,000-acre tract derived from eighteenth-century grants. Almost overnight the N & W called into being the cities of Bluefield in the Bluestone region and Welch on the upper Tug Fork, along with dozens of smaller places. By 1888, when national attention was focused on the Hatfields and McCoys, N & W surveyors were combing the length of the feud region, with land, timber, and coal prospectors not far behind. Two years later construction crews were at work, townsites and coal camps were being platted, and whiskey was being sold ''at the mouth of every ravine along the line,'' according to the *Banner*, Logan Court House's new newspaper.[7] In 1891 a syndicate of Huntington, Charleston, and Kentucky businessmen laid out the new town of Williamson on the Tug Fork opposite the mouth of Pond Creek, whose headwaters held the McCoy stronghold. By 1893 Williamson had two hotels, a bank, and a

---

7. Quoted in Cubby, "Transformation of the Tug and Guyandot Valleys," p. 163.

newspaper; and smaller towns were springing up all around it, including Matewan near the site made famous by Ellison Hatfield's death and his murderers' execution a scant decade earlier. Meanwhile another Pennsylvanian William M. Ritter established a series of circular and band sawmills along the N & W, beginning at Oakvale in Mercer County in 1890. By the time the railroad reached Huntington and made connections with the midwestern rail network in 1895, Ritter's operations had entered the Tug Fork watershed and were on the way to making the firm the country's largest producer of Appalachian hardwoods. Other lumbering operations were started by the coal firms themselves, who used the timber for mine supports and railroad ties and to build miners' houses, warehouses, and stores.

Similar developments emerged during the 1880s in the upper Kanawha and New River districts traversed by the C & O and in the Greenbrier Valley, where timbermen harvested white pine to feed a giant new band mill established at Ronceverte in 1884. Farther north the B & O became the jumping-off place for feeder railroads penetrating southward into the interior. The West Virginia Central Railroad, which inched its way south along the eastern border between 1880 and 1900, formed the backbone of a family empire developed by Henry G. Davis, a shrewd and taciturn Baltimorean, and his son-in-law, Stephen B. Elkins, a territorial politician and land speculator from New Mexico who settled in New York after his marriage to Hallie Davis in 1875. On the opposite side of the state another north-south railroad was developed by Johnson N. Camden of Parkersburg, who built the Ohio River Railroad from Wheeling to Huntington with profits earned in the oil industry. Camden's West Virginia & Pittsburgh Railroad, started in 1879, extended south from Clarksburg toward the timber resources of the upper Monongahela, Elk, and Gauley watersheds; his Monongahela River Railroad led in the opposite direction, opening another north-south corridor and tapping important new coal deposits in the Clarksburg-Fairmont region, which Camden helped to develop in partnership with James O. and Clarence W. Watson of Fairmont. The modern Consolidation Coal Company traces one of its ancestral lines back to mines that Camden and the Watsons opened in 1886. Davis and Elkins were also active in the central interior and gave Charleston its most direct access to the B & O region with their Coal & Coke Railroad, completed in 1906. In the south, Henry H. Rogers of New York, one of Camden's Standard Oil Company associates, extended his Virginian Railway from the Kanawha across the coal-rich plateau drained by the New and Guyandot rivers to Flat Top Mountain, where the road turned eastward toward the seaboard along a line engineered to take advantage of the fall in altitude from the coalfields to the ports. Except for branches developed by the trunk lines, the Virginian's completion closed the era of railroad building in 1910.

There were some less spectacular but equally important developments in other industries during this era. Petroleum and natural-gas production spread rapidly during the 1890s, producing oil booms in the Sistersville and Mannington districts, although these had generally less effect on population and transportation patterns than other extractive industries. The Northern Panhandle's steel, glass, and pottery industries expanded in step with those of neighboring Ohio and Pennsylvania and provided an important stimulus to coal mining in the Wheeling hinterland. Charleston, Huntington, Clarksburg, and Parkersburg attracted service industries related to the coal and lumber boom, along with some processing industries such as the manufacture of staves, handles, packing crates, and planing-mill products; Charleston, Huntington, and Point Pleasant also developed boatyards. A fuller assessment of the age would find abundant evidence of modernization in agriculture as well as in industry, but in the long run the most important changes were the most remarkable ones. The transformation of the interior shifted the centers of population and wealth in West Virginia away from the northern and western edges of the state toward the central and southern counties, while extension of the rail network gave the state a geographic unity that it had never known before. These developments led to other shifts as people moved to towns from the country and from the older agricultural towns to the new industrial centers. Although West Virginia was only thirteen percent urban according to the census definition in 1900, nearly all of the new settlements that grew up around coal mines, sawmills, and tanneries were urban in their conditions of life if not in their size. The face of the land changed even more drastically. People rarely failed to notice the novelty of locomotives whistling in once-lonely valleys and the rise of coal towns in hollows where men had never lived before. The greatest change of all, however, was the disappearance of the Appalachian forest. Men had been hacking at the forest since pioneer times, of course, but as late as 1870 there were at least ten million acres of virgin forest in West Virginia, covering nearly two-thirds of the state's surface. In 1900 this figure had been reduced by half; in 1910, by more than four-fifths. The virgin forest was gone by 1920. In its place were many acres of welcome new pasture lands, but more typical was a stubble of stumps and culls that naturally gave birth to a less valuable and less attractive second growth. In the unluckiest places, such as the high-altitude plateaus and canyons around Blackwater Falls, visitors saw blackened wastelands where the fires that nearly always followed the lumbermen and their locomotives had swept across the cutover debris and burned down through the centuries' accumulation of humus to the rocky subsoil beneath. For the first time in its history, West Virginia came to be thought of as a place of ugliness as well as of beauty.

"The change, apparent to ordinary persons, was in the material development, in the mode of education, in roads and cities and farms, but underlying this change and not so well apparent was the real change, which was the political change." So wrote William A. MacCorkle, governor of West Virginia from 1893 to 1897 and a man who knew what he was talking about. "I mean political in a very wide sense," the governor added.[8] It was less a change of party loyalties, although the Republicans benefited sufficiently to reclaim control of the state in the elec-

8. William A. MacCorkle, *Recollections of Fifty Years of West Virginia* (New York: G. P. Putnam's Sons, 1928), p. 193.

tions of 1894 and 1896. The essential differences lay in the way party loyalties were formed and exercised, in the cost and character of election campaigns, and in the types of leaders who were most successful. The cumulative effect of these changes was to move West Virginia beyond the preindustrial political culture with its regional networks of kinship and influence to a modern politics dominated by pressure groups, mass media, and professional organization. The day of the circuit rider yielded to the day of the boss.

At the head of the new political order were West Virginia's leading industrialists, Camden and Davis, who were Democrats, and Elkins, a Republican who transferred his political address from New Mexico to West Virginia during the campaign of 1888. While each of these men had different reasons for embarking upon political careers in the first place, their sustained interest in politics derived from their business enterprises. They were not so much concerned with the impact of local government—there were always plenty of smaller fry who were eager to serve, indeed to anticipate, the political needs of their West Virginia firms. But all three were involved in business projects that stretched far beyond the boundaries of a single state and so were vitally interested in national economic policies, particularly with tariff policies that had an important bearing on prices and markets for timber, petroleum products, and bituminous coal. The United States Senate was an advantageous point from which to intervene in national politics and it had the further appeal of being a prestigious office that did not require aspirants to seek a stamp of popular approval, since the state legislature continued to choose senators until 1915. To become senators, the industrialists had to intervene in local legislative elections all over West Virginia. Thus their exertions gave them a statewide perspective and influence notwithstanding their national focus. In effect, two of every three legislative elections under this system became senatorial canvasses. The ex-Confederate "redeemers" who competed with Camden and Davis during the 1870s had never thought of seeking senatorial seats in this way, and even after it became a standard practice, few other candidates could afford to. Among the other states of the Union,

only Nevada matched the extent to which West Virginia supplied the Senate with millionaire businessmen during these
years.

When Davis first appeared in West Virginia politics after the
Civil War, it was as lobbyist for the B & O and his own enterprises. He carried a supply of railroad passes "for friends"
and found that members of all parties and factions were eager
to have the free train rides.[9] When he bid for the senatorship in
1871, however, there were cries of scorn and surprise, for the
inarticulate and businesslike Davis affronted traditional Virginia
notions of statesmanship. The same scorn often dogged Camden, though he had a more polished air and a distinguished family background. Neither man was an effective speaker on the
platform or in debate, but both Camden and Davis could buy
newspapers and newspaper editors whose polishing lent their
ideas an eloquence in print that they failed to project in person.
They also had on tap what contemporary political slang called a
"barrel." Besides the ubiquitous railroad passes, the barrels
held campaign contributions, private loans to politicians and editors, legal jobs and other forms of private patronage generated
by the industrialists' firms, plus assorted incidental favors such
as the free carload of coal with which Camden annually provi-
sioned Judge Jackson. Another valuable form of private patronage was the tycoons' ability to place small investments with
key followers who were engaged in banking, insurance, or local
development projects in various places in West Virginia. Partly
for this reason, Davis and Elkins acquired stock in more than
twenty West Virginia banks. They also provided local developers with personal introductions to metropolitan suppliers of
capital. The local men were usually only too happy to do favors
for the industrialists in return, just as Camden, Davis, and
Elkins often ran errands in Washington for such national business leaders as John D. Rockefeller, Andrew Carnegie, and
Collis P. Huntington.

Behind the industrialists' rise to power lay some important

9. Henry G. Davis to John King, June 15, 1868, Henry Gassaway Davis Papers,
WVU, series 1, box 1, letterbook 1.

changes in voter behavior and political organization. In districts that had not yet been affected by the industrial boom, political alignments still derived from the Civil War. Here traditional speeches and ''a little whiskey [for] our *hill* people'' sufficed to ''get out the vote,'' since historic party allegiances and the influence of extended families invariably produced lopsided margins for one party or the other.[10] Such districts grew fewer and fewer as industrialism advanced. An influx of new jobs and people into a given district always increased the strength of the minority party, brought partisan balances closer to equality (unless the newcomers greatly outnumbered the old residents, in which case party balances changed drastically, as happened in Tucker and McDowell counties), and increased the potential payoff in campaigns of persuasion that attempted to reach critical groups of swing voters. Since the most dramatic changes took place in the previously Democratic interior, industrial growth and population redistribution tended to favor the GOP although there were a few districts where the reverse was true. Swing voters were also of increasing importance in the state's largest cities, where they were probably as much a product of growing sophistication as of industrial change. As the predictability of voters diminished, the cost of campaigning climbed; politicians bent every effort to reach the critical groups that might decide an election. Whether the methods of persuasion employed were legal or illegal, rising costs increased the weight of the industrialists' barrel.

Politics also became an increasingly specialized activity, as did other areas of endeavor during this period. Professional politicians were much more dependent upon a steady supply of jobs and campaign funds than the gentlemen-politicos of preindustrial times. Professional politicians also made it their business to control the permanently functioning party machinery that both Democrats and Republicans set up after the Civil War, and since the industrialists were the most accessible source of the funds needed to keep this machinery turning, here was another

10. J. V. Cunningham to Johnson N. Camden, September 22, 1894, Johnson N. Camden Papers, WVU, box ''1894-Politics,'' folder C.

boost to their influence. Although Davis and Camden were often stymied by factionalism within the Democratic party, they controlled the Democratic state committee throughout this period. Since this committee decided when and where conventions that nominated candidates for statewide office would meet and distributed campaign funds that came from the national party, it was a considerable source of leverage. Jointly or singly, Davis and Camden themselves represented West Virginia Democrats at all but two of the national party conventions held between 1868 and 1908. One of the first things Elkins did after he took over the West Virginia Republican party was to replace the state chairman, George W. Atkinson, with his own man, William M. O. Dawson of Kingwood, who was regarded by other politicians of his day as a professional's professional. During the campaign of 1892, Dawson gave the GOP its first thorough campaign organization extending from the state to the precinct level. When the party swept into power in 1896, Atkinson won the office of governor, but Elkins made sure that Dawson went with him to Charleston in the lucrative and politically sensitive post of secretary of state. There Dawson introduced another innovation, using the party legislative caucus—which previously had been important only in senatorial matters—as an instrument for formulating and expediting bills.

These changes in the political process introduced costly and recurrent activities that could be sustained in only two ways: through the money supplied by rich contributors like Camden, Davis, and Elkins, or through the services and cash contributions exacted from government workers as a condition of their employment. During the nineteenth century, the federal government was the primary source of patronage. Camden generally managed to control the distribution of federal jobs during the two Cleveland administrations, while Elkins enjoyed a similar privilege under Presidents Harrison, McKinley, Theodore Roosevelt, and Taft. Without this advantage, Elkins's conquest of West Virginia Republicans would have been neither as swift nor as bloodless as it was. Atkinson, for example, had little sympathy for Elkins or his organization, and the feeling was mutual. The governor longed for a federal judgeship, however, and so by dangling the job like a carrot on a stick, Elkins was able to keep him in line for a decade before Atkinson finally ascended the bench in 1905.

"I had not the remotest idea that every man, woman, and child in West Virginia wanted a government position, but I believe they do," wrote the Wheeling industrialist Nathan B. Scott when he became Elkins's junior Republican colleague in the Senate in 1899.[11] Scott exaggerated West Virginians' office hunger, but not by much. Public employment had become an informal welfare system for the poor and unfortunate, at least for unfortunates who held the proper party credentials. But government jobs also appealed to young men on their way up, to mature men seeking a new career, to the widows and heirs of earlier officeholders, and to just about anyone who desired a steadier income or a fresh start in life. Job seekers came from every level of society and generated humor as well as pathos in their quest. "He wants an office very, very, very bad," Dawson remarked of a Charleston lawyer in 1900. "I can't make it any *badder* than it is; and he wants it instanter . . . a Judgeship, district attorneyship, or a Marshalship, or any old thing." [12]

To a significant extent, the scramble for office reflected the incomplete nature of West Virginia's industrialization. Extractive industries created disproportionately few managerial positions, with the result that aspiring professional men and other white-collar workers who could not land a railroad or coal-company job had to turn to the government. "The bar is crowded and the business is small," remarked a Morgantown lawyer of his quest for patronage.[13] As for wage earners, mining and lumbering jobs were seasonal in character and even railroad employment was affected by the seasonal rise and fall of demand in the coal industry. In addition, every industry was affected by the cycle of boom and bust in the national economy. Govern-

11. Nathan B. Scott to A. B. White, February 18, 1899, A. B. White Papers, WVU, box 3.

12. William M. O. Dawson to Stephen B. Elkins, April 23, 1900, Stephen B. Elkins Papers, WVU, box 7.

13. John M. Hagans to Waitman T. Willey, March 21, 1881, Willey Papers, WVU, box 3.

ment jobs did not always pay as well, but they had the advantage of being steadier, easier, and safer. On the state as well as the federal level, the number of applicants for even very minor positions always outran the demand. MacCorkle received 3,760 applications for around one hundred jobs when he took office in 1893, for example. When state jobs were scarce, the politicians guarded them jealously. In 1897 West Virginia University brought in a bright young president from one of the innovative new universities of the Midwest who began hiring professors on the basis of academic credentials instead of political recommendations. Legislators were almost unanimous in their outrage at this departure and in 1901 voted to withhold the university's appropriation until the offending president was replaced by someone more attuned to West Virginia realities. During the subsequent decade, when all manner of "progressive" proposals for reforming state government were under debate, advocates of civil-service reform were conspicuously lacking in West Virginia. "I am perfectly willing to go into the fight and do all I can actively," wrote a West Virginia member of Theodore Roosevelt's Progressive Party in 1912, "but should our side win, then I want something for it. I have always been . . . bitterly opposed to Civil Service." [14] Government programs adopted in West Virginia after 1880, whatever their purpose, invariably had one thing in common: They increased the number of political jobs.

During the nineteenth century, West Virginia had no large state or municipal bureaucracy that might have served as a counterweight to the senators' control of federal patronage. With the growth of population and public business, this began to change. Already the traditional prizes of courthouse politics, especially the fees that clerks and sheriffs collected, were fat enough in some counties to sustain local political organizations with which statewide leaders were forced to reckon. Kanawha County, for example, generated a Democratic "Kanawha Ring," headed by a group of Charleston lawyers—MacCorkle,

14. C. A. Swearingen to William E. Glasscock, February 10, 1912, William E. Glasscock Papers, WVU, box 20.

John E. Kenna, Cornelius C. Watts, and William E. Chilton—who were able to bargain from strength with Davis and Camden. When Republicans took over the county during the 1890s, a similar organization emerged called the "Hog Combine." It became an important component in the Elkins machine. The largest growth in local jobs came later, however, with the expansion of school, highway, and other public-service programs. For the time being, interest in patronage centered upon the federal payrolls and this strengthened the hands of the industrialists. They had the jobs to dispense and were free in their own private lives from the insecurity that led so many West Virginians to seek them.

Under these circumstances most West Virginia politicians active between 1880 and 1910 made some sort of accommodation with Davis and Camden or Elkins. The only important exceptions were both named Wilson. Representative William L. Wilson, who became a prominent and admired figure in national Democratic circles during these years, worked well with Camden, but Davis mistrusted Wilson on the tariff issue. After relations between the two became openly hostile during the passage of the Wilson-Gorman tariff of 1894, Davis joined forces with Elkins's Republicans to help drive Wilson from office. After 1894 West Virginia's congressional delegation was known collectively as "Elkins's Orphans."

The second Wilson, a distant cousin of the first, was E. Willis Wilson, a fiery but humorless orator who, in 1884, rode a wave of farmer discontent over taxes into the governorship. In 1887 he managed to gather a mixed bag of twelve maverick legislators who, by the use of filibustering tactics, blocked Camden's re-election to the Senate. But the tactic rebounded against Wilson, and a year later the Democrats were under Camden's control more tightly than ever. The 1888 convention nominated the industrialists' handpicked candidate for governor, A. Brooks Fleming of Fairmont, a corporation lawyer and business associate of Camden. His election inaugurated a string of six West Virginia governors who were either picked directly by one or more of the industrialists or who, like MacCorkle and Atkinson, were chosen with their approval after certain understandings were reached. Thus while Governor Wilson raised some important modern issues, such as mining and railroad regulation and fiscal reform, his administration was really the last stand of the traditional politics. Wilson "was not a good organizer of a machine," MacCorkle explained. "His great forte was in getting hold of the people at mass meetings. Of course this plan was good at times but very ineffective in later-day ideas of politics." [15]

We have come a long way from the Hatfield-McCoy feud, but not so far as it might seem. There are two connections between the feud and the political changes of this era. One is the change in governors from Wilson to Fleming, which had a direct bearing on the end of the feud. The other is the background of Henry D. Hatfield, one of the major figures of twentieth-century West Virginia politics. The place to start exploring both these connections is with a Logan County patriarch named George Rogers Clark Floyd. It goes without saying that in 1888 this 78-year-old gentleman was known by the title of Colonel.

Colonel Floyd's grandfather had surveyed along the Kanawha and Ohio and had also been at Point Pleasant in 1774; his father had been governor of Virginia and so had his brother. His great-grandson would become one of the more celebrated county political bosses in West Virginia during the 1960s. Floyd himself was not celebrated at all, in his day or later, but he had been touched by many of the changes that occurred in his lifetime. He had come to the Tug Fork Valley in 1853. The region was well known to his family from earlier hunting expeditions, and he was seeking a new start after disappointments in the West. Floyd quickly became Logan County's largest resident landowner, patenting some 20,000 acres in the county by 1860, together with other large acreages in nearby Kentucky. Most of the land was gone by 1880, sold for debts to speculators like Stuart Wood, the sewing-machine salesman, but Floyd retained other attributes of preindustrial traditions of leadership. One was an aristocrat's passion for learning. As grandchildren recalled it,

15. MacCorkle, *Recollections,* p. 101.

his library lined the walls of one room in the four-room log house where he spent his last years. He also saw to it that, no matter how poorly, even primitively, his family lived back in the hills, his children got a good education. The girls went to convent school in Wheeling, the boys to colleges in Virginia and Maryland. Another attribute was political influence, not the sort that derived from a machine but from his standing as "first among equals" among the Logan backwoodsmen. Floyd had been the first Democrat elected to the legislature by Logan County after ex-Confederate political rights were restored in 1871, and he remained as its first delegate under the new constitution in 1872. In 1880 this influence had passed on to his eldest son, John B. Floyd, who entered the House of Delegates at the age of 25 and two years later went on to the state senate. A reporter who accompanied the younger Floyd to Anse Hatfield's Island Creek stronghold in 1888 wrote that Floyd had "the absolute confidence of all the people of this region." [16] This turned out to be something of an exaggeration, but it is evident that the Floyds retained the confidence of the Hatfields, and for very good reasons.

It was John B. Floyd who linked the gubernatorial politics of the 1880s with the Hatfield-McCoy feud. While in the legislature, Floyd had befriended E. Willis Wilson and had helped to swing Logan County behind his gubernatorial candidacy in 1884. Consequently he went along when Wilson entered the statehouse, becoming assistant secretary of state in 1885. It was in this capacity that he extended his protection over the Hatfields when Kentucky demanded their extradition in 1887, and it was he, also, who persuaded the governor to issue warrants and rewards for the capture of the raiders who harassed the feudists that winter. Anse Hatfield's gratitude was expressed in the name of the eighth of his nine sons; born just a month after the New Year's Night raid of 1888, the child was named E. Willis Wilson Hatfield, or informally, Willis. The accolade turned out to

16. T. C. Crawford, "An American Vendetta," reprinted in Jim Comstock and Bronson McClung, eds., *West Virginia Heritage* (Richwood, W. Va.: West Virginia Heritage Foundation, 1969), p. 25.

be somewhat premature. Like Anse, the people might still follow Wilson and Floyd, but in the county conventions where political decisions were made, industrious lobbying by Kanawha Ring lawyers supplied from Camden's barrel had already captured Logan County for Camden. In 1886 the county's seat in the House of Delegates went to H. Clay Ragland, a relative newcomer and ardent promoter of development whose Democratic principles were characterized by Colonel George R. C. Floyd as those of a tomtit, a bird that could peck with equal facility whether its tail was pointing uphill or down. The state senator elected from the Logan district was a lawyer affiliated with the Kanawha Ring; in the senatorial contest of 1887, both he and Ragland sided with Camden. After another local struggle the following year, Logan sent a Democratic state convention delegation composed of ''all our friends,'' as a Camden man put it.[17] John B. Floyd made a feeble effort to oppose Fleming's nomination for governor, but the Camden organization simply brushed him aside. A few years later, he switched to the Republican party and tried with no better success to challenge the Elkins machine. Like many minor politicians of the day who struggled to keep abreast of shifting political currents, Floyd gradually sank out of sight.

Still Floyd managed to stay afloat long enough to be of real value to his most famous constituents. The added weight of Elkins's barrel on the GOP side made the election of 1888 the closest in West Virginia history and, though the Democrats retained a narrow edge in the legislature, it took them over a year to arrange a convincing recount in the gubernatorial race. As a result, Wilson and Floyd got an extra year in their offices. When Fleming took over in February 1890, the Hatfields' official protection in West Virginia came to an end, but the memories of the New Year's Night raid had faded considerably. Thus when Fleming dismissed Floyd and initiated contacts with Kentucky officials looking toward a settlement of the feud's interstate repercussions, the results were not as drastic for the Hat-

17. B. H. Oxley to Johnson N. Camden, July 5, 1888, A. B. Fleming Papers, WVU, box 14.

fields as they might otherwise have been. Ellison Mounts had already been hanged in Kentucky, but he was only an illegitimate relation and was a half-wit to boot. By September Fleming had withdrawn Wilson's rewards and extradition warrants against the Kentucky raiders, and newspapers in both states were discussing an end to the feud. The general understanding seems to have been that while the indictments would remain on the books, feudists on both sides of the border would be left unmolested by authorities so long as they behaved themselves. And they were ready to behave. Early in 1891, Anse Hatfield sent word to the press through his son Cap that "The war spirit in me has abated, and I sincerely rejoice at the prospect of peace." [18] Locally the growth of mining and population along the N & W's Tug Fork extension led to demands for the division of Logan County, which was finally done when the legislature created Mingo County in 1895. The new local officials were more attuned to the needs of the mining communities than to the traditional networks of influence on which the Hatfields had relied. When Cap Hatfield got involved in another election-day shooting in 1896, he found himself spending some time in the new Williamson jail.

Other members of the Hatfield family made better terms with the new age. While some of Anse's sons continued to lead turbulent lives, most of the younger generation settled down to respectable modes of existence. Unlike many of their less prominent neighbors, Hatfields tended to wear white collars in the industrial era. Johnse became a land agent for the Island Creek Coal Company, for example; young Willis, after a youthful brush with the law, also went to work for a coal firm. Joe, another of the younger sons, became the first Republican sheriff of Logan County in 1924 and, despite the generally scandalous character of his term, was succeeded in office by another brother Tennyson Hatfield ("Tennis"). Among the sons of Anse's brother Elias, Greenway Hatfield shook off his early reputation as a moonshiner and feudist to become a deputy U.S. marshal and a three-term sheriff of Mingo County, where during

18. Quoted in Jones, *Hatfields and McCoys* p. 192.

the 1920s his sons supplied Williamson with its postmaster, jailer, and mayor. Other Hatfields on the public payroll by this time included county officials in McDowell County along with an assortment of lesser functionaries—such as school-bus drivers and state policemen—scattered all over southwestern West Virginia. As for Anse, he got religion in his old age, as patriarchs often do who have enjoyed themselves in their prime, and died quietly, surrounded by his generations at his log house on Island Creek in 1921. His survivors erected an imposing Italian-marble monument over his grave.

The best terms of all were those won by Henry D. Hatfield, the second son of Elias. Henry had been a child of seven when the feud began, but if he retained many memories of the time when his father and brother and cousins went everywhere armed and always sat where they could face a room's windows and doorways, he had little to say about these memories except to claim for himself "all the courage of his feudist kinsman [*sic*] of an earlier day." [19] His most interesting memories of youth centered upon Colonel George Rogers Clark Floyd. After Elias moved his family away from the Tug Fork to safer quarters near Logan Court House, young Henry became something of a pet of the old colonel. He visited him nearly every day and often tagged along when the old man went to the village to pick up his mail and to talk politics with the men who gathered in front of the post office. Hatfield did not imbibe Colonel Floyd's Jeffersonian principles; like other members of his generation, he abandoned the ancestral Democratic party for the Republicanism of McCoys. But Hatfield did absorb the Colonel's fondness for learning and later credited the old man with starting him out on a quest that took him out of the backwoods while still in his teens, first to college in Ohio, then to medical school in Louisville. In 1895 young Hatfield returned to the Mingo County village of Thacker, not far from his birthplace on Mate Creek. Here he embarked upon a political as well as a medical career.

If Dr. Hatfield credited his start in life to the traditional system of backwoods patronage as represented by old Colonel

---

19. Draft manuscript, Henry Drury Hatfield Papers, WVU, series 1, box 12.

Floyd, his later success owed to his understanding of the modern system. His first job was with the Norfolk & Western, which he served as a company doctor until 1913 while simultaneously holding a number of political posts. In 1895 he secured the job of health commissioner in the new Mingo County government. Four years later he moved up the valley and became director and chief surgeon of a newly established state hospital for miners at Welch. He became a member of the McDowell County Court in 1906 at a time when this body was the envy of every professional politician in West Virginia because of its control over the lucrative saloon-licensing business in thirsty mining communities and also the huge Republican majorities regularly turned out by the county's five thousand black miners. In 1908 Hatfield went to the state senate, where he quickly came to Elkins's attention by opposing Prohibition and the direct election of U.S. senators, two things that were not high on Elkins's list. Soon Elkins was urging his lieutenants to "get closer to Senator Hatfield," [20] But Hatfield did not need Elkins to tap him for leadership; he tapped himself. It was an opportune time for a new man. During the campaign of 1910 the West Virginia Republican party became entangled in a vortex of factional conflicts, some of them local in origin, others national, and Elkins, dying of cancer, was no longer able to hold the party together. In the disorganization that followed Elkins's death and the division of the national party into progressive and conservative wings, Hatfield was able to present himself to voters and to party professionals who were preoccupied with the national conflict as a leader free of factional commitments but one who was wholeheartedly devoted to the spoils system, as the doctor took every occasion to emphasize. Given the distinctive combination of his professional status and his celebrated family name, Hatfield made an attractive gubernatorial prospect. Taking on two more experienced candidates in the state's first primary in June 1912, Hatfield trounced his rivals easily and went on to become West Virginia's fourteenth governor in the fall election. He was then 37 years old.

20. Stephen B. Elkins to William E. Glasscock, July 7, 1910, Elkins Papers, WVU, box 9.

Hatfield was not the youngest governor ever elected in West Virginia, but he was the first to have been born in the state after its admission to the Union in 1863, and he was fitted in other ways to preside over its fiftieth birthday celebration in 1913. He had come to maturity with a new generation of middlemen who linked the people and resources of West Virginia to the distant centers of wealth and power where the owners of those resources lived. Like the land lawyers of Colonel Floyd's youth, Hatfield's power combined both the influence of an extended family and his mastery of the system of political patronage that prevailed in his day. The antebellum leadership of western Virginia had used its control of the local political system to assert control over absentee-owned resources, which in preindustrial times primarily consisted of wilderness land. The Civil War, the dearth of local development capital, the work of the federal courts and of local leaders who were content to serve only as middlemen, had negated much of this achievement. By 1900 the largest part of West Virginia's resources was again subject to absentee ownership. Governor Hatfield and other leaders of the "progressive era" in West Virginia attempted by various means to reassert local control over these resources. The resistance they encountered was much more bitter than that preindustrial leaders had met. Unfortunately for West Virginia's future, it was also much more successful.

5

Paint Creek

*O*n March 5, 1913, his first full day in office, Governor Henry D. Hatfield got up early and slipped out of Charleston on an eastbound C & O train. He traveled alone and carried only the small black bag that identified him as a medical man. Carrying his doctor's kit was more than a practical gesture, for Hatfield wanted to heal in both the literal and figurative senses of the word. In common with many American public men in this "progressive era," he believed that it was government's duty to search out and hold middle ground between the contending interest groups, such as business and labor, that modern industrial society had spawned. In states where the conflicts between these groups were sufficiently manageable, the progressive spirit led to an impressive array of reforms. But West Virginia was different. Hatfield soon found that the middle ground between the forces contending for control of the state's new industrial economy was as narrow as the labyrinthine valleys where some of the bitterest conflicts were fought.

Hatfield journeyed toward one of these industrial battlegrounds on his postinaugural tour. Paint Creek and Cabin Creek are neighboring streams that wind northward toward the Kanawha River some 25 miles east of Charleston, carving the interior plateau into characteristic narrow defiles and defining the eastern edge of the Kanawha coalfield. Coal mines lined both valleys in 1913, along with the company-owned hamlets, or camps, that usually clustered nearby. There was also a new type of community along both of the creeks, one that became distressingly familiar in West Virginia as time went on. These were the tent colonies that housed miners and their families who had been evicted from company housing during a strike. The tents that Hatfield saw were of the sturdy military variety, but after a winter of use, the floorboards were greasy with mud, and families who lived in them had grown weary of bundling children into sodden blankets and of cooking on outdoor stoves that smoked and sizzled in the damp West Virginia air. Hatfield found "small pox, diptheria [*sic*], measles and every other conceivable form of disease" in one cluster of tents on Cabin Creek.[1] Conditions in other colonies were nearly as bad.

The doctor's kit came in handy, but the governor's special mission was the healing of social wounds, and these posed a more difficult problem. Paint Creek miners had been on strike for nearly a year when Hatfield took office, their Cabin Creek comrades since the previous summer. At issue were recognition of the union, the United Mine Workers of America (UMWA), and the adoption by Paint Creek and Cabin Creek mine operators of a union contract such as had been in force in other districts of the Kanawha field since 1902. As the strike wore on, however, it grew into a full-fledged mine war. Wholesale evictions from company houses began along Paint Creek in May 1912, accompanied by the importation of strikebreakers and of heavily armed mine guards to protect them and to police the mines and company towns. These developments led to tense confrontations and eventually to violence between strikers and guards. By midsummer of 1912, the surrounding hills routinely echoed the crack of gunfire, even the rattle of machine guns, which the guards posted in ironclad forts they built near some of the company towns. Miners took to the woods where they lay in wait to draw beads on the guards or to fire down into the towns and at trains carrying strikebreakers. The guards manned their forts, patrolled the surrounding woods and pathways, and even armored a train from which they blazed away at one of the tent

1. Memorandum, n.d., Hatfield Papers, WVU, series 1, box 12.

colonies. Governor William E. Glasscock sent National Guard units into the strike zone in July and proclaimed martial law there in September. These measures clamped a lid on the violence as the soldiers confiscated thousands of weapons and set up military courts to deal summarily with persons—usually strikers—accused of violating the governor's proclamations. But each time Glasscock tried to withdraw the Guard, violence flared anew, and so when Hatfield took office, the soldiers were still there, along with the tent colonies. At least twenty and perhaps as many as fifty men had been killed in the mine war by this time.

As Hatfield told the story in later years, he spent two days in the strike zone, treating the sick, consoling the bereaved, and spreading goodwill. One of the patients he treated was the strike's most famous participant, Mary Harris "Mother" Jones. At the age of 83, Mother Jones was a grandmotherly figure with a sweet face and a salty tongue that delighted working-class audiences as much as it offended the guardians of "law and order." Although she had ranged widely across the country during forty years of labor struggles, West Virginia—"Medieval West Virginia!" as she called it [2]—came as close as any place to being her adopted home. She had first come here in 1897, the year of the UMWA's first big organizing drive in the state, and she had returned often. In 1902 she took part in the statewide strike that won the union its first foothold in the Kanawha field, and she was back in 1912 soon after the first shots rang out along Paint Creek. On both occasions corporation lawyers hired stenographers to follow her around, hoping to hear something incendiary. They were not disappointed. But Mother Jones's forte was her ability to dramatize the miners' plight, creating solidarity among the workers and their families and winning support in the world beyond the hills. West Virginia military authorities gave her an even more expansive stage to tread in February 1913, when they seized her on the streets of Charleston and hauled her before a court-martial sitting at Pratt, a

2. Mary H. Jones, *The Autobiography of Mother Jones*, ed. by Mary Field Parton (Chicago: Charles H. Kerr & Company, edn. 1972), p. 235.

railroad junction at the mouth of Paint Creek where military trials were held in a makeshift courtroom in the local Odd Fellows Hall.

Pending trial on charges of conspiring to murder, Mother Jones was held either in "a pleasant boarding house . . . on the banks of the Kanawha River," as Governor Hatfield told inquisitive congressmen in 1913, or in a "plank cottage," as Hatfield recalled the story for a labor audience in 1932.[3] In any case, when the governor visited Mother Jones on March 6, he found her dangerously ill with pneumonia and had her taken to Charleston and placed under medical care. But Hatfield did not set her free as soon as she recovered, as he sometimes claimed in later years. Instead, she went back into custody at Pratt, where she helped fan a growing national controversy over the arbitrary means of her seizure and the obviously trumped-up character of the charges she faced. "I can raise just as much hell in jail as anywhere," Mother Jones told a visiting journalist,[4] and she proved true to her word by winning widespread attention in the press and provoking a debate in Congress over the character and causes of the West Virginia war. Under pressure of this publicity, Hatfield released her from custody on May 8. Mother Jones then embarked on a speaking tour of eastern cities and a lobbying trip to Washington, whence she returned to Charleston a month later, bringing in tow an investigating subcommittee of the United States Senate Committee on Education and Labor. This was the first of many official expeditions from Washington that pried into West Virginia problems local officials would just as soon have kept out of the headlines. Hatfield protested the investigation indignantly but in vain. On the battlefield of public opinion, Mother Jones easily outmaneuvered her captors, which is perhaps why her autobiographical account of the Paint Creek conflict refers to it as a victory for her side.[5]

3. Dale Fetherling, *Mother Jones, The Miners' Angel: A Portrait* (Carbondale: Southern Illinois University Press, 1974), p. 101; "Address of Senator Henry D. Hatfield . . . May 1, 1932," Hatfield Papers, WVU, series 1, box 11.

4. Cora Older, "Answering a Question," *Colliers* 51(April 1913):28.

5. Jones, *Autobiography,* pp. 148–167 *passim.*

Other UMWA leaders were less satisfied with the settlement that Hatfield eventually imposed. Observers who saw Hatfield in action in the strike zone were impressed by his personal goodwill toward the miners and his desire to deal fairly with both sides in the dispute. But like many progressives, the governor tended to pressure the weaker contenders when he was unable to translate his personal goodwill into effective social policy. He initiated negotiations between operators and the union at Charleston on March 13, serving as a go-between because the operators refused to sit down face to face. When these talks failed to produce an agreement, Hatfield issued a unilateral "compromise proposition" on April 14, wherein he proposed to give the miners a nine-hour workday, the right to employ "checkweighmen" to safeguard the calculation of wages, the right to spend wages at places other than company stores, and an amorphous "right to organize" that was unsecured by contract or by any other formal recognition of the union on the operators' part. He also condemned, but provided no sanctions against, the continuing employment of mine guards. It would be presumptuous of him, he explained, to tell the mine owners how to look after their properties.[6] However, he made known his disapproval of the military courts and the numerous and lengthy prison terms they had imposed on the strikers and took credit for the workmen's-compensation bill that the legislature had recently enacted.

Since these proposals offered no real gains for the union, the operators promptly accepted them, but from the union leaders' standpoint the governor's conception of middle ground proved narrow indeed. A nine-hour workday was already common in nonunion mines. The new workmen's-compensation scheme was optional so far as company participation was concerned, and the compensation fund was nearly exhausted by the next big mining disaster. The military courts at Pratt operated in spite of severe restrictions on such courts in the state constitution (a legacy of Confederate and Copperhead anger over the use of courts-martial to try civilians during the Civil War). Then, too,

6. *Charleston Daily Mail,* April 15, 1913.

the safeguards on calculating and spending wages that Hatfield proposed were already written into laws that the operators had freely violated for years. It was a measure of the cynical tradition of West Virginia justice and politics that Hatfield considered it a breakthrough to promise enforcement of laws already on the books, but this gave the union leaders cold comfort. Rank-and-file miners, especially members of the Socialist Party, which had flourished in some coalfield districts in recent years, openly scorned the governor's propositions, but Hatfield refused to negotiate further. Displaying the explosive temper he shared with some of his feudist kinsmen, the governor issued an ultimatum on April 25, telling the UMWA leaders to accept his program or to face draconian measures against the union and themselves. Putting the best interpretation they could on this "Hatfield agreement," the union leaders capitulated. On May 1, the governor was once again touring the strike zone, leading a brace of intimidated union leaders and proclaiming an end to the strike.

In point of fact, the strike sputtered on for another few weeks along Cabin and Paint creeks, fanned by socialist agitators whom Hatfield, true to his threats, sought to harry from the state. Dissatisfaction with the Hatfield agreement was one of the factors that brought a more militant union leadership to the fore in West Virginia in subsequent years, setting the stage for a renewal of the mine wars soon after World War I. But it also helped to give the West Virginia coal industry an interlude of relative calm that bridged the economically uncertain years before the war and carried into a phenomenal wartime boom that sent profits, wages, and the volume of production soaring. Meanwhile, Hatfield gradually withdrew the National Guard from the strike zone, formally suspended the sentences of the military courts, and waited patiently in Charleston as the U.S. Senate investigators accumulated some two thousand pages of testimony on the causes and course of the strike. The senators went back to Washington on June 18, 1913, just in time to allow Governor Hatfield to get up to Wheeling for West Virginia's fiftieth birthday celebration on June 20. As the semicentennial observance got under way, the "war-born state," as

West Virginia patriots sometimes called it, was once more at peace.

It was one of the embarrassments that seem to plague patriotic celebrations in West Virginia that the state's first and bloodiest mine war coincided with its fiftieth anniversary of statehood. The semicentennial observance at Wheeling was the culminating event in a series of jubilees that had begun with the sprouting of Civil War monuments in several communities at the turn of the century. These rituals celebrated the geographic unity that completion of the railroad network brought to West Virginia and expressed the satisfaction of many citizens in the achievements of industrialization. Thus, the semicentennial organizers chose Henry G. Davis, the "Grand Old Man" of West Virginia business and politics, to preside over the festivities, passing over men with a more direct claim to involvement in the achievement of statehood. Governor Hatfield stressed industrial progress in his Wheeling speech, ignoring the industrial problems that had so recently absorbed his attention.

One function of the jubilees was to bolster state pride. As Charles Ambler explained, West Virginia "is unique in that she has few state traditions and little authentic history of the kind out of which state pride and patriotism grow." The bitter divisions that had attended West Virginia's birth had deprived its people of "common heroes." [7] Ambler set out to remedy this situation by writing scholarly monographs and biographies, but most people preferred to pass over what he called "authentic history" in favor of history that contained a large dose of romance. A good example was the celebration that took place at Point Pleasant in 1909, when a committee of boosters dedicated a monument on the battlefield of 1774. Over the protests of Virgil A. Lewis, a local editor and politician who had become the first "state historian" and director of the recently established State Department of Archives and History, the monument sponsors insisted on making the battle something more

7. Charles H. Ambler, "Preface," in Anna Pierpont Siviter, *Recollections of War and Peace, 1861–1868* (New York: G. P. Putnam's Sons, 1938), pp. vii, ix.

than "the chief event of Lord Dunmore's War," as Lewis described it. They wanted state and federal authorities to declare the battle to have been "the first battle of the American Revolution," not by virtue of its diplomatic repercussions but on the basis of an unproven and rather simple-minded notion that Lord Dunmore, peering into the future course of human events to anticipate the Revolution, had somehow conspired with the Indians against the frontiersmen. Lewis managed to keep this "atrociously false" version of "manufactured history" off the monument itself, but he encountered the "first battle" claim everywhere else at Point Pleasant, even on "a banner stretched across the street directly in front of the speakers stand" where he had to sit and stare at it all through the dedication ceremony. "State pride—a love for my native State and that of a long line of ancestry—would naturally prompt me to claim for her all honors to which she is entitled," he wrote dejectedly on his return to Charleston, "but never could I do this at a sacrifice of historic truth." [8]

Lewis obviously missed the point. The jubilees of the "progressive era" in West Virginia had little to do with "historic truth," if by this phrase Lewis meant history as it had actually happened. Rather they celebrated history as people preferred to remember it, as something called "heritage," consisting of events cleansed of their sweat and blood and of historical actors who had lost their power to anger and wound. It is revealing that although the fiftieth anniversary of the Harpers Ferry raid occurred within a week of the Point Pleasant ceremony, the occasion received no official notice in West Virginia. John Brown and the principle of racial equality that his name evoked among black people had not yet become "heritage" as far as whites were concerned.

Another function of the jubilees was to put to rest the sectional animosities left over from the statehood movement and

8. Virgil A. Lewis, "An Explanation to History Students," draft manuscript, October 20, 1909; "An Address to All Students of American History," n.d.; "The Battle of Point Pleasant Not a Battle of the American Revolution," unpublished ms.; all in Virgil A. Lewis Papers, West Virginia Department of Archives and History, Charleston.

the Civil War. The veneration of Stonewall Jackson as a West Virginia hero dates from this period; a statue of Jackson was put in place on the capitol lawn in 1910. A generation earlier angry Union veterans had blocked attempts to honor Jackson officially. Now the only untoward incident occurred when the parade marshal placed a contingent of Virginia Military Institute cadets in line ahead of the national colors, leading the West Virginia National Guard unit to withdraw from the parade in a huff. Another once-controversial figure Francis H. Pierpont was also enshrined in stone in 1910. "West Virginia, child of Freedom! Lift your happy head on high," exclaimed Anna Pierpont Siviter, the state maker's daughter, in a poem written for the occasion. "Truth and justice are your birthright, . . ." [9] ("There is never peace in West Virginia because there is never justice," said Mother Jones.) [10] In a 1913 poem read at the semicentennial observance, Siviter proclaimed without conscious irony that West Virginia was a land of "Peace and plenty," where love now prevailed over the "fierce hatreds" of her father's day. [11]

The truth was, of course, that new hatreds were at large in West Virginia in 1913, hatreds just as fierce and threatening as those of 1863 and just as subversive of the state's pride and its sense of community. Like quarreling families who gather to smile grimly into cameras on birthdays, Hatfield and other speakers at Wheeling might ignore the new divisions, but ignoring them would not drive them away. The Paint Creek strike was not the first outbreak of industrial warfare in the state, but it was the worst thus far, and it was the first to attract nationwide attention. Thus the mine war dealt a double blow to the jubilee mood of 1913. It raised questions about the character of West Virginia's economy that singers of paeans about "progress" were not able to answer, and instead of the positive image that official spokesmen strained to project, it gave the state an "unsavoury reputation," in Governor Hatfield's words, [12] thus rein-

9. Siviter, *Recollections of War and Peace*, p. 367.
10. Jones, *Autobiography*, p. 234.
11. Siviter, *Recollections of War and Peace*, p. 367.
12. *Charleston Daily Mail*, April 15, 1913.

forcing the defensive posture that was one of the less fortunate legacies of statehood days.

An adequate assessment of the economic and social ills that plagued West Virginia through much of the twentieth century must begin with the coal industry and the peculiar types of communities that it spread through this and other Appalachian states. In some parts of the country coal mining developed slowly in the midst of established communities that cushioned some of the industry's social impacts. This was true of the Northern Panhandle and, to a lesser extent, of parts of the Monongahela Valley. Elsewhere in West Virginia, however, mining developed in precisely those rugged interior districts that had been least attractive to agricultural settlement. Consequently, coal operators had no choice but to build their own towns. A federal study completed in 1924 showed that around eighty percent of West Virginia miners lived in company-owned communities, compared with sixty-four percent in Kentucky and nine percent in Indiana and Illinois. In southern West Virginia the proportion was even higher.

The coal towns were a total social environment, one that involved workers and employers in many daily transactions besides those involved in the digging of coal. "Thus the operators are not only the miner's employer," wrote Winthrop Lane, a journalist whose *Civil War in West Virginia* sought to interpret the mine wars to metropolitan audiences in 1921; "they are his landlord, his merchant, the provider of his amusements, the sanitary officer of his town, sometimes the source of his police protection and the patron of his physician, his minister, and his schoolteacher." [13] The transactions that rankled most involved housing and the company stores. The miner's inability to own his own home or even to enjoy the security available to other classes of tenants in West Virginia denied him one of the most deeply cherished dreams of American workingmen. The stores were notoriously exploitative, and even the minority that tried to

13. Winthrop D. Lane, *Civil War in West Virginia* (1921; reprinted New York: The Arno Press, 1969), p. 17.

deal fairly with consumers passed along the higher overhead costs and narrower selections that the distribution of goods to such remote and scattered localities entailed.

There were model towns in the West Virginia coalfields, notably Widen in Clay County and Holden near Logan, and there were ramshackle camps with unspeakable living conditions that were well publicized by investigators like Lane. Somewhere in between were towns like Justus Collins's Winding Gulf in Raleigh County and the nearby town of Tams. Collins was an absentee owner, living in Cincinnati or Charleston, while Walter P. Tams lived all his life in his town. Collins insisted upon an "absolutely nonunion" operation and employed private detectives to watch and infiltrate his work force.[14] Tams had no love for the union, but also disliked the brutality of the guards and kept them away from his town. He governed his town directly, taking a paternal interest in the personal and social lives of his workers and providing them with the district's best recreational facilities. Collins built saloons or, after Prohibition took effect in West Virginia in 1914, "thirst parlors," and pretty much left it at that. It was his policy to ignore those personal matters that did not impinge directly upon the company's economic functions. As he explained to the superintendent of his first mine in Mercer County in 1896, "we are not running a Christian Endeavor Camp Meeting or a Sunday School. . . ."[15]

From the standpoint of the people who lived there, the common features of Tams and Winding Gulf were as important as their differences. Both towns were nestled in isolated wilderness valleys and built largely from green lumber sawn on the spot. The houses here as in nearly every coal camp had open post foundations, board-and-batten siding, and tar-paper roofs: even Collins called some of his houses "shanties."[16] Tams painted

14. Justus Collins to H. H. Rogers, June 3, 1909, Justus Collins Papers, WVU, series 1, box 4, folder 26.

15. Justus Collins to Jairus Collins, September 18, 1896, Collins Papers, WVU, series 1, box 1, folder 1.

16. Justus Collins to Isaac T. Mann, September 14, 1909, Collins Papers, WVU, series 1, box 5, folder 29.

his houses white; other operators preferred yellow; some houses were painted red or green, but whatever the color scheme, the towns were monotonous in appearance and always begrimed by the gritty black mud that seemed a special curse of coalfield communities. Each town was divided into distinct clusters, one for blacks, one for foreign-born workers, one for native whites. Even if there were no guards, the local constables and other county officials were usually involved in the coal companies in some way or another. Allowing for the very best of circumstances, miners still enjoyed none of the privacy and few of the options that other classes of industrial workers enjoyed.

The mine guards were the most visible and the most fiercely resented symbol of the captive character of the company towns. The most celebrated supplier of private police in the coalfields was the Bluefield firm of Baldwin-Felts. To judge from the reports this firm passed on to Collins, the undercover men were often as preoccupied by gossip, grumbling, and Saturday-night sprees as by the real or imagined doings of union men, but the guards who openly exercised their authority were easily the most hated men in the camps. At best they were symbols of the miner's complete lack of control over his living and working conditions. At worst they were swaggering bullies who tyrannized the camps from petty thrones tilted back on the porches of the company stores. After the Paint Creek mine war, Baldwin-Felts men became so controversial that some operators, particularly in northern West Virginia, hired and trained their own guards, while others switched to deputy sheriffs commissioned by the counties but paid from company funds. The more enlightened mine operators pressed West Virginia to emulate Pennsylvania by establishing a state police. Despite the bitter opposition of labor leaders, the legislature established a state constabulary in 1919, but it was too poorly organized and patronage-ridden to be a very effective force in the mine wars, which resumed in that year.

"People living in two-story houses," as one journalist identified the company doctors, clerks, and other middle-class people she encountered along Paint Creek in 1913, managed to convince themselves that conditions in the coal camps were no worse than most miners deserved. "The men were lazy and fond of drink," the women were unthrifty and had too many children. The same people who voiced these attitudes usually added that miners were content with their lot until disturbed by "outside agitators" like Mother Jones.[17] This set of ideas has cropped up nearly every time and every place in American history that ordinary people have banded together to better their lot, but a great many West Virginians who had no stake in the matter and who should have known better accepted the operators' views. Many people who lived in the comfortable new industrial cities and railroad towns could not believe that conditions in the company towns were as bad as the critics described and, as usual, the mountainous terrain shielded uninquisitive eyes from uncomfortable realities.

The miners themselves knew better than to accept the "outside agitator" line. Many of their demands antedated the UMWA's formation in 1890. "Screen and scrip" laws, both having to do with the way wages were calculated and paid, first went on the books in 1887, but the companies ignored them. It was the same with mine-safety legislation, which dated back to 1883. The union did not have to lobby for these laws. The periodic mine explosions kept pressure on the legislature, and the device of appointing mine inspectors afforded a harmless way to relieve it, for it was an open secret among politicians that the inspectorships were intended to pad the patronage rolls and only incidentally to promote safety in coal mining. The number of inspectors thus increased steadily and so did the number of disasters, with the worst coming at Monongah in 1907 (361 dead) and Eccles in 1914 (188). Another grievance that became the subject of legislation was the appointment of mine guards as deputy sheriffs or the subsidization of deputies' salaries by the coal operators. This became illegal in 1913, by virtue of a law that lacked an enforcement clause! It was easy to bamboozle labor spokesmen, a Barbour County legislator explained to A. B. Fleming in 1904. "As you will remember, in order to placate the labor interests, certain of their bills were allowed to pass the House. In permitting their passage, we knew full well

17. Cora Older, "Answering a Question," *Colliers,* 51:26–27.

there would be no time for them to be considered in the Senate." Consequently, he added, labor representatives had gone home empty-handed, while "the House, and especially some of its officers, received credit for being very favorable to labor interests. . . ." [18]

Such attitudes were typical among the state's elected officials, and so it is not surprising that the mine workers turned to the unions. The union organizers, venturing into the coal camps at the risk of beatings and even death at the hands of the guards, found a receptive audience. They did not create discontent. They tapped it, gave it voice, shaped it into goals that related in concrete ways to their members' working and living conditions. With the union, men felt less alone. Company recognition of the union was an important psychological breach in the isolated and autocratic character of the mining towns.

The UMWA succeeded in realizing many of its goals during the years around World War I. The boom in coal production and the attendant labor shortage enabled the union to negotiate from strength, while the friendly attitude of wartime federal agencies inhibited antiunion activities. A new West Virginia union leadership, headed by C. Frank Keeney and Fred Mooney, two Cabin Creek miners who became the top officials of the union's District 17 in 1917, pressed these advantages forcefully. As a result the union rolls grew from six thousand to fifty-three thousand during the war, incorporating over half the state's miners and embracing the Fairmont, Elkins, Kanawha, New River, and Northern Panhandle fields. The Pocahontas, Winding Gulf, Logan, and Tug Fork fields remained unorganized, however, and it was here that production had expanded most rapidly during the war. The UMWA was as anxious to organize these districts as the operators were to defend them. By mid-1919 conditions for a new mine war were brewing, with the battle line now located south of Cabin and Paint creeks, along the ridges that separated the Guyandot watershed from that of the Kanawha.

While the miners' view of West Virginia's labor problems was shaped by the peculiar character of the mining communi-

18. F. P. Moats to A. B. Fleming, March 1, 1904, Fleming Papers, WVU, box 32b.

ties, the operators' perspective was based on the structure of the nation's bituminous coal industry. Most West Virginia coal was sold to consumers outside the state, and no matter which way it was shipped, it had to cross the territory of competing producers who were located closer to the most lucrative markets. Although West Virginia producers had some compensating advantages, such as generally superior qualities of coal, their chief competitive weapon was a lower wage scale than prevailed in Pennsylvania or the midwestern coal regions. Historical patterns of development had given the state, especially southern West Virginia, more than its share of small operators whose obsolete and inefficient mines might well go out of business if they gave up the wage differential. But the state also had some of the newest, largest, and best-equipped mines in the country, and these companies saw an industry-wide wage scale as a form of subsidy that enabled their northern competitors to hang on to markets that West Virginia coal might otherwise claim.

Regional wage differentials seemed all the more important given certain long-range market trends in the coal industry. After 1910 coal consumption in the United States ceased to expand as rapidly as the nation's economy because alternative energy sources and more efficient energy use ate into older consumption patterns. World War I and the hothouse growth of coal exports that accompanied it postponed the reckoning that these trends forecast, but since the boom also called into existence a great increase in coal-mining capacity, it only helped to make the reckoning more severe when it finally came in the mid-1920s. By then the U.S. bituminous industry was able to produce nearly a billion tons of coal annually, while demand fluctuated around 550 million tons. The industry was too decentralized, had too many firms spread out over too many states to agree on a program for cutting back on this excess capacity. Thus a great scramble for markets ensued, with disastrous implications for prices, profits, and wages alike.

The United Mine Workers, from its inception in 1890, recognized the chronic instability of coal prices and offered the industry a solution: put a uniform floor under wages, and prices would firm up on this base. It was an unspoken but obvious corollary that marginal producers would go out of business if uniform wage scales were the rule. The problem was: who was marginal? Was it the older, less efficient operators or those most distant from the market? No matter how the question was answered, a significant proportion of West Virginia producers, especially those in the south, felt that the UMWA program treated them unfairly. In fact, West Virginia operators habitually insisted that the union was the pawn of its competitors, that it represented a conspiracy between operators and miners in Pennsylvania and the Midwest to put West Virginia mines out of business and West Virginia miners out of work. This argument had a sufficient kernel of truth to persuade many middle-class West Virginians who might otherwise have been neutral or supported the union. The "conspiracy" thesis reinforced the "outside agitator" argument. In this light, the UMWA program looked like a plot aimed at the state's general prosperity by inhibiting the exploitation of its premier resource.

In this atmosphere, the progressive impulse gave way after 1913 to the election of public officials who deemed it a patriotic duty to defend the coal operators against the union assaults. State and local judges routinely granted coal-company requests for blanket injunctions against union organizers, making it illegal for them even to mention the existence of a strike in some mining counties. Ira E. Robinson of Grafton, the sole supreme court judge to condemn the Paint Creek military tribunal of 1912–1913, ran with Hatfield's blessing as the Republican gubernatorial candidate in 1916, but lost the election to a conservative Democrat John J. Cornwell. Hatfield and Robinson credited the loss to coal-company influence, although the outcome was so close that it is hard to be sure precisely how it came about. Cornwell was followed in office by a trio of lackluster Republican governors with conservative views. Meanwhile the senatorial election of 1918 pitted two coal-company presidents: Davis Elkins, the Republican heir to his father's and grandfather's fortunes, against Democrat Clarence W. Watson of Consolidation Coal, with Elkins prevailing. Another Davis (no relation), John W. Davis of Clarksburg, won election to Congress as a progressive Democrat in 1910 but soon left the state for a successful career as a diplomat in the Wilson administration and a lawyer in New York. Davis returned to touch base in Clarksburg in 1924, when he ran as the Democrats' spectacularly unsuccessful presidential candidate against Calvin Coolidge, but he had little impact on West Virginia politics. His successor in Congress was another matter, however. Matthew M. Neely, a Democratic lawyer from Fairmont, managed to exploit Republican divisions during the "progressive era" to create a permanent base in the GOP's former northern West Virginia stronghold and went on from there to win a Senate seat with UMWA backing in 1922. The antiunion reaction of the 1920s led Neely to trim his sails considerably in order to win industry backing during his re-election campaign in 1928. This tactic left his opponent, ex-Governor Hatfield, full of resentment even though Hatfield squeaked through to victory on the coattails of Herbert Hoover, the Republican presidential nominee. Hatfield believed that his effort to apply "even-handed justice" between miners and operators had gone unappreciated, and to a significant extent he was right.[19] The logic of this realization was that Hatfield's middle ground was untenable: West Virginia's leaders had to choose between the union and its enemies. It was Neely, however, not Hatfield, who learned this lesson and applied it to great advantage in subsequent years.

Even if the politicians had come up with a plausible compromise formula neither side was in a mood to apply it in the years following World War I. The UMWA was anxious to expand and consolidate its gains in West Virginia. Nonunion operators were equally anxious to draw the line, while some who had submitted to unionization during the war hoped to go back to prewar conditions. The result was an almost continuous struggle as the union sought first to break into the nonunion coalfields south of the Kanawha and then, failing there, to defend its position in central and northern West Virginia.

The struggle produced some of the most dramatic episodes in American labor history. On four separate occasions in

---

19. ———— to Gordon Blizzard, October 15, 1928, Hatfield Papers, WVU, box 1, folder 1.

1920–1921, West Virginia governors asked for federal troops to patrol Mingo and Logan counties, where they joined an already impressive array of police agencies that included Baldwin-Felts men, deputy sheriffs, all of the new state police force, National Guardsmen, and a host of "special police"—vigilantes recruited from businessmen and white-collar workers in coalfield towns. With so much firepower, bloodshed was certain. The "Matewan Massacre" on May 19, 1920, claimed ten lives and involved Baldwin-Felts agents, union men, and prounion local officials. One of the latter, "Two Gun" Sid Hatfield, a tough, diminutive character who lived up to all the romantic potential in the Hatfield name, became the miners' most prominent hero in the Mingo County war. Thus when he was gunned down on the steps of the courthouse at Welch on August 1, 1921, by a Baldwin-Felts man who claimed self-defense, an angry reaction developed in the coalfields, culminating in an armed march of some three thousand miners from the Kanawha River to Blair Mountain in northern Logan County. Here, on the border between union and nonunion territory, the miners skirmished for five days with a Logan County sheriff's posse until federal soldiers forced the two "armies" apart on September 4. One of the most bizarre features of this March on Logan was the participation of a squadron of army airmen who came down from Washington to see how air power could be deployed in civil disturbances. The army planes never made it to Blair Mountain. Six of them got lost and crashed in the mountains, leaving the booted and beribboned survivors grounded in Charleston with nothing to do. However, Logan officials borrowed a plane and dropped a homemade bomb near the battlefield, thus making airborne history anyway. As one participant put it, the March on Logan "wasn't no cap-buster parade." [20]

The aftermath of the Logan march was scarcely less remarkable. A Logan grand jury indicted nearly six hundred alleged participants, fifty-four of them for murder and treason. The

20. Quoted in Anne Lawrence et al., *On Dark and Bloody Ground, An Oral History of the U.M.W.A. in Central Appalachia, 1920–1945* (Charleston: The Miners' Voice, 1973), p. 16.

"treason trials" that followed in 1922 took place under changes of venue in the agricultural Greenbrier and Potomac counties and resulted in few convictions while they won much favorable national publicity for the union cause. But the publicity came too late to help the striking miners in Mingo County. In October 1922 the UMWA formally abandoned the Mingo strike and began a long and unsuccessful rear-guard action to retain its bases in the Kanawha, New River, and Fairmont fields. John L. Lewis, the union's dynamic national president since 1919, insisted that existing wage rates be maintained in the unionized districts, despite the disastrous slump in coal sales and prices after 1923. When West Virginia leaders such as Frank Keeney protested this policy, Lewis replaced them with "provisional" district officials of his own choosing in 1924.

By this time the focal point of the struggle had shifted to the northern coalfields, where a strike against nonunion operators began on April 1, 1924. Evictions began that spring on Scotts Run near Morgantown; here and in other coal-blackened valleys with pioneer names a sullen and bitter struggle dragged on for three years. In 1925 Consolidation Coal, the region's largest producer, abrogated its union contract, claiming that coal could no longer be sold at prices that the union wage scale required. The union leaders widened the strike and worked valiantly to sustain it, but in the end the union miners had to scramble to fill a declining supply of jobs just as operators competed for a share of the shrinking market. Gradually the union hold on West Virginia disintegrated. By 1930 the bituminous industry was sliding toward bankruptcy as the national economy caved in on top of an already depressed coal market. When national attention again turned to the West Virginia coalfields in 1931 and 1932, it was not drawn by labor violence but by the plight of destitute people who lingered on in the camps that bankrupt companies left behind.

The dislocations of the coal industry were part of a larger set of problems in West Virginia, problems that came to be grouped under the heading of a "colonial economy." During the nineteenth century, as the new extractive industries helped themselves to the state's timber and industrial fuels, local leaders were confident that this was only the first stage of development. It was "an axiom of political economy," Governor MacCorkle explained to a Chicago audience in 1893, that manufacturing clustered around the sources of coal and other "heavier products." [21] Raw materials assured that West Virginia would become a great manufacturing center—it was a matter of destiny, nothing more, nothing less. But by the turn of the century it had become apparent to thoughtful observers that a mature economy was not materializing, that the "boundless" resources of which promoters boasted were being taken out swiftly and recklessly and that, as a Huntington man complained in 1901, "after they are gone we will have only the worthless lands now yielding them, without the benefits they ought to give us as the golden stream flows out." [22]

Economic statistics supported these fears. Apart from the long-established iron and steel, glass, and pottery industries of the Northern Panhandle, West Virginia's manufacturing sector developed as an offshoot of extractive industry. Such factories as there were specialized in products auxiliary to resource extraction—mine cars, for example. A related form of manufacturing involved simple processing operations such as the manufacture of coke from coal or lumber or wood pulp from logs. The capital-intensive, technologically complex industries that provided the heftiest payrolls and profits and whose taxes supported the highest levels of public services remained scarce south of the Wheeling region. Since this had also been the most developed district in western Virginia in 1860, the opening of the interior and its resources clearly had a disappointing effect on local manufacturing growth. With no home market, the resources sped away by rail, barge, and pipeline to the manufacturing centers of other states. Estimates on the proportion of coal shipped out of the state during this period vary from fifty to ninety percent, depending upon whether they include coal sold

21. "Address of Governor William A. MacCorkle . . . August 23, 1893," in Cometti and Summers, *The Thirty-Fifth State*, p. 480.
22. E. A. Bennett to A. B. White, March 19, 1901, White Papers, WVU, box 9.

as fuel to railroads or manufactured locally into coke before it was shipped. West Virginia became an important producer of natural gas after 1890 and the country's largest producer between 1910 and 1924, but two-thirds to three-fourths of this valuable fuel left the state. In the forest industries, West Virginia produced an abundance of wood pulp but little paper, lots of ax handles and clothespins but not much furniture, tannery products but no finished leather goods. And even in the Wheeling area, local steel mills and glass factories tended to turn out cheaper and less complex products than their Pittsburgh or Toledo counterparts.

Thus while industrialization wrought dramatic changes in the state, it did not make West Virginia "one of the wealthiest states in the Union," as the boosters had so confidently predicted.[23] It remained one of the poorer states, a hewer of wood and supplier of energy to its richer neighbors on the north, east, and west. The term "colonial economy" had not been invented in 1900, but the characteristic features were already present in West Virginia by this time. These included a high degree of absentee ownership, which took on a new and increasingly controversial form as large corporations displaced the smaller firms and individuals who pioneered in industrial development; heavy dependence upon extractive industries oriented to distant markets; and a relative lack of those manufacturing industries that provided the greatest stimuli to material growth and welfare in the nation at large. This was not the economy that the founders of West Virginia had dreamed of, nor was it what most citizens wanted. Consequently, some questions emerged at the turn of the century that have haunted West Virginians ever since: Why had a colonial economy developed here and what could be done about it?

The colonial economy developed primarily because of environmental and historical factors that were beyond the power of local leaders to control. Mountainous terrain retarded transportation development, added to the overhead costs of railroads after they were built, and restricted the level land most suitable

23. "Wealthy West Virginia," *The West Virginian* 2, no. 5 (May 1900):7.

to modern manufacturing installations. West Virginia's natural resources, although basic to modern industry, were neither intrinsically valuable nor particularly scarce, and so as manufacturing processes grew more complex, requiring a greater variety of raw materials, urban market locations began to exert a stronger pull than raw-materials sites. Generally it made more economic sense to take West Virginia's fuels to the factories than to bring the factories to the fuels.

This is not to say that the colonial economy was a purely impersonal development. West Virginia business and political leaders could react in different ways to these trends, depending upon the dictates of their individual interests and understandings. As early as 1875, for example, Johnson N. Camden faced the choice of defending the autonomy and markets of his oil-refining business or of turning over control to the more powerful Standard Oil Company headed by John D. Rockefeller. Camden decided not to fight and instead collaborated with Rockefeller, who wanted the West Virginia refining industry phased out, except for a single plant at Parkersburg, and West Virginia crude-oil production shipped to Standard refineries in Cleveland, Baltimore, and New York. This decision was a profitable one for Rockefeller and Camden and a more efficient allocation of resources for Standard Oil and the American petroleum industry generally, but, of course, it cost the state in terms of actual and potential jobs, taxes, and locally reinvested profits. Nearly thirty years later, Camden and the Watson-Fleming interests of Fairmont faced a similar situation created by the expansion of Consolidation Coal, then a Baltimore-based firm whose directors interlocked with the B & O Railroad and thus enjoyed critical advantages in the shipping of coal. Again realism prevailed. Consolidation absorbed the Fairmont Coal Company, Watson moved to Baltimore to manage the expanded firm, Camden retired to enjoy an island he owned in Florida, and Fleming became the principal lawyer and political spokesman for a powerful combine of industries that included "Consol," the B & O, South Penn Oil, Hope Natural Gas, and other local subsidiaries of the Standard Oil Company. Similar decisions swept most of the Wheeling area's steel and tin-plate mills into the control of large national corporations, except for the Wheeling Steel Corporation, which the remaining local producers banded together to create in 1920.

Henry G. Davis, by contrast, was an empire builder by instinct and held control of his enterprises for as long as he could. Justus Collins was another businessman who fought domination by the trunk-line railroads in the southern part of the state. Other West Virginia entrepreneurs retained their independent status by moving to the big cities and starting large national corporations of their own. Earl W. Oglebay moved from Wheeling to Cleveland and established an influential firm in the mining and shipping end of the steel industry.Michael L. Benedum and Joseph C. Trees, young oil wildcatters who operated in Marshall and Wetzel counties around the turn of the century, sold out their holdings to Standard Oil and moved on to Wheeling and then, in 1907, to Pittsburgh, where they founded a cluster of independent oil and gas firms. "They make more deals [in Pittsburgh] in a day than are made in Wheeling in a month," Benedum explained.[24]

Such independence was the exception, not the rule, however. Most smaller coal producers were only nominally independent from the nonresident landowners and the big railroads that dominated the marketing and shipping of coal. The Paint Creek Coal Company, for example, itself a Pennsylvania-based corporation in 1913, leased its coal land from Charles M. Pratt, a Standard Oil stockholder who lived in New York, and shipped and sold its product only on terms acceptable to the C & O. And the relative independence that forceful men like Davis managed to retain rarely survived for more than a generation. Consolidation into larger and larger firms with remote managements remained a lively trend in all West Virginia industries during the twentieth century.

Political leaders faced a similarly restricted range of choices. Barring a radical transformation in national economic priorities, West Virginia could have done little on its own to reverse the

24. Sam T. Mallison, *The Great Wildcatter* (Charleston: Educational Foundation, 1953), p. 175.

trends that concentrated investment capital and manufacturing payrolls in the nation's metropolitan centers, but state fiscal policies might have mitigated the worst effects of economic colonialism. Tax reform as a means of extracting more local benefits from "the boundless resources" and their absentee owners had been discussed in agrarian circles since the 1880s, but the most comprehensive reform program emerged from a curious alliance of progressive Republicans and the Elkins political machine early in the new century. As advanced by the Tax Commission of 1903, a body created at Elkins's suggestion and numbering Davis as its most prominent member, the reform program called for a complete overhaul of fiscal administration, larger corporation license taxes, and severance taxes on the production of coal, oil, and natural gas.

Cynics at the time suggested that tax reform represented the Elkins machine's desire for a larger state payroll and also a Davis-Elkins business alliance with the Western Maryland Railroad against the B & O–Consolidation Coal–Standard Oil combine. There was some merit in the former suggestion, but as to the latter, the Western Maryland fought alongside other corporations opposing the program while Davis and Elkins themselves shied away from endorsing it publicly once it became controversial. Elkins's governors—White, Dawson, and Glasscock—became tax reform's most vigorous advocates. Hatfield along with other progressives who were independent of the machine endorsed the program, as did the voters in every election where it became an issue at the polls.

Middle ground in the tax-reform controversy was as narrow as in labor relations, however. Corporate interests strenuously opposed the program, especially the severance taxes. Directed by Fleming, who in turn took his cues from Standard Oil executives in the Rockefeller headquarters (26 Broadway) in New York, lobbyists representing all of the state's major railroads and extractive industries met in Washington in June 1903 to organize a massive and well-financed "antitax" campaign that effectively stymied the tax-reform movement, although agitation persisted for over a decade. A private agreement between Elkins, Dawson, and Fleming produced a compromise in 1904, which enacted certain of the Tax Commission's administrative proposals, the most significant of which established the office of state tax commissioner. This was the limit of change as far as Fleming was concerned. "We are doing everything we can to deal justly with the great interests of the State but the people representing them seem to concede nothing in the world," Elkins complained to Fleming during a stormy legislative session in 1905. "This is all very embarrassing; we should give and take in going through life." [25] But the corporation men had no interest in compromise nor any need to do so as long as they could successfully manipulate the right legislators and legislative committees. Hatfield appealed to coal producers in similar terms a decade later, with similar results as far as severance taxes were concerned. However, the legislatures of 1915 and 1917 adopted excise taxes on corporate incomes, which were, in turn, replaced in 1921 by a modified form of corporate license tax, called a gross sales tax, that operated upon the gross receipts of firms and partnerships doing business in the state. Coal operators preferred this tax to severance taxes because it was pegged to coal prices rather than to the volume of production and because it automatically made allies of the thousands of small businesses that were also subject to the tax. The Hope Natural Gas Company fought the tax as it applied to interstate gas shipments, but the U.S. Supreme Court upheld the gross sales tax in 1925. By this time the peak years of gas production had passed, but the legislature did what it could to catch up by hiking the tax rate on gas sales to more than four times the rate on coal, which was twice that on manufacturers. The gross sales tax rested most lightly on railroads and other public utilities, according to a study published in 1930. By then "the railroad crowd were the big toads in the puddle" as far as leading resistance to corporate taxation was concerned, according to Senator Hatfield, who was especially disdainful of "the C. & O. and its bunch of political bums." [26]

25. Stephen B. Elkins to A. B. Fleming, February 17, 1905, Fleming Papers, WVU, box 40.

26. Henry D. Hatfield to Walter S. Hallanan, June 28, 1929, Hatfield to Herman Gieske, June 5, 1930, Hatfield Papers, WVU, series 1, box 6, series 3, box 20.

The gross sales tax was something of a breakthrough in spite of its imperfections, but the state's fiscal administration remained a jerry-built structure, especially as it applied to the assessment and collection of property taxes. This situation led to unfortunate results when the Great Depression produced a twin demand for greater welfare services and tax relief for small property owners. The Tax Limitation Amendment added to the constitution in 1932 permitted classification of property for taxation at differential rates, but it also imposed low ceilings on those rates and made it difficult to raise tax rates for special purposes. The amendment forced the state government to assume much of the financial burden that counties had previously borne, especially in the support of roads and schools. This greatly enlarged the possibilities of state patronage, but the conservative Democrats who took over the statehouse in 1933 decided to pay for it in the usual regressive way, by enacting a consumer sales tax imposed on all products, even on medicines and food. Although the depression years inspired a new batch of proposals for severance taxes, West Virginia taxation remained regressive, while public services remained patronage-ridden and chronically underfinanced. In words that Charles Ambler applied to the educational system, public services generally acquired a "poverty complex" that, in turn, generated an "inferiority complex," both of which, like the mine wars, served to reinforce West Virginia's characteristic defensive mentality.[27]

In the final analysis, the worst features of West Virginia's colonial economy endured because men like Fleming, who were content with their roles and their profits as middlemen for the absentee owners of the state's natural wealth, prevailed over those who, like Hatfield, sought to impose a degree of local control over local resources. The most advantageous middle ground in West Virginia was held by those who occupied the social space between the big nonresident firms that dominated the state's economy and the farmers and townsmen who made up the overwhelming majority of West Virginia property own-

27. Charles H. Ambler, *A History of Education in West Virginia* (Huntington: Standard Printing and Publishing, 1951), p. 207.

ers. This middle ground was narrow, too, but it was capacious enough to hold the local owners of coal and gas lands left over after the absentee owners took their share, the bankers and wholesalers who reached out from Charleston, Huntington, Bluefield, Clarksburg, and other cities to serve the coalfields with floating capital and nondurable goods, the men who owned the public utilities of these cities and who developed their new residential suburbs and built the new office buildings that lined their narrow downtown streets. Not least among the middlemen were the expensive lawyers who so successfully plied the courts and the legislature in their corporate clients' behalf.

A representative sample of this type of leadership could be found on any working day in downtown Charleston housed in the handsome new headquarters of the Kanawha Valley Bank, a 20-story "skyscraper" that rose in 1928–1929 on an appropriate site formerly occupied by the state capitol. The bank itself was Charleston's oldest and represented in its directors and stockholders all of the Kanawha Valley's historic sources of wealth: saltmaking, agriculture, land speculation, coal, timber, and processing. When the building was formally opened on September 6, 1929, other tenants included Justus Collins, the Cabin Creek Consolidated Coal Company, the Kanawha Coal Operators Association and more than twenty other coal firms and operators. The Chesapeake & Potomac Telephone Company offices spread over four floors and represented the great utility holding companies that were beginning to exert much influence through their local subsidiaries. Brown, Jackson & Knight, West Virginia's oldest and most prestigious law firm, took over the entire sixteenth floor of the new building. It was through this firm that the first mine guards had been recruited on Paint Creek in 1912; the firm had also hired the stenographer who shadowed Mother Jones and had used his notes as well as copious additional sources of information to prepare the briefs and interrogatories with which it had guided Kanawha coal operators through the several state and federal investigations that the mine wars inspired. A lawyer could be born into a firm like this; he could work his way into it, combining strength of intellect with the proper amounts of deference and tact toward his superiors; or he could be selected for preferment from among the scores of ambitious politicians who crowded into the capital year by year. However he made the grade, the man who made it was not likely to quibble about the defects in West Virginia's economy, for that economy assuredly worked for him. West Virginia thus remained the way it was because the most powerful West Virginians liked it that way.

"I smiled and the money came," ex-Governor MacCorkle noted cheerfully as a millionaire writing his memoirs in 1928.[28] And money brought other rewards. On top of a hill overlooking Charleston, MacCorkle built Sunrise, a mansion whose tall white columns remind us that a large proportion of West Virginia's middlemen, especially those in the southern part of the state, were descended from Confederate Virginians who had had West Virginia thrust on them and who felt no particular personal loyalty to the new state. Perhaps inherited attitudes helped to explain the general civic indifference of southern West Virginia's elite. In the field of education, for example, the most eminent lawyers and businessmen of the south were more likely to have attended the University of Virginia or Washington & Lee than West Virginia University or Bethany College (although coal operators who wanted their sons trained as engineers tended to prefer V.M.I.). These same people often complained about the "high" level of West Virginia's educational expenditures and taxes, while sending their own children to private schools in the Old Dominion. As in every period and every other state, wealthy conservatives usually found a way of escaping personally from the negative social consequences of the public policies they espoused.

It seems appropriate, then, that this era's finest expression of nostalgia and social escapism took the form of a pious monument to the imagined graces of the Old South. This was The Greenbrier, a palatial new hotel built at White Sulphur Springs in 1913 after MacCorkle and a Huntington associate persuaded the C & O Railroad to rescue the historic spa from the genteel decay that had overtaken other traditional mountain resorts.

28. MacCorkle, *Recollections,* p. 618.

Most West Virginians came to think of The Greenbrier as a place apart from the gritty realities of the state's mining and industrial districts, and so it was, from the standpoint of the comforts and pleasures that guests learned to expect. But though the walls of the new hotel glistened white and pristine amid its alpine surroundings, the social foundations on which it rose were as black as the coal-laden trains that chugged past its gate. The coal operators' associations came to White Sulphur twice a year during the mine wars to talk over prices and freight rates and to plot their successful battle against the union. Their bankers and lawyers and railroad friends came even more frequently to play golf (an unknown sport in antebellum times but an indispensable one for the enjoyment of modern businessmen), to mingle with their wives and children among the metropolitan rich who patronized the new hotel, and to sample the prohibited joys of the Jazz Age in speakeasies and casinos that nestled discreetly on the edges of The Greenbrier's six-thousand-acre estate. Notwithstanding its air of cultivated Southern nostalgia, the new White Sulphur was supremely a place of the 1920s, reflecting its mood of carefree indifference to social concerns. During the early 1930s, as the blight of depression spread from the coalfields over the industrial and farming districts of the state, the hotel undertook a program of expansion that doubled its size and inaugurated an annual week-long festival devoted to the memory of Robert E. Lee. It is hard to envision a finer monument to the urge to escape through historical fantasy from West Virginia's uncomfortable truths.

6

Hawks Nest

*F*EW places have been more a part of West Virginia history than Hawks Nest, the towering cliff formation that guards the western entrance to New River Gorge. The soldiers of Andrew Lewis's army passed nearby in 1774, as had generations of Indian warriors and hunters before them. Ninety years later, Civil War soldiers followed the same route between the Kanawha and Greenbrier valleys. Ambrose Bierce, the Ohio-born writer who marched into western Virginia with General Cox in 1861, set one of his gloomy war stories at Hawks Nest. Another writer-soldier, David Hunter Strother, won a bottle of wine by throwing a stone across the canyon there after the Lynchburg Raid of 1864. The Chesapeake & Ohio Railroad's completion along the floor of the canyon in 1873 ended a century-long search for a more easily traveled route across southern West Virginia; mining began in the coal measures along the canyon's lower walls soon afterward. The first sustained strike of West Virginia coal miners occurred at the Hawks Nest Coal Company in 1880, as did the first use of state militia in a coal strike. The appearance of mining communities in the canyon did not ruin the scenery when viewed from above, however, and so when the growth of automobile traffic redirected the stream of travelers back to the canyon rim, Hawks Nest became a favorite stopping place. In 1935 the state of West Virginia acquired the overlook and developed it into one of the first and most popular

159

of a new system of state parks. Its location, roughly halfway between White Sulphur Springs and Huntington, made it a convenient place for visitors crossing the state to stop and admire the scenery, as generations of travelers before them had done.

From the overlook at Hawks Nest today, visitors can see something far below that looks like a gigantic door in the northern wall of the canyon. This is a part of the twentieth century's most imposing landmark at Hawks Nest, a tunnel that burrows through the south flank of Gauley Mountain, cutting across the top of a double horseshoe curve of New River and diverting its water through the mountain to a hydroelectric generating station three miles away. Union Carbide Chemicals Corporation, one of West Virginia's largest industrial employers, owns the tunnel and power facilities, and uses the electricity in electrometallurgical and chemical plants in the nearby Kanawha Valley. The tunnel was constructed over a four-year period beginning in 1930 and began producing electricity in 1935. A roadside historical marker about a mile from the overlook recites the engineering statistics.

There is nothing on the marker or anywhere else at Hawks Nest to tell visitors that the construction of this tunnel led to one of the great tragedies of West Virginia history, perhaps the greatest in terms of total loss of life. No one knows precisely how many men died as a result of digging the Hawks Nest tunnel; the most frequently cited number of victims is 476, but this number does not include those victims who may have lingered for years before dying. The cause of these deaths was silicosis, a disease contracted when abrasive particles of silica dust are trapped in the lungs, impairing and eventually destroying the victim's ability to breathe. Some silicosis victims die quickly from obvious respiratory complications; others die slowly over a period of years, even decades. It is often difficult to diagnose the disease or to explain its varying degrees of incidence among workers exposed to the same conditions. For these reasons, the precise number of silicosis victims was never established, nor was the disease proven to be the cause of death except in the cases of a handful of men whose lungs were examined by autopsy. What is certain is that the rock under Gauley Mountain turned out to have a silica content of up to ninety-nine percent, so pure, in fact, that Union Carbide used the rock to make fer-rosilicon, a steel alloy, without further refining. It is also known that the contracting firm that built the tunnel paid some $130,000 to settle damage suits brought by some three hundred tunnel workers and their survivors in 1933 and that half of this sum went to the victims' lawyers. Neither the contractors nor Union Carbide ever admitted liability for the tragedy, however, nor did the state of West Virginia, although workmen's-compensation legislation was later adopted, making silicosis a compensable disease. Civic leaders at Gauley Bridge, which gained an unwelcome notoriety as "the town of the living dead" because of the numbers of debilitated silicosis victims lingering in the neighborhood during the 1930s, traced the problem to "undesirables, mainly Negroes" who flocked to Fayette County to work on the tunnel and to "troublemakers" who subsequently exploited the tunnel workers' distress.[1]

The Hawks Nest tunnel was not a battlefield like Point Pleasant or Droop Mountain, although it claimed many more victims. Nor was it a disaster like West Virginia's numerous mine explosions or the flash floods that periodically brought sudden death sweeping down out of the hills. The tunnel victims died slowly, without a cause to dignify their passing or an enemy to blame. Their tragedy was neither an act of God nor one for which identifiable men could be held responsible. It was both unanticipated and foreseeable, an event governed by the same laws of probability that explain the incidence of traffic accidents and stuck elevators. Or as one of the victims put it, the Hawks Nest tragedy was "just one of those things that happens in some people's lives."[2]

The Hawks Nest tunnel is a symbol of life as well as death in mid-twentieth-century West Virginia, for it was part of a project that expressed some of the most important social and technological developments of the age. As an engineering achievement,

1. Quoted in Alicia Tyler, "Dust to Dust," *Washington Monthly* 6, no. 11 (January 1975):57.
2. Quoted in Tyler, "Dust to Dust," p. 58.

the Hawks Nest project was one of those modern technological marvels that, in West Virginia, usually involve the conquest of mountains in one way or another. As a social achievement, it was a landmark of an age of bureaucracies, the large, complex organizations that the management of modern technologies seems to require. In theory, bureaucracy and technology were neutral instruments, in themselves neither good nor bad. They can be credited with many of the most desirable accomplishments of the age as well as with some of its defects: with the park and highway on top of Gauley Mountain, for example, along with the murderous tunnel in the mountain's heart. Yet the use of bureaucratic and technological means in the pursuit of social objectives has increasingly required the mobilization of power and information on a scale far beyond the reach of ordinary individuals, sometimes beyond the reach even of the traditional means of social control embodied in state and local political systems. The achievements of the age were therefore often won at the expense of local control over vital social decisions, in effect a form of "depoliticizing" state and local governments, even when the growth of government and the rise of other bureaucracies ostensibly offered "countervailing power" against the influence once wielded by corporations alone. Typically, the most strenuous and sustained governmental interest in Hawks Nest was administrative, not political: a thirty-year campaign by the Federal Power Commission to bring the power project under its licensing authority. The Commission finally won its campaign in 1965, which means that in 1991 Congress will have the option of purchasing the Hawks Nest project at its original cost in the name of the American people. In the meantime the Hawks Nest tunnel remains an appropriately ambiguous symbol for an ambiguous era in the history of the state.

In the fall of 1939 Governor Homer A. "Rocky" Holt examined the manuscript of *West Virginia: A Guide to the Mountain State,* then being prepared for publication by the Federal Writers' Project, an arm of one of the relief agencies established by President Franklin D. Roosevelt's New Deal. The manuscript contained a lengthy discussion of the silicosis problem at

Hawks Nest, together with other material chiefly relating to labor and black history that, in Holt's words, "may be distinctly discreditable to the State and its people." [3] The governor, therefore, refused to sanction the guide and ordered withheld from it the reproduction of the state seal or any other mark of official approval. Officials of the Writers' Project were distressed but unapologetic. "To omit adequate treatment of labor questions in a state that is widely known for its labor history . . . would subject our book to attack as being a 'white-wash' job," wrote Bruce Crawford, the Writers' Project's West Virginia director. [4] The controversy continued acrimoniously for some weeks and then ended in an ambiguous compromise that toned down some parts of the book and left others standing. Finally, in February 1941, the final version went to the printers. A week later Crawford left the Writers' Project to join the liberal administration of Governor Matthew M. Neely, while Holt joined the Charleston law firm of Brown, Jackson & Knight. Later Crawford became a newspaperman, while Holt moved on to New York as chief counsel for Union Carbide. Their quarrel like many others during this period illustrated that West Virginia's social landscape, like its mountain terrain, looked different according to who made the observation and from what angle of vision.

The guidebook episode was also a minor skirmish in a major war, an intermittent struggle for control of West Virginia's future as well as of its past. Generally the combatants were, like Holt and Crawford, the local representatives of rival metropolitan elites: the leaders of big business and organized labor or officials of the federal bureaucracy. Alliances and enmities between these groups varied according to time and to issues, but, by and large, labor and the federal government intervened as "liberal" forces seeking to modify West Virginia's economic and political dependence upon extractive industry and to bring

3. Homer A. Holt to W. W. Trent, September 21, 1939, Writers' Project Collection WVU, box 123, folder 2. See also edited ms. material in Homer A. Holt Papers, WVU, box 2, folder 3.
4. Bruce Crawford to W. W. Trent, October 10, 1939, Writers' Project Collection, WVU, box 123, folder 2.

local government and social services up to national norms. Although this effort was far from successful, it exerted a trans-
forming effect on the state's political life, particularly during the
age of the Great Depression and the Second World War.

The depression hit West Virginia harder than most parts of
the country, affecting nearly every segment of industry, farming, and commerce, but striking its greatest blow in the coalfields, already depressed by the coal slump of the preceding decade. Coal production fell another forty percent from 1929 to
1933, but since demand slackened proportionately, reduced output did not boost wages or prices. Unemployed or un-
deremployed miners made up a significant share of the Hawks
Nest tunnel work force, while nearby abandoned mining towns
provided shelter for the workers who came from afar. Not far
away along Cabin Creek and in similar mining districts from
McDowell County to Morgantown, Red Cross workers and religious and volunteer groups organized emergency food programs, while state officials, unable to agree upon and finance an
adequate welfare program themselves, appealed for larger dona-
tions of food and clothing and for more volunteers.

Beginning with Herbert Hoover's Reconstruction Finance
Corporation in 1931, federal agencies gradually displaced the
volunteer relief workers. After Roosevelt took command, alpha-
bet agencies sprouted in Washington like mushrooms after a
warm rain: there were FERA (Federal Emergency Relief Administration), CWA (Civil Works Administration), PWA (Public Works Administration), WPA (Works Progress Administration), CCC (Civilian Conservation Corps), AAA (Agricultural
Adjustment Administration), NRA (National Recovery Administration), and FSA (Farm Security Administration), to name
only the most important. Each had its West Virginia program
and payrolls. FERA put 60,000 unemployed West Virginians to
work and spent $51,000,000 in West Virginia between 1933
and 1936, mostly to build roads and highways. CWA and PWA
spent millions to build major public improvements such as
Charleston's Kanawha Boulevard and campus buildings at Marshall College and West Virginia Tech. WPA undertook over
4,000 smaller projects, including the Writers' Project and other
research projects designed to employ white-collar workers; its

total payroll reached 36,000 by 1936. CCC workers built recreational facilities and ran surveys in the new state parks and national forests and joined forces with WPA and private philanthropy to develop Wheeling's Oglebay Park into one of the best in the nation. FSA chose Arthurdale in Preston County as the site of a unique and celebrated experiment in resettling unemployed workers (in this case miners from the squalid coal camps around Morgantown) into "subsistence homesteads" where, in theory at least, they might support themselves through a combination of farming and handicrafts. Other homestead communities were built in Randolph and Putnam counties.

The tangled character of state and local finances in the early 1930s prevented West Virginia from meeting all the requirements of federal relief and public works programs. Consequently the state failed to claim its full share of available federal funds. The financial picture improved by 1935, however, and in 1937 the legislature created the necessary machinery for participation in the welfare and unemployment-compensation programs established by the federal Social Security Act. The result of all this activity blunted the depression's worst features and made President Roosevelt a popular hero. It also made his Democratic party the majority party in the state, as in the nation, and gave its leaders an unprecedented number of patronage jobs to hand out. Of course, federal law strictly prohibited the use of political tests in awarding jobs, relief, and contracts under these programs, but this injunction was routinely ignored. Even when political recommendations were not primary criteria, they were commonly employed when selecting from among applicants of equal qualifications or need. Nevertheless the demand for jobs always outran the supply. Matthew M. Neely, who had regained a U.S. Senate seat in 1930, reported in July 1933 that "the number of job hunters on my back considerably exceeds fourteen thousand, with nearly six hundred from my own county [Marion] besieging me and actually following me to my bathroom. . . ." [5] Six weeks later Neely's list of applicants had grown to twenty-one thousand and was still growing.

5. Matthew M. Neely to William E. Chilton, June 1, 1933, William E. Chilton Papers, WVU, box 8, folder N.

The spreading of this feast before a party starved by long years out of office led swiftly to factional combat among Democrats. As the New Deal took shape in Washington, a "federal," or "liberal," faction emerged to take charge of its operations in West Virginia, headed by Neely in close collaboration with labor leaders, especially Van A. Bittner and William M. Blizzard of the UMWA. Opposing them was a "statehouse" faction led by Governor H. Guy Kump and his attorney-general and successor, "Rocky" Holt, two Southern-style Democrats bred in the party's traditional strongholds along the Virginia border, and Robert G. Kelly, a Charleston corporation lawyer whom Kump made Democratic state chairman in 1932. Although they respected Roosevelt's popularity, these conservatives had little sympathy for the leftward drift of the New Deal, for which they blamed "a small group of labor leaders and social workers." [6] And they had patronage resources of their own to counter the weight of the federal payrolls. The change brought about by the Tax Limitation Amendment greatly increased statehouse control over highway construction and payrolls, while the newly constituted county boards of education were heavily dependent upon the state's financial aid and so provided a Charleston-oriented counterweight to the local courthouse machines that had frustrated ambitious governors in the past. The repeal of federal and state Prohibition led to the creation of a system of state-owned liquor stores which provided not only payrolls but purchasing contracts, leasing arrangements, insurance and banking requirements, plus other plums not yet dreamed of in these comparatively innocent early years. The expansion of welfare and conservation programs, although instigated and partly financed by Washington, placed another new source of jobs under statehouse control. Upon these resources the conservatives laid the foundations of what became known as the Democratic statehouse machine.

After a number of preliminary skirmishes, the two Democratic factions clashed head-on in the primary election of 1940,

6. Robert G. Kelly to James A. Farley, October 29, 1935, Robert G. Kelly Papers, WVU, box 1, folder 3.

one of the most bitterly contested election battles in the history of the state. The contest got under way in January, when the statehouse faction put together a slate of conservative Democrats headed by former governor Kump, who went after the junior Senate seat. The identity of the liberal opposition remained in doubt until April, barely a month before the party primary. Then Senator Neely astonished the state by announcing his candidacy for the governorship, a move that observers logically credited to the persuasion of UMWA leaders. Almost as surprising was the designation of Harley M. Kilgore, an obscure Beckley judge, as the liberal candidate in the Senate race. A whirlwind campaign followed, dominated by Neely's Bible-quoting, tub-thumping oratory, culminating on May 14 with a sweeping victory for the liberal slate. Neely carried the interior coal counties by nearly a two-thirds vote, ran well in interior farming districts, and held his own everywhere else except in the cities and in the conservative Greenbrier and Potomac counties. The general election in November ratified these results with the same geographic pattern—the Republicans running strong where the statehouse Democrats had run well except in the eastern counties, which returned habitual, if somewhat diminished Democratic majorities. These outcomes marked an enduring realignment of the electorate and constituted an impressive victory for Neely and his friends.

The election returns of 1940 were above all else a vindication of organized labor in West Virginia and this, too, was an outgrowth of federal influence. In 1931 the West Virginia Federation of Labor reached its lowest ebb since its founding in 1903; there were fewer than a thousand dues-paying members in the federation's largest constituent union, the UMWA. A decade later unions enrolled some 290,000 workers and, though this strength was divided among affiliates of two national federations, the older American Federation of Labor (AFL) and the new Congress of Industrial Organizations (CIO), the unions' power was sufficient to convince most West Virginia politicians after 1940 that labor's basic interests could no longer be violated with impunity.

Friendly and hostile observers both gave much credit for labor's remarkable transformation to John L. Lewis, a stormy and overbearing figure who left a controversial imprint on the history of both the nation and the state. Working effectively with Roosevelt and Democratic leaders in Congress, Lewis exploited friendly provisions of newly framed federal laws to rebuild the UMWA and then to organize the CIO. A majority of West Virginia coal operators, caught off balance and willing to try anything to alleviate the industry's desperate situation in 1933, at first submitted tamely to Lewis's whirlwind organizing campaign. On September 21, 1933, the UMWA signed the first of a series of industry-wide contracts known as Appalachian Agreements, which among other features provided for the gradual narrowing and then the elimination of the regional wage differentials that had kept West Virginia miners' earnings near the bottom of earlier wage scales. By the time the operators began to regroup in opposition to these changes, Lewis confronted them with other achievements, notably the Wagner Labor Relations Act of 1935, which became the basis of CIO organizing drives among the nation's mass-production workers, and the Guffey Coal Acts of 1935 and 1936, which enacted in separate and somewhat different form the bituminous coal price and wage stabilization features of Roosevelt's National Industrial Recovery Act of 1933. In 1939, notwithstanding Governor Holt's opposition, the UMWA succeeded in forcing recalcitrant southern West Virginia operators to accept a closed-shop agreement that required union membership as a condition of employment. Two years later the union organized the "captive" mines belonging to steel corporations in a strike that featured a breakthrough of sorts in West Virginia labor history: When violence flared on a picket line at Gary in McDowell County, Governor Neely disciplined the state policemen involved instead of jailing the picketers. There were advantages to having friends in the statehouse.

The miners' achievements and the gains of other CIO unions made Lewis a popular figure in West Virginia, but he had to share credit with Roosevelt. When the labor leader denounced the president's bid for a third term in the White House late in the 1940 campaign, coalfield voters stuck with Roosevelt, which led to Lewis's resignation as head of the CIO. Two years later he took the UMWA out of the CIO, rejoined the AFL in 1946, and withdrew from it again in 1947. These moves, combined with a series of defiant wartime strikes, cost the union some of its earlier public support and led Neely, Kilgore, and other politicians to draw back from their earlier close alliance with Lewis. Thus the long-term consequences of the 1940 contest were not as far-reaching as conservatives initially feared.

The Neely administration restructured the statehouse machine but did not make it liberal, only less conservative. Neely succeeded in establishing organized labor on a par with business and agricultural pressure groups as a "veto group" able to block most policy measures to which it strongly objected. He also gave more recognition to other groups, such as Negroes and public schoolteachers, who aspired to future "veto group" status. But the ability of these groups to initiate policies instead of merely blocking the ones they opposed did not increase appreciably. In fact it was becoming harder for anyone in Charleston to make policy in the sense of initiating and executing significant departures from already established procedures and programs. Rather, the test of state government had become how well it responded to initiatives that originated at the federal level or in the national headquarters of corporations or unions. Thus the governors who followed Neely were judged not by their ideological commitments but by the efficiency with which they tuned the state bureaucracy to respond to such initiatives. In the postwar era, the skills of the manager were more relevant than those of the leader or boss.

Another outcome of these years was the enlargement of that official cynicism that was one of West Virginia's oldest if least praiseworthy traditions. Governor Neely's scramble to appoint his own Senate successor and to return to the Senate himself after only two years in Charleston affords one example. The practice of appointing legislators to state jobs in defiance of the spirit if not the letter of the state constitution did not originate in Neely's governorship, but it became more common then, and thereafter remained a standard feature of the statehouse machine. The machine's ideological neutrality further contributed to its cynicism. Following his unsuccessful Senate race in 1942, Neely moved away from his reliance on the labor vote and Rooseveltian liberalism and accepted a compromise gubernatorial candidate in 1944—Clarence W. Meadows of Beckley, a former attorney-general whose service bridged the Holt and Neely regimes. Meadows's successors kept carefully in the ideological middle, defeating both liberal and conservative rivals in the primaries of 1948 and 1952, and relying for their success on the web of obligations created by the state and federal payrolls, school and highway contracts, bank deposits, and liquor accounts. At the center of the web sat Homer W. Hanna, a quiet and affable political organizer whom Neely had brought to Charleston in 1940 via the WPA and UMWA payrolls. Hanna remained there for twenty years, keeping in the background, efficiently making and unmaking slates of candidates, perfecting the party's machinery, and, not incidentally, selling insurance to the state. The accumulated scandals and dissatisfactions of the Hanna years cost the Democrats the governorship in 1956, but they retained control of the legislature and other state offices. By 1960 the statehouse machine was ready to enter an even more cynical and scandalous phase of its career.

The seamier side of West Virginia's postwar political system featured nepotism, ballot-box stuffing, vote-buying, and a dozen varieties of petty and not-so-petty graft. There were higher levels of politics, however, involving the overwhelming majority of citizens who did not sell their votes and those prominent and respectable leaders who chose to remain innocent of the arrangements that sustained lesser lights. At this level, the webs of obligation revolved around a different sort of patronage, the sort that nineteenth-century cynics nicknamed "pork barrel." This type of politics was as old as the country, but the twentieth-century expansion of government services greatly augmented its impact at both the state and federal levels. Nearly every citizen was in potential need of advice or intervention involving some government program; nearly every community wanted a place at the public-works banquets that the New Deal and subsequent state and federal administrations served up. A politician who paid careful attention to these needs could win supporters without risk or impropriety. Thus the most widely admired postwar leaders were those who were able to secure federal money for such things as dams, post office buildings, and airports and to deploy their personal staffs effectively on what was called casework: helping individuals to deal with the military, welfare, and other bureaucracies. Senator Kilgore, for example, became ,a widely known and respected leader of this type.

The success of postwar politicians in putting together disparate but effective coalitions of business and labor, of "payrollers" and bureaucrats, reflected the ambiguous character of West Virginia society during the quarter century after 1945. For much of the state, the depression returned as the wartime boom subsided, but some districts entered into a period of unprecedented prosperity. As usual in West Virginia, whether the view was good or bad depended upon where one stood.

Perhaps one reason people found it hard to believe the dimensions of the Hawks Nest tragedy was that the project that produced it also brought together three of the most hopeful elements in modern West Virginia's economy. These were the chemical, primary-metals, and electrical-power industries, whose growth during the interwar period helped take up some of the economic slack caused by the decline of coal mining. Of the three, the chemical industry produced the most striking changes. It tied electrical and metals production together and it provided the manufacturing capstone on industrial development that southern West Virginia had previously lacked.

In a small way, chemical production in West Virginia is as old as the salt industry, but its great modern growth derived primarily from four interrelated developments of the early-twentieth century: the application of scientific research to industrial processes, the development of electrochemistry and electrolytic methods of producing metals and alloys, the discovery of nitrogen-fixation processes, and the effect of World War I, which greatly stimulated demand for chemical products while cutting off previously dominant German sources of supply. The first impact of these developments in West Virginia was the es-

tablishment of a small aluminum-reduction plant at Kanawha
Falls in 1901, where the same firm also established the state's
first hydroelectric generating station and built the town of Glen
Ferris. The Electrometallurgical Company absorbed and expanded this operation in 1907 and laid plans for the hydroelectric project at Hawks Nest. The war disrupted these plans, however, and they were not reactivated until 1928. Meanwhile,
Electrometallurgical and three other companies merged in 1917
to form Union Carbide, which embarked on a major program of
expansion in West Virginia during the next two decades. A pilot
petrochemical plant at Clendenin in 1920 led in 1925 to the development of the corporation's huge South Charleston works.
Five years later, Carbide broke ground at Alloy, five miles from
Glen Ferris, for a larger electrometallurgical plant, which was
designed to use power from Hawks Nest in producing steel
alloys. During World War II, a government contract for the
production of synthetic rubber ingredients led to expansion of
the South Charleston plant and the building of another large
works downriver at Institute in Kanawha County. By this time,
E. I. du Pont de Nemours & Company, Monsanto Chemical
Company, and other major American chemical firms had discovered the Kanawha Valley and had lined the river bottomlands for fifty miles west of Gauley Bridge with more than
two dozen chemical plants producing a great variety of products
and filling the narrow valley with a great variety of odors and
fumes. Manufacturing employment in the chemical districts
grew at two to three times the state rate during the Great Depression, doubling from 3,000 in 1930 to 6,000 in 1940, then
mushrooming to 25,000 in 1948. Since over two-thirds of these
workers were concentrated along the Kanawha, it is not surprising that Charleston boosters began to describe their region as a
"magic valley."

Chemical production continued to expand after World War II,
but the locus of growth shifted from the Kanawha to the Ohio
Valley. Here the broad and accessible bottomlands that captured
Washington's eye in 1770 proved equally attractive to industry,
with the Parkersburg and Moundsville districts providing the
most active centers of growth. By 1960, West Virginia had

nearly fifty major chemical-process plants, representing all of the country's important producers. Moreover, as they penetrated the Northern Panhandle, chemical producers encountered and, to some extent, interlocked with three long-established West Virginia industries: steel, glass, and pottery manufacture. Pottery remained localized in northern Hancock County and, with the more dispersed glass tableware industry, entered into a period of gradual decline during the 1930s, owing to the impact of foreign competitors. Industrial glassmaking expanded, however, with the Charleston, Clarksburg-Fairmont, and—after World War II—Parkersburg areas setting the pace.

The most notable development in the steel industry during this period was the rise of the Weirton Steel Corporation, which displaced Wheeling Steel as the state's largest integrated steel producer during the 1940s. Weirton had its beginnings at Clarksburg, where Ernest T. Weir of Pittsburgh and his partners bought a bankrupt tin-plate mill in 1905. Four years later, Weir picked out a more advantageous site for expansion near the Northern Panhandle community of Hollidays Cove. Here in a broad, crescent-shaped segment of the Ohio flood plain Weir built one of the nation's most modern steel-making complexes and with it the new town of Weirton. In 1929 Weir merged his company with others to create the National Steel Corporation and moved to Pittsburgh to manage the new firm. But Weirton Steel continued to flourish and so did the town, putting it in a unique position for a steel-making town during the depression. Strictly speaking, Weirton was not a company town, since the company owned no real estate or stores. The Weirton Improvement Association, a Weirton Steel subsidiary, provided streets, sewerage, safety, and other community services without charge to the residents until 1947. Then Weirton gave up its claim of being "the country's largest unincorporated town" and became the state's eighth largest city, with the president of Weirton Steel as the first mayor. The large number of immigrant workers who flocked to Weirton after World War I made it West Virginia's most colorful and diverse community in terms of ethnicity, a distinction it still retains.

If it could not match Weirton's phenomenal growth, the

Wheeling district's steel industry at least kept pace with the national rate of expansion, and there was growth in other sectors of the primary-metals industry. The establishment of the International Nickel Company's Huntington works in 1922 marked that city's first big step away from dependence upon glassmaking and industries auxiliary to railroads and coal mining. As with the chemical producers and steel makers, government contracts provided an expansionary stimulus to INCO during World War II. The use of electric-arc furnaces made alloy production an integral part of the state's chemical industry, while electrochemistry was essential to aluminum production. The announcement in 1955 that Kaiser Aluminum and Chemical Corporation would build a huge aluminum-reduction and manufacturing installation on the Ohio at Ravenswood excited West Virginia boosters at a time when the state's economy was especially hard hit by the coal slump. But though many political and business leaders stepped forward to claim credit for the new plant, its arrival was due to the same factors that stimulated industrial growth generally during the interwar and postwar years. This growth rested on a solid base of locational assets, including the central geographic location and "boundless natural resources" about which promoters had boasted so loudly and vainly in earlier times. The revival of waterborne traffic along the navigable rivers during and after World War I benefited West Virginia greatly and helped to make up for deficient highway and rail networks. Coal and natural gas provided both fuels and raw materials to the chemical producers, while coal also fed the power plants that supplied the metals producers with the copious amounts of energy they required. The increasing size of the state's industrial establishment and its contiguity with a system of inland waterways was itself a locational asset that attracted smaller suppliers and fabricators who served as satellites of the larger firms.

The growth of this manufacturing complex posed another challenge to organized labor. The CIO's Steel Workers Organizing Committee (SWOC) brought Wheeling Steel and INCO into the union fold, but failed signally at Weirton, where an extended contest with a company union ended in defeat in 1950. A drive to organize Kanawha Valley chemical workers also failed during the 1940s, partly because of competition between rival unions but mostly because the largest employers, Union Carbide and DuPont, were practitioners of "welfare capitalism," which provided wages and other benefits attractive enough to blunt union appeals. However, the Oil, Chemical, and Atomic Workers Union managed to establish locals at Alloy and at some of the Ohio Valley plants. Another breakthrough came in 1964 when Carbide workers succeeded in establishing a local of the International Association of Machinists at the South Charleston "mother" plant. Meanwhile, the Wheeling and Huntington districts' historic concentrations of craft unions provided a basis for the resurgence of the AFL in West Virginia from 1938 to 1956, when the craft and industrial unions reunited in the present AFL-CIO.

The spread of industry along the rivers naturally led to population changes. In 1930 the twelve Ohio River counties, plus Putnam and Kanawha, accounted for a third of West Virginia's population. By 1970 their share had risen to forty-three percent. A related shift drew more people to cities, although West Virginia cities grew slowly and remained small by national standards. Huntington became the state's largest city in 1930, but Charleston remained the most populous metropolitan area, while Wheeling seemed to many visitors to be the only *real* city in terms of the things that make a city urbane. Population growth in these and in other cities came to an end during the 1960s, but it continued in nearby suburban areas. Putnam County, straddling the suburban Teays Valley corridor linking Huntington and Charleston, became the state's fastest-growing county, followed closely by Jefferson, whose mountain-rimmed farmlands were taken gradually into the embrace of metropolitan Washington-Baltimore. Federal census takers in 1970 counted only thirty-nine percent of the population as urban, but the statistic was misleading in that West Virginia was by no means a rural state in the traditional sense that equates rusticity with farming. Less than six percent of West Virginians in 1970 actually lived on farms.

Along with population changes came more subtle changes in

West Virginia's social geography. For generations "the people who lived in the bottom looked down on the people on top," according to a mountain aphorism meaning, of course, that the most valuable level land tended to be occupied by the most affluent people. This held true in the cities as well as in agricultural districts. Wheeling provides a classic example. As the city overspread its riverside bench during the late nineteenth century, the best housing was built on flat land on Wheeling Island or along the flood plain of Wheeling Creek, while slum housing and narrow, unpaved lanes climbed the steep hills next to the downtown business district. Charleston enjoyed a more spacious townsite, but here, too, expensive housing spread out across the bottomlands east of the business section while poorer housing pressed into the hills along the hollows that divided them or concentrated in the less convenient bottomlands west of the Elk. Even in hilly interior cities like Clarksburg and Fairmont the finest housing occupied the most accessible land. The reason was simple. Men who could afford a choice preferred to walk to their downtown places of business or at least to avoid the hazards and inconveniences that beset pedestrians, horses, and streetcars in hilly terrain.

The automobile changed all this. Or, more precisely, the expansion of business districts and of noisy and smelly factories along the rivers provided the stimuli to escape to the hills, and automobiles provided convenient means to do so. Eminences like William A. MacCorkle in Charleston and Earl W. Oglebay in Wheeling built hilltop suburban estates before World War I, but the largest growth of hilltop suburbs came later: during the 1920s and especially during the twenty-five-year real estate boom that followed World War II. In every West Virginia city, middle- and upper-income families fled the flatlands as fast as the factories moved in, exchanging their older two-story houses for models of the latest approved suburban styles located in new neighborhoods with names that were often borrowed from fashionable metropolitan suburbs. In Weirton, executives of the steel corporation left the neat, terraced residential blocks next to the mills for Marland Heights, a suburb whose most privileged residents nestled close to a company-sponsored country club with a commanding view of the Ohio River and the smoggy industrial valley below. In Charleston, developers started from the heads of hollows already filled with cheap housing and drove roads upward into the steep surrounding hills to create the South Hills complex of neighborhoods, a miniature version of an affluent Pittsburgh district. Even Huntington, whose shady boulevards and wide, level lawns enchanted earlier generations of hill-bred West Virginians, began to move from the bottomland to the hills, while in Ravenswood, Kaiser Aluminum executives occupied the higher elevations from the start, mingling there with local bankers and lawyers in a ridgetop location jocularly known as Martini Row. The importance of the automobile in the new suburbs was witnessed by the almost total absence of pedestrian sidewalks and by an architecture that devoted from one-eighth to one-third of each residence to space for a garage.

The people who lived in the new hilltop suburbs and in prosperous corners of smaller towns and cities throughout the state enjoyed a way of life that differed sharply from that of the people who lingered on in mountain coves and hollows, in the coal camps, and in the abandoned urban bottomlands or the old hillside slums. Prosperous West Virginians lived in the same type of houses, shopped in the same stores, dreamed the same dreams for themselves and their children that affluent Americans did in other parts of the country. Urban West Virginia was a part of urban America, and its citizens were quick to resent any suggestion that local departures from national norms were anything more than minor variations on a dominant harmonious chord. From the perspective of the new suburbs and the industrial valleys they overlooked, this attitude was surely correct, and yet West Virginia as a whole was still different from the rest of the country, in this age as in every other. The interior plateau was still the dominant factor in the state's economy and in the image that the state projected abroad.

Traditionally Hawks Nest marked for travelers a transition between the rivers and the hills, between the smooth passage afforded by the Kanawha and Ohio and the rugged paths of the interior. During the 1950s this transition was again as much economic as geographic, for it carried between riverside towns with expanding populations and payrolls and an interior plateau once more filled with unemployment and hardship. The welfare programs established during the 1930s cushioned the shock of this postwar depression, but a more potent meliorative factor was the availability of jobs in nearby metropolitan centers. The slump precipitated a great migration of West Virginians to other states, draining the interior of over one-fourth of its people and lowering the population of the state by thirteen percent between 1950 and 1970, a time when the nation at large grew rapidly. In the growth-oriented context of traditional West Virginia boosterism, the migration dealt a blow to pride as well as to pocketbooks.

The migration started in the farm counties during the 1940s, especially in the Little Kanawha region and in mountain counties such as Pendleton, Pocahontas, and Tucker, but, as usual, the greatest calamities were reserved for the coalfields. McDowell County lost almost half of its population between 1950 and 1970; Logan and Fayette declined by over forty percent, while all but one of the other major coal-producing counties declined by smaller proportions. The exception was Monongalia, where the growth of West Virginia University and related research institutions balanced the decline in the coal towns, though it created few opportunities for unemployed coal miners. An official study reported in 1955 that the migration was "heavily weighted with relatively young people of working age," precisely the people the state least wanted to lose.[7]

The people who left were in a very real sense cast out of their homeland because their labor was no longer needed, but the decision to go or stay was made on a personal basis and was usually carried through with the determination of westering pioneers. "I said to Clara and all my kids that they should say goodbye to those mountains—goodbye, period, the end," one man recalled of his family's move to Chicago; "you don't want to leave because of the strangeness ahead of you, but you know

7. Arthur D. Little, Inc., *Report to the State of West Virginia,* 2 vols. (Cambridge, Mass.: The Author, 1955), 1:6.

you leave or you near die, just about, and you know that your kids might find something in the cities, though God knows what, so you wrench yourself away. . . ." [8] Many emigrants tried first to find work in West Virginia cities, but the opportunities close to home were simply too few for the many who sought them. Even Huntington, with its diversified economy, was overwhelmed by jobless men drifting in from the coalfields. And so they left, often leaving their families at home at the outset. Special buses ran between Huntington and Detroit during the 1950s, bringing migrants home for 24-hour weekends. Eventually the families migrated also, and weekends at home came to be confined mainly to holidays; then the streets of West Virginia communities would be crowded with cars bearing Ohio or Michigan or Maryland tags. For the grandchildren, West Virginia became just a place to visit in the summer. "My boy likes the woods, and playing with his cousins," a former Raleigh County man told Robert Coles. "But on the way home he always tells me that he's glad we're leaving and he's glad I left a long time ago." "My grandchildren are city children," reported a Logan County man who moved to Pittsburgh. They had learned the streets and byways of an urban neighborhood the way their parents and aunts and uncles had learned the hillside paths behind their West Virginia home. [9]

Individual stories like these, which were collected and published by Coles in *The South Goes North,* resolve in the aggregate into a mountain of social statistics, a sort of numerical gob pile that gradually rose out of the coalfields to overshadow the entire state. In addition to the declining population figures, West Virginia's unemployment rate was two to three times the national norm, and its per-capita income hovered around seventy-five percent of the national average. Prosperous West Virginians sometimes grew tired of hearing such statistics recited, but the grim portrait they painted was essentially correct, as a growing volume of expert social and economic inquiry tes-

8. Quoted in Robert Coles, *The South Goes North* (vol. 3) of *The Children of Crisis,* 3 vols. (Boston: Little, Brown, 1970), p. 618.

9. Coles, *The South Goes North,* pp. 345, 366.

tified. By 1960 the experts, at least, were in widespread agreement that something was desperately wrong in West Virginia and that something ought to be done.

What was wrong was more than simply another slump in the coal industry. West Virginia coal production fell off by 35 percent between 1947 and 1954, but the number of mining jobs fell even more rapidly, from 125,000 to 65,000. Moreover, while production leveled off and even increased during peak years of national economic activity, the number of jobs continued to fall—to 49,000 in 1960 and 41,000 in 1968, the lowest number of miners employed in West Virginia since 1903. The causes behind this decline were mechanization and consolidation in the bituminous coal industry, two trends that had the United Mine Workers' wholehearted approval. The union's quid pro quo was a welfare fund created from royalties collected on each ton of coal produced in union mines. The fund was established after a bitter strike in 1946 but not fully accepted by the companies until 1950. As John L. Lewis explained it, high wages and a seniority system would protect the miners' share of the massive productivity gains that mechanization made possible, while the welfare fund's pension and health-care provisions would take up the slack of a slowly diminishing job supply. That was the theory; in practice it did not work out that way. The industry's experts predicted a healthy, long-range future for coal as the nation came to depend on it more and more for electrical-power production. But this future was a long way off, while the economic recessions of 1958–1962 were soon at hand. The recessions sent production down to 1954 levels and deprived the welfare fund of badly needed royalties. As a result, in 1961 the union closed down or sold a chain of ten shiny new welfare-fund hospitals it had opened only five years earlier. Pensions were reduced and the pension rolls shaved by the adoption of hairsplitting eligibility requirements. Behind the scenes, Lewis and his successors transformed the UMWA from a citadel of labor militancy into a "sweetheart union" that routinely entered into furtive and illegal deals with the largest coal companies. Lewis's destruction of union democracy, carried out in the name of unity and efficiency in the 1920s and 1930s, now came home to haunt the miners as it stifled the discussion and criticism that might have moved the union leaders away from their disastrous course.

It should be noted that there would still have been a great migration from West Virginia even if the UMWA program had worked out according to plan, for though there would have been less hardship for veteran miners, young persons would still have had to leave the mining communities to find other jobs. Throughout the long period of negotiations that preceded the welfare and mechanization agreements, there had been only one proposal put forward the purpose of which was primarily to protect the coal communities. This was a clause in one of the Guffey bills of the 1930s that would have provided redevelopment and retraining funds for mining towns hit hard by unemployment. The idea originated with some of President Roosevelt's economic advisors, but it died in Congress, not so much because of opposition as because no interested party was strongly in favor, not John L. Lewis or Senator Neely or the companies who, after all, still owned most of the mining towns. The incident showed that a remote and autocratic union bureaucracy could be just as unresponsive to unorganized local constituencies as absentee corporations or landlords. If any doubt remained on this point in the postwar era, it was speedily cleared up by the inept and dishonest union leadership that took over after Lewis retired in 1961.

In the end the big coal companies benefited more from mechanization than anyone else. While dozens of small firms sold out or went out of business because they could not afford the outlays that high wages and equipment costs entailed, corporations like Consolidation Coal began aggressive programs of expansion. Already northern West Virginia's largest producer, Consol merged with Pittsburgh Coal, the giant of the western Pennsylvania fields, and then moved into the south with the acquisition of Pocahontas Coal in 1956. Of the firms historically rooted in southern West Virginia, only one—Island Creek—survived as one of the larger producers in 1970. The big companies were able to modernize their plants, get rid of their surplus workers, liquidate the company towns (which had become more a nuisance than a convenience after unionization eliminated their value in disciplining workers), and in general to prepare to take advantage of the prosperous future that coal economists forecast. Of course the well-paid miners who kept their jobs would share in that future, but they paid a higher price for productivity than did the companies. One price was "black lung," or pneumoconiosis, a disease resembling silicosis in its disabling effects, the incidence of which increased with the greater amounts of coal dust that mechanized equipment threw into the air. Another drawback for workers was the industry's deplorable safety record, which the union abetted by declining to press for mine-safety improvements after 1952.

It was therefore clear that if something was to be done about West Virginia's predicament, it would not be done by the coal companies or the UMWA. The most logical source of relief was government. In 1953, Governor William C. Marland, the most controversial governor of the Neely-Hanna regime, revived with Neely's support the severance-tax idea as a means of financing better welfare and educational programs, but the proposal met short shrift in a legislature full of friends of the coal industry. After a brief and vituperative debate, Marland dropped the idea. Subsequently he staged a series of well-publicized but generally ineffective "industrial recruitment" campaigns in New York and other cities. A more successful program of the Marland years was an expansion and modernization of the state park system, which, it was hoped, might serve to attract a larger volume of tourists.

Most leaders looked to Washington rather than to Charleston for help. The state's congressional delegation led an effort during the 1950s to restrict foreign oil imports and to promote natural-gas "conservation" in hopes of limiting these fuels' inroads on the electrical-generating market, but oil's lobby proved much more powerful than coal's. After oil companies bought control of Consolidation and Island Creek Coal during the 1960s, the effort was dropped. More promising routes to recovery were special "area redevelopment" programs, wherein federal funds and agencies would deploy to attract new jobs to the coalfields and to retrain workers to fill them. These proposals made headway in Congress as Democratic majorities increased after 1958, but they lacked the essential support of President Dwight D. Eisenhower. In hopes of winning support from Eisenhower's successor, the governor of Maryland summoned a Conference of Appalachian Governors to meet at Annapolis early in 1960. The governors decided to invite each candidate to take a stand on the region's economic problems in the course of the coming presidential campaign.

Only one of the presidential contenders made a significant response to the governors' initiative, but he was the one who counted most: John F. Kennedy. During a brief but masterful campaign that won West Virginia's presidential primary in May, Kennedy visited the state frequently and personally confronted its problems, which he promised, if elected, to solve. He later described his victory in West Virginia as the most important step in his path to the White House, since it demonstrated that a Roman Catholic could win in a predominantly Protestant state. Although Kennedy emphasized this religious angle, the shrewdest observers concluded that religion had actually played a relatively small role in the campaign compared with economic issues and the candidate's engaging personal style and lavish campaign expenditures. In any event, this "primary that made a president" gave West Virginians a sense of participation in the national destiny that they had not enjoyed for many long years.

If President Kennedy had done nothing more than revive the flagging spirits of West Virginians, that was no mean achievement. But he did more. While his interest in the state produced few concrete changes during his brief presidency, Kennedy set in motion some developments that had important repercussions after his death. The Appalachian Regional Commission, established by Congress in 1965, grew out of pilot programs established by Kennedy in response to his 1960 campaign commitments. The complex of agencies and programs known as "the war on poverty," though they were partly a product of President Lyndon Johnson's desire for "his own program" after Kennedy's assassination, grew out of commitments and concepts of the Kennedy years. One such concept—the idea that poor people should participate in shaping and running programs designed to help them—would give a thorough shaking up to a number of West Virginia courthouses before the poverty warriors were finally driven off. Finally, the glare of national attention that Kennedy originally helped to focus continued to shine on West Virginia and its region during the subsequent decade. "Appalachia," once a specialized term used mainly by geologists, became a code word that summed up all the things that made West Virginia different from the rest of the nation, the good things as well as the bad. Intermingled with the state's economic disadvantages, which politicians, academics, and bureaucrats promised to change, was much that seemed worthy of preservation. This included the remnants of an Appalachian folk culture that specialists had been searching out in the hollows and hills since the 1920s and which now became an increasingly fashionable part of metropolitan popular culture. No matter how it was defined, Appalachia always included more of West Virginia than of any other state. And while affluent citizens found it hard to identify with any form of "Appalachian consciousness," by 1970 growing numbers of people, especially young people, hoped to see the region's cultural distinctiveness preserved.

Yet there was a dark side to the Kennedy legacy in West Virginia. The same primary campaign that catapulted Kennedy toward the White House also launched W. W. "Wally" Barron as the rebuilder of the Democratic statehouse machine and, while there was no formal alliance of the two candidates, an obvious symbiotic relationship was fostered in many counties by Kennedy's supply of money and Barron's equally lavish promises of political jobs. Barron subsequently put together the most corrupt administration in the history of the state, an administration whose misdeeds left even hardened West Virginians aghast. Barron himself became the first governor to go to prison; with him went thirteen former officials in his or the succeeding Democratic administration, plus five of their friends, relatives, and business associates. Another official was placed on probation and others were still awaiting trial in 1975. Most of the convictions grew out of bribery or related conspiracy, tax-evasion, and falsification-of-records charges, although Barron himself was convicted of jury tampering. The trials began in March 1965, and continued for a decade. It was in keeping with the cruelest traditions of West Virginia politics that the first indictments involved a scheme by statehouse insiders to make money from a disaster, specifically a flash flood that killed twenty-two persons in the hollows of Charleston in 1961. Altogether, the Barron administration was an outstanding entry on West Virginia's already formidable list of "worsts."

It thus seemed fitting that President Kennedy and Governor Barron—representing the best and worst of West Virginia, one articulating hope for the future, the other embodying the deep-seated cynicism of the past—presided jointly over the state's centennial celebration in 1963. This time the birthday party was no weekend affair, as in 1913. Barron launched painstaking preparations for the event at a special "centennial conference" held at The Greenbrier in November 1961. Here it was resolved that the celebration must be more than fun and frolic.[10] It was. The observance lasted a year and served up a whopping helping of the usual historical fantasies. Some parts of the celebration unintentionally told more about the state than others, however. For example, one of the events specifically designed to counteract the state's poverty-stricken and "hillbilly" images was an art competition with a distinguished panel of "outside" judges; they awarded first prize to a harshly realistic portrayal of Appalachian poverty, outraging those citizens who wanted the winning painting to depict something "pretty." Similarly, the Centennial Commission adopted as an official symbol an outline of a giant radio-astronomy telescope of a type then under construction by federal authorities in Pendleton and Pocahontas counties. The idea was to convey West Virginia's readiness to enter the Space Age, but the notion was considerably tarnished when the sponsors decided not to complete one telescope and moved the administrative headquarters of the other to Charlottesville, Virginia, because the highly trained scientists who manned it were unwilling to

---

10. W. W. Barron to John D. Hoblitzell, Jr., November 1, 1961, John D. Hoblitzell, Jr., Papers, WVU, series 1, box 1, folder B; *Charleston Gazette,* November 17, 1961.

expose their families to West Virginia social services and schools. Although these incidents attracted nationwide attention, they failed to dampen the enjoyment that most West Virginians derived from the centennial events. Nevertheless they served once again to remind us that, in West Virginia, unpleasant realities have a way of undermining romance.

7

Buffalo Creek

N the autumn of 1971, West Virginians were pleasantly surprised to hear their radios playing a popular ballad called "Take Me Home, Country Roads" whose refrain opened with the words, "Almost heaven, West Virginia . . ." [1] Hearing their state's praises sung in a nationally popular song might be a routine occurrence for residents of California or Georgia, but for West Virginia it was a unique and gratifying experience. The song quickly became a semiofficial anthem, while "Almost Heaven" became a popular and ubiquitous slogan, posted on everything from billboards to swizzle sticks. State officials and boosters eagerly expropriated the phrase, asserting that West Virginia was "almost heaven" for tourists and industry as well as for the scenery, moonshine, and "mountain mamas" celebrated by the lyrics of the song.

The response to "Take Me Home, Country Roads" was all the more noteworthy in that the song was written by a trio of popular entertainers then living in Washington, D.C., whose acquaintance with the state was obviously limited. The lyrics evoked a number of hillbilly and coalfield stereotypes that normally provoked an angry or defensive response and, most insulting of all, confused West Virginia geography with that of Virginia. But most people, if they took note of these defects at all, tended to overlook them. Whether or not it said the right things, the song came along at just the right time. Unlike the slogans that boosters cranked out in the past, "Almost Heaven" was not an attempt to create pride where pride was lacking. Rather it reflected a growing feeling of satisfaction shared by many, if not most, citizens, a feeling that one of the worst chapters in West Virginia's history was closing at last.

This feeling had a substantial basis in fact, for by the beginning of the 1970s there was an abundance of tangible evidence that things were not so bad as they had been. Measurements that had once inspired gloomy prognoses now provided statistical glimmers of hope. Unemployment, which had fluctuated between two and three times the national average during the worst years of the preceding decades, had fallen to within one percentage point of the national average by 1970. Migration diminished, and while the 1970 census registered another drop in the state's overall population, official estimates for 1971 and 1972 showed a slight population increase, the first since 1950. Per-capita income, which dipped below seventy-five percent of the national average during the early 1960s, rose to eighty percent by 1972. These signs were all the more encouraging in that they were no longer confined to industrial and suburban districts. The coal industry's long-promised upsurge was well under way by 1971, while the eastern mountain counties were on the verge of a boom in recreational industries and lands.

An expansive public-works program offered further evidence of prosperity. New libraries, schools, parks, and public buildings appeared in every corner of the state, but here, as in other states, the most popular monuments to "progress" were new highways. West Virginia's share in the original interstate-highway system designed in 1956 was small, but local business, labor, and political leaders worked hard to expand it and were rewarded by the designation of two additional routes, Interstates 77 and 79, crossing the state from north to south. Another network of highways, "Appalachian development corridors" planned and partly funded by the Appalachian Regional Commission, provided a supplementary 450-mile system to the 500 miles of interstate roads. While construction of these expressways was a slow and costly process in West Virginia's rugged terrain, enough mileage had been built by 1971 to amply illustrate their advantages. As far as most citizens were concerned, West Virginia seemed all the more heavenly the less it was bound by its older system of romantic but dangerous country roads.

Federal assistance to the states in areas such as highway construction dated back to the time of the First World War, but the scope of this aid greatly increased during the 1960s and extended to a vastly greater array of programs. Federal funds available to West Virginia more than tripled between 1960 and 1970, which was roughly the national rate of expansion, and while there were plenty of local leaders who stepped forward to claim credit for this largesse, essentially it flowed from the same sort of government agencies and pressure groups that had produced most significant initiatives in public policy since the New Deal. It was such an alliance, for example, that produced the interstate program and which also brought pressure to bear upon West Virginia's patronage-ridden and inexpertly managed State Road Commission during the program's early years; as a result, in 1965 the legislature reorganized the commission as a state department of highways and took steps to insulate its most critical jobs and financial decisions from the influence of "payrollers." In public education, the West Virginia Education Association, reorganized as a pressure group during the 1940s, campaigned steadily to raise teachers' salaries and benefits and to remove their jobs from the patronage system, while the National Education Association worked to unlock the key to the national treasury. Partial success on both fronts modernized school systems in some of the wealthier counties during the late 1950s, notably Hancock and Kanawha, but the big breakthrough for the "school lobby" did not come until 1965, when both Congress and the legislature voted substantial increases in public-school aid. Although the provisions of the Tax Limitation Amendment of 1932 continued to inhibit the raising of matching funds on the county level, a school building boom followed that affected more than half of West Virginia's counties. The new funds stimulated modernization and expansion at every educational level, from preschool to the university, but the characteristic landmarks of the boom were sprawling new "consolidated" high schools that appeared in both rural and suburban districts during these years. Although they were more controversial (and much less costly) than the new expressways, the new high schools were also prominent symbols of progress.

Modernization was the watchword in other areas of state government during the postcentennial era and here, too, the federal government was the most consistently effective prod. The number of state employees protected by a merit system of recruitment and promotion steadily increased under the pressure of federal agencies interested in a stable and efficient state bureaucracy; by 1971 roughly a third of state employees were covered by civil service, compared with one-sixth ten years before. In a related area federal courts undertook to supervise congressional redistricting and the reapportionment of the legislature, county courts, and municipal councils. The reapportioned legislature in turn sponsored constitutional amendments in 1968 and 1970 that provided for extended annual sessions of the legislature, prohibited public employees from serving as legislators, and deflated the perennial political football of legislative salaries by turning the job over to a special commission. Other changes centralized budgetary responsibility in the governor's office and made incumbent governors eligible for re-election to a second term. Arch A. Moore, Jr., a Republican elected in 1968 in the wake of the Barron scandals, took advantage of this last provision to become West Virginia's first two-term governor in the election of 1972.

The U. S. Supreme Court inaugurated another string of important changes in its school-desegregation decision of May 1954. Since West Virginia state leaders promptly announced compliance with the decision, local affiliates of the National Association for the Advancement of Colored People were initially content to work through the courts to pressure those counties that offered some resistance to the decree. Many younger blacks found this mode of desegregation too slow, however, and so in

March 1960 a group of Bluefield State College students turned to the "direct action" techniques that labor organizers had used in an earlier day. Beginning in Bluefield, a city that black activists referred to as West Virginia's Mississippi, a series of nonviolent demonstrations and "sit ins" spread to Huntington and Charleston and eventually led to a number of integrated theaters and eating-places in these and other major cities across the state. The accumulated pressure generated by these tactics around the country led first to federal (1964) and then state (1967) public-accommodations laws that banned racial discrimination in such places as restaurants, hotels, and parks. These developments, plus the absence of racial violence at a time when it was common in many parts of the country, encouraged a self-congratulatory feeling among many white West Virginians. However most private social and recreational associations remained segregated, while surveys at the end of the decade showed that discrimination was standard practice in the fields of employment and housing. What passed for racial harmony was often more nearly a mood of indifference. Blacks had left West Virginia at a rate three times greater than whites during the great migration. This reduced their proportion of the population to just over four percent in the census of 1970, the lowest black proportion in a century. In these circumstances other issues generally overshadowed the controversies and resistance that black aspirations stirred elsewhere, except in a few eastern and southern West Virginia communities where Southern traditions died hard.

The methods of the civil-rights movement may have had a greater impact on West Virginia than the issues it raised, for the success of "direct action" led to its adoption by other dissident groups. The most spectacular example was the Black Lung Association (BLA), an organization of rank-and-file miners and ex-miners who joined forces in December 1968 to seek workmen's-compensation benefits for pneumoconiosis victims. Although a group of coalfield doctors lent medical authority to the crusade, the UMWA's national leaders treated BLA with open hostility, while other conventional liberal pressure groups turned an indifferent ear to the miners' pleas. Consequently BLA turned to direct action, rocking the state with a dramatic series of wildcat strikes and Charleston demonstrations until finally, in February 1969, a reluctant legislature and an even more reluctant Governor Moore approved the new compensation law. The BLA then moved on to Washington to push the Federal Coal Mine Health and Safety Act through Congress later in the year. This created an even more expansive program of pneumoconiosis benefits under federal auspices. Encouraged by these victories, the BLA leaders joined with other dissident miners to challenge the corrupt leadership that had governed the UMWA since John L. Lewis's departure in 1961. After a long, tough, and frequently violent campaign waged throughout the coalfields, this Miners for Democracy (MFD) movement succeeded in electing Arnold Miller, a Cabin Creek miner and BLA activist, to the union presidency in December 1972. As it did with the black-lung movement, the federal government played a critical role in the later stages of the MFD campaign, but in both cases the initiative came from the coalfields, not from Washington. Perhaps more than any other events, these manifestations of an insurgent coalfield democracy contributed to the sense of new possibilities that prevailed in liberal circles in West Virginia at the turn of the decade.

Linking the civil-rights activism of the early 1960s with the insurgent miners of 1969 was the Kennedy and Johnson administrations' "war" on Appalachian poverty. While the Appalachian Regional Commission followed a conservative course, spending most of its money on highways and working only through established state and local authorities, the federal "war on poverty" as established in 1964 and administered through the Office of Economic Opportunity (OEO), sought to infuse its complex of programs with the ethic of "participatory democracy." The poverty warriors pursued this objective in two ways: first, by requiring community participation in the design and execution of specific social programs, and second, by harnessing the energies of youthful activists to work as VISTA (Volunteers In Service To America) or Appalachian Volunteers. The primary objective was "community organizing," an effort to mobilize hitherto passive communities of poor people, arousing them to an awareness of their needs and creating a sustained and active demand for government policies that could help them. Although the untested social theories upon which this approach rested later came in for much criticism, from the standpoint of many West Virginia politicians the idea worked only too well. Mingo County, as Huey Perry recounts in a detailed and entertaining fashion in *They'll Cut Off Your Project,* provided a classic example of how the poverty program unsettled established authorities. The Mingo program started out modestly enough by sponsoring some twenty-six local "community action" groups that initially concerned themselves with such seemingly tame objectives as school-bus service and road repairs. But any goals involving better service to the poor— however minimal—quickly led to confrontation with the county's notoriously corrupt political structure headed by state senator Noah Floyd. Thus in 1967 the "community action" groups organized a biracial Political Action League. "The strategy was to direct the energies of the poor away from development and implementation of federal programs, which usually treated only the symptoms of poverty, toward the building of a political base from which the poor could attack poverty itself." [2] The reformers met with many frustrations, for Floyd had powerful connections in Charleston and Washington. They managed, however, to purge the voting rolls of several thousand dead and other illegally registered voters. (Mingo was one of a number of West Virginia counties whose registration totals increased as the overall population shrank.) They also set in motion a series of grand-jury investigations and political realignments that eventually led to Floyd's defeat for re-election in the 1970 primary. Considering all the hard work, time, and personal risk the Mingo reformers had invested, these achievements were modest enough, as Perry admitted. Yet the effort provided a valuable civics lesson about the seamier side of West Virginia politics and helped to create the conditions that made for the insurgent miners' success in later years.

Courthouse politicians who eyed local OEO budgets and payrolls enviously tended to welcome the program itself and to

---

2. Huey Perry, *They'll Cut Off Your Project: A Mingo County Chronicle* (New York: Praeger, 1972), p. 135.

cast the blame elsewhere for the unsettling things that it did. Usually the blame fell on the young volunteers. "They are dirty, nasty; they won't shave," a Mingo politico complained, while many officials accused them of teaching communism.[3] Moreover, since the majority of the volunteers were young white college students recruited outside the state, they were subject to the traditional label of "outside agitator." Actually no more than 150 of the volunteers served in West Virginia at any one time between 1965 and the end of the poverty program in 1972, and the majority of these served quietly in uncontroversial roles with mental-health agencies. The rest of them, however, more than made up for their small numbers by an energetic approach to their task. In Mercer County volunteer organizers effected a coalition of urban black and rural white communities that defeated a school building program that promised to perpetuate segregation and other inequities. School controversies also engaged the volunteers in Nicholas, while in Kanawha they helped to carry the largest "community action" program into the slums and hollows around Charleston. Beginning in 1968, volunteers in Mingo, Clay, Boone, Kanawha, and Wyoming counties promoted the spread of the National Welfare Rights Organization, while a number of VISTA and AV "alumni" participated in the black-lung and MFD campaigns of 1969. In a less controversial but equally valuable endeavor, Kanawha volunteers helped organize Cabin Creek Quilts, a co-operative formed to take advantage of the growing commercial interest in traditional Appalachian crafts. Another development of potentially far-reaching impact was the appearance of young activist lawyers who staffed federally funded legal-aid offices around the state and who also manned a "public interest" law firm established at Charleston in 1970. Proclaiming itself "a countervailing force to the heavy influences of the special interest groups" that had traditionally dominated West Virginia politics and government,[4] this Appalachian Research and Defense Fund

3. Perry, *They'll Cut Off Your Project,* p. 145.
4. Quoted in Neal R. Pierce, *The Border South States, People, Politics and Power in the Five Border South States* (New York: W. W. Norton, 1974), p. 157.

promptly set to work on OEO-financed studies of tax reform, strip-mining, air and water pollution, and other controversial issues that were expected to come before the legislature in 1971.

This particular legislature, the sixtieth to assemble since 1863, embodied all of the forces that stirred hope and anger in the postcentennial decade. By 1971 the public-works program of the past few years had raised public expectations about the scope and quality of government services, while the end of the economic decline bolstered faith in the state's ability to finance further improvements. Reapportionment, reorganization, and the recent success of coalfield insurgency all enhanced this mood of expectancy. Divided partisan control of the statehouse, with Governor Moore facing an overwhelmingly Democratic legislature, made for divided accountability. Given the low level of trust that most West Virginians placed in their politicians, however, many people were glad to have the governor and legislature check each other. And since Moore's occupation of the statehouse had sharply curtailed the amount of patronage available to county Democratic organizations, liberal, issue-oriented Democrats had been correspondingly strengthened. Headed by House Speaker Ivor Boiarsky of Charleston, a leader widely admired for both competence and integrity, the liberals were in a stronger position than at any time in recent decades.

In these circumstances, the 1971 session emerged as one of the most productive of the twentieth century. Its output contained something for everyone: a labor-relations act of the type that organized labor had sought since 1941; a civil-rights act that banned housing and job discrimination; more money for roads, schools, legislators, and teachers; measures that reformed the state's drug laws and lowered the voting age to 18; extensions of the civil service; and new regulations governing mine safety and air pollution. The most controversial measure of the session, a comprehensive tax-reform package that had been five years in the making, met with a gubernatorial veto, but later the governor and legislative leaders agreed on a compromise that raised business and occupation taxes—as the gross sales tax was formally known—and added a severance tax that raised the levy on coal sales by 159 percent. Another compromise evolved when a proposal to abolish strip-mining failed of passage, but a moratorium on stripping in twenty-two counties was adopted along with stiffer regulations governing the reclamation of strip-mined land. The unexpected death of Speaker Boiarsky in the closing days of the session added a poignant note to the sense of accomplishment that these enactments entailed.

It must be admitted that few of the achievements of the post-centennial years set West Virginia apart from the other states of the Union. The period produced a few outstanding projects or measures: the workmen's-compensation law of 1969, a luxurious new state park—Pipestem in Summers County, innovative high schools in a number of counties, an architecturally distinctive public library at Clarksburg, a record-shattering highway bridge over New River Gorge. Generally, however, West Virginia was not yet a leader among the states. It was still a follower, struggling to catch up with most of the others. The most that could be said in 1971 was that this struggle had become somewhat less desperate than before. By almost any standard of measurement, West Virginia had drawn perceptibly closer to national norms, and this was important. For fifty years, even longer if one looked all the way back to the start of the mine wars, West Virginians had repeatedly found their state being examined in the national limelight as some place different, a bad example, a backward, unprosperous, violent island in the rich and placid current of American life. Most West Virginians were tired of a limelight that showed only blemishes; even those who were most critical of the state's continuing deficiencies sometimes longed to be thought of as typical, ordinary, normal Americans. In 1971 these feelings did not seem so unrealistic as they had in earlier years. For most people it was a time of satisfaction and optimism, a well-deserved and long-awaited moment. And the moment found a perfect mode of expression in the friendly lyrics and lilting tune of "Take Me Home, Country Roads."

Then came the disaster at Buffalo Creek.

There are at least ten streams called Buffalo Creek in West Virginia. Nearly every major river has a tributary of that name.

George Washington camped near the mouth of the Ohio's Buffalo Creek on his way down the river in 1770. Subsequently he acquired lands surrounding the junction of another Buffalo Creek with the Kanawha. The town of Widen, a model coal camp of the 1920s and the scene of bitter labor struggles from 1933 to 1954, stands at the head of a Buffalo Creek that flows into Elk River, while another landmark of coalfield history, a Consolidation Coal Company mine that exploded and killed seventy-eight men in November 1968, lies in the valley of the Monongahela Buffalo Creek near Farmington. The Guyandot Buffalo Creek in Logan County had not found its way into history before the morning of February 26, 1972. Then, in the space of a few short and terrible hours, this Buffalo Creek became more famous—or infamous—than all the rest.

What happened that morning was called a flood, but the disaster was something much more deadly than an ordinary flood. At the head of Buffalo Creek hollow—as in the hollow at Widen and in more than two dozen other places in West Virginia at this time—stood a giant mound of "gob," or mine refuse, which the Buffalo Mining Company had formed into a dam impounding water used in its coal-washing operations. The failure of this dam on February 26 sent 135 million gallons of water crashing through the narrow, winding hollow below. The flood killed 125 people and destroyed the homes of 4,000. Most of the victims had little warning other than a weird dancing of the overhead utility wires and a roar moving down the valley—warnings they did not comprehend until too late. The devastation was as complete as it was sudden.

The Buffalo Creek flood led to the usual investigations: one by federal authorities, another by a gubernatorial commission filled with coal industry spokesmen and clients, a third by a self-constituted group of liberals and Buffalo Creek residents who were certain that the other two groups would concoct a whitewash. All three inquiries were surprisingly unanimous in their conclusions. The impoundment that caused the flood had been built in defiance of law and of proper engineering procedures. Moreover, there had been many warnings of the impending disaster, warnings that officials of Buffalo Mining and the state and federal agencies charged with policing such structures had ignored. Although heavy rains preceded the flood, they were neither unusual nor unseasonable. Consequently the disaster was entirely man-made and preventable. Even the governor's commission concluded that the Pittston Company, the parent firm of Buffalo Mining and the nation's largest independent coal producer, had "shown flagrant disregard for the safety of residents of Buffalo Creek and other persons who live near coal-refuse impoundments." However, the Pittston Company called the disaster "an Act of God." [5]

What happened at Buffalo Creek demonstrated forcefully that the shadow of West Virginia's tragic and violent history was longer than could be whistled away by a single popular song. Of course, not all West Virginians were willing to learn this lesson. In a move that attracted nationwide attention, Governor Moore closed the Buffalo Creek area to journalists for a period after the flood because he objected to their "irresponsible reporting." Subsequently Moore relented on the news blackout, but he continued to complain about the "terrible beating" that West Virginia's image took as a result of the flood. [6] Far better than all the statistics that churned out of government offices, such attitudes showed just how far West Virginia still had to go.

5. Governor's Ad Hoc Commission of Inquiry, *The Buffalo Creek Flood and Disaster* (Charleston: The Commission, 1973), p. 6.6; Tom Nugent, *Death at Buffalo Creek: The 1972 West Virginia Flood Disaster* (New York: W. W. Norton, 1973), p. 155.

6. Nugent, *Death at Buffalo Creek*, p. 156; *Washington Post*, February 29, 1972; *Charleston Gazette*, March 8, 9, 1972.

8

Montani semper. . . .

F West Virginia history has a central theme, it was sounded at the very beginning by the explorers who described it as a "pleasing tho' dreadful" land. The rugged face of this land has provided every generation with a rich source of sentimental attachment to West Virginia homes. West Virginians have always loved their mountains. They have proclaimed that love loudly and often, agreeing with the English poet William Blake that "Great things are done when men & mountains meet." [1]

This is the first line of a couplet, however, and Blake's second line—"This is not done by Jostling in the Street"—is rarely quoted in West Virginia, for it illustrates a persistent and unpleasant situation: the antithesis that is nearly always found between mountainous terrain and the economic uses of modern urban-industrial society. Poets and singers have treated mountain people and mountain themes with such affection precisely because they stood apart from the main currents of modern development, and yet this distinctiveness came at a price. The picturesque qualities of West Virginia mountain life began attracting attention from lowlanders as early as the 1840s, but visitors

---

1. William Blake, couplet from "Songs of Experience," in Northrop Frye, ed., *The Poetry of William Blake*, Modern Library Edition (New York: Random House, 1953), p. 79.

noticed the poverty of mountain people even earlier. Whether or
not mountaineers were always free, they were almost always
poor. Consequently most West Virginians—particularly the
leaders who have acted in their collective behalf—have tried to
become part of the mainstream. They have tried in every age to
find their way around, over, under, or through the barriers to
economic prosperity that the mountains raised. Thus notwithstanding protestations of love, their actual behavior toward the
face of the land suggests something more akin to hate.

Had West Virginia been nothing more than a mountainous
bulwark around which rushed the main currents of American
life, its fate would probably have resembled that of Vermont. In
fact, Rutherford B. Hayes made this comparison and concluded
that there was "Nothing finer in Vermont or New Hampshire"
than the western Virginia scenery he enjoyed.[2] If the resemblance had continued to hold, West Virginia would have remained a backwater during the agricultural and industrial revo-
lutions of the nineteenth century but still would have enjoyed
two compensating mid-twentieth-century trends: the federal policies and programs that have worked to iron out differences in
material standards of living among the various states, and the
rise of tourist and recreational industries. Even today, notwithstanding all the violence that has been visited on the landscape,
West Virginia's scenery and the recreational potential of its
mountains, forests, and streams have proved its most enduring
economic resources. Thus for states like Vermont and for those
small portions of eastern West Virginia that have nothing but
scenery to depend on, modern affluence and aesthetic values
may finally break down the barriers that once separated mountain regions from full participation in the nation's economic life.

Yet most of West Virginia's hills and mountains overlie deposits of coal. Herein lies another theme of West Virginia history, one in which the sour notes vastly outnumber the sweet.
Persons who have studied the impact of coal mining on different
societies from Silesia to northern Japan have usually concluded

2. Rutherford B. Hayes to Lucy Hayes, September 5, 1861, in Williams, *Diary and
Letters of Hayes*, 4: 86.

that coal has been a curse upon the land that yielded it. West Virginia is no exception. In its repetitive cycle of boom and bust, its savage exploitation of men and nature, in its seemingly endless series of disasters, the coal industry has brought grief and hardship to all but a small proportion of the people whose lives it touched. There has been, of course, a tiny elite of smaller producers and middlemen who grew rich from coal exploitation although not so rich as the nonresident owners in whose shadow the local elite worked. For those West Virginians who lived at a remove from the industry, its impact has been more ambiguous. Certainly coal created opportunities that were not there in the agricultural era, but it also created new problems, especially as the owners of the industry have always tried and have usually succeeded in passing off the external or social costs of coal production to the public at large. Moreover, the industry called into being a larger population than West Virginia's other economic resources can support so that, even after the great migration of postwar years, the position of the state is like that of an addict. West Virginia is "hooked" on coal, for better or for worse. In the past it has generally been for the worst.

The dilemma of coal promises to become all the more painful in the near future because of two developments of the 1970s: the increased importance of strip-, or surface, mining as a means of removing coal and growing national concern over potential energy shortages that makes coal production a patriotic task as well as an extremely profitable one. In terms of short-run market considerations, strip-mining is the swiftest and cheapest way to expand coal production at a time when demand is high. Stripping is the most costly method of producing coal, however, if social and environmental factors are calculated. Many experts have argued that West Virginia as a whole would be much better off if strip-mining were abolished. This is particularly true if the interests of future West Virginians are weighed. Nor is it true only of the coalfields. Nearly every part of the state has some strippable resource. The mountains of eastern West Virginia, for example, contain low-grade iron ore and manganese deposits that have already been mapped for stripping should a change in demand justify it commercially. The future of tourism and recreation depends to a significant extent on what is done about surface mining and other environmental issues, such as the clear-cutting of forests and water and air pollution. Yet the political impact of recreation industries is diffuse, and the aesthetic and human values that environmental degradation subverts are difficult to measure. By contrast, the coal industry retains much of its old-time political power in West Virginia and can readily deploy it to defend immediate and specific economic concerns. Thus environmental controversies promise to generate the most lively and probably the most crucial debates that West Virginia faces in the last quarter of the twentieth century.

Much of West Virginia's history has revolved around a struggle for control of the state's resources. During the first century or so of white settlement, this struggle focused upon the land. Later the focus shifted to natural resources during the struggles over regulation and taxation of extractive industries in the early industrial era and to human resources during the mine wars. Neither of the latter struggles can be regarded as finished, and yet the most critical conflicts today concern a new prize—control of environmental resources. West Virginians do not own the state's most valuable resources; by and large, they never have. Beginning with the land grants of the Revolutionary period, governments and local owners traded away ownership of these resources in return for development capital. And while the development itself has always fallen short of what the capitalists promised, few West Virginians have challenged the rights of absentee owners except when such challenges could be mounted within a framework of law, as in the case of land reform in antebellum times. The enduring issue is not ownership as such but the extent to which the use of West Virginia resources will be governed by considerations of local benefits and needs.

Today absentee ownership still predominates. In fact, a 1974 study by Tom D. Miller, a Huntington journalist, concluded that absentee owners "own or control at least two-thirds of the privately held land in West Virginia," including most of the resource-bearing land. One-third of the land is owned by large corporations based in Baltimore, Boston, Philadelphia, Pittsburgh, and New York.[3] The managers and stockholders of these corporations obviously have little to gain and much to lose by preservation of West Virginia's environmental resources, and yet the reverse is true for the overwhelming majority of residents of the state. Thus the environment battles of the future, like the taxation and labor struggles of the past, are likely to pit weak and poorly organized coalitions of local reformers and interest groups against powerful and well-disciplined combinations of absentee owners and middlemen. If the past is any guide, there will always be plenty of middlemen.

In their attempts to cope with such problems, West Virginians have always been hampered by their lack of cohesion. Many visitors think that West Virginia is remarkably homogeneous compared with most other states. The state is relatively small, its terrain is nearly all hilly, while the people are predominantly white, north European in ancestry, Protestant in faith. Yet in every generation West Virginians have quarreled bitterly among themselves. Some of the quarrels have been rooted in economic divisions, reflecting differences in the quality and accessibility of land, and later, in the industrial era, the conflicts generated by the spread of coal mining. Other divisions are geographic in origin. The state owes its very existence to its border location between the North and South; it is also a borderland between the nation's industrial heartland and the distinctive economic and cultural regions of Appalachia. The result has been an enduring and complex sectionalism. Most outside observers see the Appalachian characteristics of West Virginia as the defining ones, but these are only the most striking features, not the most representative. Appalachian attributes—whether they be those of the quaint and stalwart mountaineer, the ignorant and impoverished hillbilly, the oppressed and violent coal miner, or some combination of the three—have always been ambiguous badges of identity as far as West Virginians were concerned. Indeed, far from uniting the state, the economic and cultural peculiarities of Appalachia have contributed to West Virginia's his-

3. Tom D. Miller, *Who Owns West Virginia?* (Huntington: Huntington Herald-Advertiser and Herald-Dispatch, 1974), p. 2.

toric divisiveness. A recent instance is the controversy over
school textbooks that rocked Kanawha and nearby counties during 1974–1975, which pitted the fundamentalist—and traditional Appalachian—religious values of people living in the
hollows around Charleston against the cosmopolitan outlooks of
the city and its suburbs. During the same years an unrelated but
equally revealing controversy developed over medical education, specifically over prescriptions for remedying a shortage of
doctors in the state's rural and coalfield communities. Instead of
bolstering the existing medical school at West Virginia University, which was less than twenty years old and still financially
shaky, the legislature of 1975 ignored the advice of most experts and sought to create two competing centers, a medical
school at Huntington and an osteopathic school at Lewisburg.
The new facilities, one in the southwestern corner of the state
and the other near the Virginia border, would be no more cen-
trally located than the older school at Morgantown, nor would
they be better able to guarantee improved standards and distribution of rural medical care (although, of course, their promoters promised this). But their establishment was in keeping
with the sectional logrolling that often governed the distribution
of public funds and facilities in the past and so served to remind
a more prosperous generation of West Virginians that wealth
does not automatically confer maturity.

West Virginians have hidden their weak sense of community
behind a particularly strident form of state patriotism, but the
disguise is very thin. The characteristic expressions are boasts,
slogans, and distortions of historical fact. Traditionally school-
books adopted what might be called the ''Soviet Encyclopedia''
approach to local history, recalling the Stalinist propaganda that
sought to establish a Russian inventor or setting for every important development of the modern world. West Virginia
boosters have not gone quite so far, but West Virginia children
are still expected to believe that James Rumsey, not Robert Ful-
ton, invented the steamboat; that Amos Dolbear, not Alexander
Graham Bell, invented the telephone; that Point Pleasant, not
Lexington, was the first battle of the American Revolution, and
so on. They are also taught to memorize the West Virginia loca-

tions of such items as the world's largest clothespin factory, the world's largest ashtray, and the world's oldest plant, and to make an inordinate fuss about West Virginia natives who have become prominent nationally. With a background like this, "Almost Heaven" bumper stickers represent a great leap forward. The point is not the merits of specific boasts but their cumulative psychological effect. Perceptive visitors usually see through the disguise right away and conclude, as with defensive individuals who seek to mask a sense of inferiority by boastfulness, that there is something about West Virginia that its citizens are ashamed of. As for West Virginians themselves, this form of indoctrination manages only to persuade most people that there is something phony about history, that it has nothing to do with the reality of their own lives, whereas the opposite is true. In West Virginia history often repeats itself. Perhaps the fact that our history is so painful explains why it is so poorly understood.

Epilogue: Back to Blair Mountain

Soon after this book was first published, a woman in Huntington Beach, California wrote to complain about its critical tone. She was a West Virginia native and felt that I should have emphasized sunnier themes, mentioning specifically the West Virginia origins of the golden delicious apple. Instead the book focuses on conflict and hardship, emphasizing political and economic matters that often set West Virginia apart from the national mainstream. "What you wrote may be true," she said, "but you didn't have to write it."

She was right. A historian is obligated to stick to the truth, but even within these limits, he or she faces choices about which truths to emphasize, which ones to ignore, which ones to mention only in passing. One of the twentieth century's greatest historians, William H. McNeill, has compared historians to poets in that both distill experience into more intelligible structures than simply streams of consciousness or lists of events. "The difference between poetry and history is real enough," he adds. "What happened does constrain historians' thoughts in a way that is not true for poets. Yet the role of imagination in weaving the facts of history together is nonetheless what gives a work of history its meaning and structure, for facts do not speak for themselves nor do they arrange themselves intelligibly."[1] The historian's choices add up to an interpretation: a framework that helps one sort through all of the available facts and decide which ones are important and which ones merely interesting.

The interpretive framework of this book was created to explain how West Virginia's social and economic reality of the late twentieth century came to be, and to provide an analytical tool

1. William H. McNeill, *Arnold J. Toynbee. A Life* (New York: Oxford University Press, 1989), 286.

for West Virginians to use in shaping their future. After twenty-five years, it seems reasonable to ask how well this tool worked in anticipating the West Virginia history that was then (1976) the future and is now (2001) the past. But the main purpose of this epilogue is to relate what I have learned that might make a difference if I were starting out anew to compress the state's long history into what is still a rather short book.

One thing that has changed is that I no longer live in West Virginia. Like a great many people who grew up in southern West Virginia, I now live in North Carolina. But my first move was to Washington, D.C., where for several years I held a government administrative post that involved, among other things, supervising a program that made grants for state, local and regional historical research all over the U.S. Even before I went to Washington I read widely in the historical literature of all fifty states and investigated and compared the origins of state and urban historical societies. In these endeavors I learned to place the differences that separated my approach to West Virginia history from the expectations of the reader in Huntington Beach in a broader context. There are two kinds of state history, I learned, just as there are two kinds of family history. The family history that one tells a therapist is usually very different from the history one relates to one's in-laws, and heaven help people who get these two kinds of family history confused. Similarly there is a type of state history that originates in promotional literature and that emphasizes facts and themes that bring personal satisfaction to people who were born in or who otherwise identify with that state. This is what the Huntington Beach woman expected when she bought the first edition of this book.

Few professional historians today are interested in the promotional type of history. My generation of historians rediscovered social history, not merely as a record of old-time customs and manners, but history as a sociologist might approach it, focused on groups rather than on individuals or institutions and on the social processes—such as class formation and conflict—that reflect and shape the cultural values and economic and political development of a particular society. Most of this "new social history," as it was called back in 1976, consisted then of case studies drawn from urban or community settings, and those few social historians who undertook the writing of state history generally addressed themselves to a narrow group of fellow professionals, not to the general public. This book, however, like a few others in the series of which it was originally a part, sought to bridge the gap, to address both audiences. I had a very specific reader in mind—a hypothetical newspaper editor who had moved to West Virginia from someplace else far away, a person who would be bored with dull writing or recitations of dates and events and who would have time to read only one book on West Virginia history in preparation for her or his job. I wanted my book to be that one book. The fact that Don Marsh, then the editor of the *Charleston Gazette*, although a native and long-time resident of West Virginia, praised the book privately and in print, brought me as much satisfaction as the favorable scholarly reviews. Even the *Los Angeles Times* reviewer liked the book, which must have galled the lady in Huntington Beach, but in time I came to understand and respect her sense of disappointment.

This book was also an early contribution to a field that has matured during the last twenty-five years under the rubric of Appalachian Studies, which is itself an offshoot of a movement known as American regionalism. Regionalism flourished during the twentieth century among a loose federation of historians, literature scholars, and social scientists who believed that regions, defined primarily in terms of environmental factors (such as mountainous terrain or extractive industries) offered the best conceptual framework for understanding and changing American life. I've learned a lot from Appalachian studies scholars whose research focuses on West Virginia, especially Altina Waller, Paul Salstrom, and Ronald W. Lewis. But, just as important, research on other Appalachian states illuminates related topics in West Virginia. The interpretation of antebellum western Virginia society that I put forward in Chapter 2, emphasizing a western Virginia social elite that both opposed the creation of West Virginia *and* preserved its influence in the new state after the Civil War, has been confirmed by other historians in books and articles about southwestern Virginia, eastern Kentucky, western North Carolina and East Tennessee. Understanding the history of Tennessee in the Civil War era is especially important for appreciating those political and military factors that help explain why, as I have written elsewhere, "East Tennessee remained a geographical expression, while West Virginia became the name of a state."[2] A deeper knowledge of Pennsylvania history than I possessed thirty years ago has led me to locate western Virginia, along with the rest of Appalachia, within "greater Pennsylvania" during colonial times, as well as to emphasize the southward expansion of industrialism from a predominantly Pennsylvanian base as a key factor in creating the region's—and the state's—colonial economy after the Civil War.

If I were starting out fresh on this book today, it would certainly contain more about Native Americans, African Americans and women. Not only have ethnic and women's historians raised our consciousness of the importance of these topics, they have provided many useful new publications. Raised consciousness also leads to new sources as well as new interpretations. The so-called Slave Narratives, transcripts of oral interviews with elderly survivors of slavery during the 1930s, were in existence when I was researching this book, but so far as I was able to determine none of the narratives collected in Virginia came from the western part of the state. But a new edition and index published in 1979 made it possible to locate ex-slaves from western (West) Virginia whose narratives were collected in other states—for example, the recollections of Lizzie Grant of her youth on a Kanawha Valley plantation, which an interviewer recorded in 1938 in Texas. Grant's detailed memories—and her lively resentment at the deprivation and exploitation she suffered as a slave—would have been impossible to ignore had I had access to them back in 1975.[3] Civil War records and

2. John Alexander Williams, "The Birth of a State: West Virginia in the Civil War," in Altina L. Waller, ed., *True Stories of the American Past.* New York: McGraw Hill, 1995), 253.

3. Lizzie Grant, interviewed by B. E. Davis, Madisonville, Texas, March 6, 1938, in George P. Rawick, editor, *The American Slave. A Composite Autobiography*, Supplement, Series 2, volume 5 *Texas Narratives. Part 4* (Westport, Conn.: Greenwood Press, 1979), 1553-55.

literature, when examined with a fresh eye, also yielded evidence about women guerrillas who operated in West Virginia. Joe William Trotter's book, *Coal, Class and Color: Blacks in Southern West Virginia*,[4] illuminates the roles that African American women played in the history of the southern West Virginia coalfields. Trotter also found that the white contractors who built the disastrous Hawks Nest Tunnel during the 1930s tried to avoid hiring West Virginia blacks because of their reputation for union militancy. Thus while Chapter 6 is correct in saying that unemployed men from the coalfields flocked to the tunnel operation, it is also important to note that the contractors probably brought many of the tunnel workers with them from North Carolina, where they had just completed Linville Dam on the Catawba River at the foot of the Blue Ridge. Martin Cherniak's *The Hawk's Nest Incident: America's Worst Industrial Disaster*,[5] an epidemiological study of the Hawks Nest disaster, makes available much more knowledge about the victims and their deaths than was available to researchers when this book was first published.

Another topic neglected in this book is art and artists, who were present in West Virginia as they were in nearly every other place in every other time in history. John Cuthbert's research on the important Morgantown artist Blanche Lazell and his authoritative survey of *Early Art and Artists in West Virginia*[6] would make it impossible for me to ignore this topic today. Similarly, the study of Appalachian religion has moved to center stage after many years of neglect (apart from the institutional history of churches); while most of the new research in this field focuses on other states, it is full of insights that are pertinent to West Virginia. On the other hand, the history of education in West Virginia is still the history of schools, as far as most publications are concerned. So I would probably again neglect this topic as I did when the book was first written.

Anyone who teaches as well as writes history must acknowledge how the selection and interpretation of historical facts are

4. (Urbana: University of Illinois Press, 1990).
5. (New Haven: Yale University Press, 1986).
6. (Morgantown: West Virginia University Press, 2000).

refined by classroom discussion. This is particularly true for me, because my students at Appalachian State, in contrast to those I taught at West Virginia University during the 1970s, have no inherent interest in West Virginia (apart from those whose parents or grandparents were economic migrants from the Mountain State) and therefore ask penetrating questions about why I think West Virginia is as important to Appalachian studies as parts of the region that are more familiar to them. Their questions— helped by listening to Doc Watson's rendition of "Ridin' on That New River Train"—led me to discover a north-south corridor roughly following or paralleling the New River valley that, while less important in history than the transportation corridors discussed in Chapter 1 of this book, is still worth knowing about. This corridor guided the Shawnee raiders who struck deep into southwest Virginia during the frontier wars, along with the initial efforts of Virginia frontiersmen to retaliate and of federal soldiers during the Civil War to reach and destroy the Tennessee Railroad. Later on it channeled the revised territorial strategy of this same railroad, after its reorganization as the Norfolk & Western, as it built west and north across southern West Virginia. Economic migrants followed this path north from the Carolina Blue Ridge and Piedmont into the West Virginia coalfields during the first decades of the twentieth century, and their descendants are following it south away from the coalfields two generations later after the corridor's multiple strands coalesced into Interstate 77. Among my ASU graduate students in Appalachian Studies, David Reynolds discovered numerous links between Baldwin-Felts mine guards, including the three Felts brothers, and the Galax, Virginia area, making the Matewan Massacre an episode in what amounted to an Appalachian civil war. Reynolds also used census records to determine that the men identified by Lee Felts as suspects in his brothers' killings were all West Virginia residents and/or natives, notwithstanding the proximity of Kentucky and the presence of foreign born and African American coal miners in the Matewan district. Jessica Kelley and Alex Hooker each helped me to analyze and interpret census data that illuminate the paths taken by West Virginia economic migrants moving south along I-77 in the late 1980s.

Finally, the best reason for an author to change his mind is to discover errors in the original publication. There are two such factual errors. One is found on page 49, where I attribute the relatively large numbers of slaves in antebellum Kanawha County to tobacco plantations, rather than to the salt industry. That industry's historian, John Stealey, pointed this out in his review of this book. The second error is more of a technicality. On page 190, I identify Arch A. Moore, Jr. as "West Virginia's first two-term governor." Actually the first such governor was John J. Jacob, elected in 1870 to a two-year term under the state constitution of 1863 and re-elected in 1872 to a four-year term under the new constitution adopted in that year. Moore was the first to serve two consecutive four-year terms, but he is more likely to be remembered as the first governor to serve three terms, having been elected to a non-consecutive third term in 1984, and as the second governor to go to prison, following his conviction on corruption charges in 1990. I also made an error in judgment when I described the congressional career of William L. Wilson as one "that no West Virginian has matched in distinction." (p. 93) That statement was invalidated even as the book went to press by the emergence of Robert C. Byrd as a national leader. Changing that one sentence would have complicated and perhaps delayed the book's publication, but I wish I had done so, for as Senate majority leader (1978-88) and in his ongoing unofficial role as the modern Senate's historian and constitutionalist, Byrd has clearly wielded more influence than Wilson or any other West Virginian in American public life.

Historians are not professionally charged with predicting the future. That responsibility belongs to economists, among others. During the "energy crisis" of the 1970s, William H. Miernyk, then WVU's leading economist, confidently predicted that rising demand for coal would raise West Virginia's per capita income to a point "close to the national average by the late 1980s."[7] I did not believe this then but I did not express my skepticism directly, not wishing to dispute with a distinguished colleague

7. *Charleston Gazette*, October 10, 1978, p. 5A.

nor to stray too far from the historian's certified area of competence, the past. Yet I knew that every previous coal boom in
West Virginia had been followed by a bust and I did not expect
the boom of the 70s to be any different. So I wrote in this book
only that "West Virginia is 'hooked' on coal, for better or for
worse. In the past it has generally been for the worst." (p. 201)

Now 1990 has come and gone and, by the measurements that
Miernyk and others take to define progress, West Virginia still
lags behind. Miernyk was wrong, but what about me? While I
did not venture to predict the future back in 1976, Chapter 8 of
this book asserts that several themes are central to West Virginia's history, the implication being (as was stated directly in
the chapter's last two sentences) that unless present-day West
Virginians learned from the past, they stood a good chance of
repeating its mistakes in the future. In 2001 the reader is entitled
to ask whether or not these themes remained central to the
state's history as it unfolded over the past twenty-five years. The
task of responding to this reasonable question takes up the remaining pages of this epilogue.

The notion that West Virginia's mountains and hills are
"pleasing tho' dreadful" remains a central historical theme. It
encapsulates the conflict between the appreciation and preservation of rugged and forested terrain and the practical uses of
modern societies. Many of the controversial public issues of the
1980s and '90s—mining by mountaintop removal, the clearcutting of forests, highway construction through scenic and envi-
ronmentally sensitive areas such as the route of Appalachian
Corridor H, the siting of polluting industrial facilities—embody
this conflict, and West Virginians are no closer to resolving it in
2001 than they were in 1976. Postindustrial society now has the
tools to reshape the land in ways that would have been unimag-
inable a century or even a few decades ago. Corridor H and
other ARC highways will be completed by "blowing through
mountains," at an estimated cost of seven to nine billion
dollars.[8] The same engineering and equipment that conquer
mountains to build roads, augmented by giant 100-ton "drag

8. Jones, "Appalachia's War," *Pittsburgh Post-Gazette*, November 26, 2000.

lines," make possible mountaintop removal, but also less controversial—and less drastic—changes on the land such as the expansion of airports, the construction of shopping centers (such
as those that now trail along "Corridor G"—U.S. 119—in the
suburbs of Charleston). It is one thing to sing about country
roads, quite another to drive on them. And why not?, most
people will ask. West Virginians are not alone in wanting to have
things both ways. Modern technological systems make it possible to live comfortably in icy Minnesota, the sweltering Gulf
Coast, and the parched Southwest. Why should West Virginia be
any different? Why should mountains be permitted to interfere
with claiming mountaineers' full share of the American dream?

And yet the 1970s also witnessed the beginnings of movements that embraced the limitations of mountain life and that
sought to create alternative models of achievement in closer harmony with nature. The environmental movement, although frustrated in its initial assaults on the practice of strip mining,
remained an important force in West Virginia, and its ranks were
augmented by small but significant numbers of in-migrants who
came to the state as permanent settlers, seeking to establish a
simpler and more purposeful way of living than seemed possible
in the nation's cities and suburbs. Overlapping both groups were
veterans of earlier struggles over civil and welfare rights and
labor militancy. Still another group consisted of athletes and
adventurers who pitted themselves against the personal challenges of rivers and mountains, some of whom helped to establish new outposts of tourism in some of the most rugged areas
of the state. Members of each of these groups had their own personal histories and agendas, but they all drew upon the "countercultural" values of the suburban youth culture that emerged
nationally during the adolescence of the postwar "baby boom."

Writing of his parents, who settled on a hardscrabble farm in
Calhoun County in 1974, the year of his birth, Jedediah Purdy
states that "They meant to live with few needs, to raise as much
of their own food and do as much of their own work as possible,
and to share what they could not do themselves with like-
minded neighbors. As my father once said to me, they intended
'to pick out a small corner of the world and make it as sane as

possible.' "[9] Settlers like the Purdys tended to drift in small clusters into agricultural counties where land prices were cheap. Thanks to the great migration of the 1940s, 50s and 60s, many West Virginia counties had smaller populations in 1970 than they had had in 1920, so there was plenty of room for people who planned to live modestly. The newcomers tended to avoid coal country, however. Rather they settled in the interior hill counties of the Ohio Valley, and the back valleys along the Virginia border from the New River northward. Another subset could be found near Morgantown and another near Harpers Ferry, which reflected the exurban influence of nearby Washington. Their numbers too small and scattered to be called colonies, the settlers nevertheless formed rural enclaves ranging from a handful to a few dozen households. Nearly every community exchanged stories of their encounters with the locals, for like the poverty warriors and other activists, the newcomers held allegiance to the counterculture, at least in its less commercial forms.

In due course, the settlers sorted themselves out into those who were merely sojourning in the mountains and who soon returned to conventional life in the cities and those who put down roots. Some of those who stayed drifted into Charleston, which they helped to make "one of the most interesting small cities in the United States," according to Denise Giardina, who returned to West Virginia after publishing two novels based on the history of the state. Urban settlers were abetted by other movements that emerged during this period to provide alternatives to standard forms of commercial development. Historic preservationists, for example, though they were unable to prevent in West Virginia the decline of conventional downtown retailing that afflicted central cities across the country, refurbished districts such as Capitol Street in Charleston and the Wheeling Market to house the offices, boutiques, cafes, bookstores and other speciality retailers oriented toward a burgeoning service economy. National Public Radio, another non-commercial

9. Jedediah Purdy, *For Common Things: Irony, Trust, Commitment in America Today* (2nd edition; New York: Vintage Books, 2000), ix.

creation of the 1970s, gave birth to West Virginia Public Broadcasting, which in turn established "Mountain Stage" in 1983, a musical variety show broadcast nationally each Sunday afternoon since 1990 from the stage of the Cultural Center on the capitol grounds in Charleston. The program's host performer, Larry Groce, was himself a "back-to-the-lander," commuting to Charleston from a farm in Barbour County. Davis and Elkins College's Augusta Heritage program was another manifestation of the counterculture's movement away from politics during the 1970s toward alternative forms of cultural expression. Beginning with a program of ten workshops attended by a total of ninety persons in 1973, Augusta had expanded by 2001 over a five-week summer term with an additional week each in the spring and fall, offering over a hundred workshops teaching traditional arts and crafts ranging from African American quilt-making to playing the Irish penny-whistle.

In one fashion or another, settlers became "neonatives" who came to have strong attachments to the communities they chose. Indeed, as the sociologist John Stephenson observed of a comparable phenomenon in western North Carolina, "the newcomers may now have a stronger sense of place than do the natives, who are uncertain what is happening to their place."[10] Eventually those settlers who had been part of experimental households grew more conventional. Settler families began raising children, schooled them at home, as Purdy's parents did, or packed them off to public schools whose deficiencies led some of them to run for the county school board, setting up yet another test of their local acceptance.[11]

Developments in Hollywood and in Europe in 1972 conspired to bring a different type of settler to West Virginia during the decades that followed. The film *Deliverance*, set in the mountains of north Georgia, helped draw the attention of whitewater enthusiasts to Appalachian rivers, while the Munich Olympics popularized a new style of whitewater kayaking, along with a

10. The concept of neonativity is developed in Hal K. Rothman, *Devil's Bargains: Tourism in the Twentieth-Century American West* (Lawrence: University of Kansas Press, 1998), 26, 77-78, 98, 137, 208.

11. For example, Jedediah Purdy's mother, whose school board activity eventually led to involvement in state politics and then law school (*For Common Things*, 189-91.)

new European technology for molding fiberglass kayaks. During the mid-1970s, the new European fiberglass molds became available in places like Cincinnati, Columbus (Ohio) and State College (Pennsylvania), all now within easier reach of West Virginia rivers thanks to new highways. These developments created a class of young experts who provided the guidance that untrained recreationists needed in order to avoid whitewater disaster. Some of those who came as recreational canoeists or kayakers became river guides and stayed on to found rafting companies. After a period of rapid growth during the 1980s, such firms now serve hundreds of thousands of visitors, bringing millions of dollars into the mountains.

Along with the rafters came rock climbers, mountain bikers, skiers, hang gliders and divers, all of whom thrived on the personal challenges presented by Appalachian terrain and waters. "My mother cried when we told her we were moving to West Virginia," recalls Chris Dragan, who with his older brothers Jon and Tom established the first commercially successful rafting company in New River Gorge. But the Dragans along with many others like them settled into new homes and started families. One whitewater professional even ran for the school board.[12] These adventurous neonatives were not always environmentalists in the activist sense of the term. But through their stewardship of the rivers they plied and the demonstration they offered of an entire new tourist market developing on the basis of scenic resources, they strengthened by example the arguments of those activists who argued that Appalachia's future would be better if only the spoliations of extractive industries could be abolished or curbed.

Some recreation industries required large capital investments. For example, the ski resort at Snowshoe, atop Cheat Mountain in Pocahontas County, between its launching in 1974 and its acquisition by a Canadian company in 1995, passed through the hands of a number of undercapitalized corporate investors. Yet for every Snowshoe and Silver Creek, there were hundreds of smaller entrepreneurial opportunities—for sports equipment and

12. Interviews with Dave Arnold, Chris Dragan, C. R. "Bud" Hill, and Jack Gannon, Lansing WV, January 31-February 1, 2001; *Fayette Tribune*, December 3, 2000.

rental shops, bed-and-breakfast accommodations for tourists, restaurants and cafes, crafts shops and art galleries. One of the most striking zones of countercultural entrepreneurship can be found in the courthouse town of Fayetteville, perched near the south rim of New River Gorge. Fayette County lost 25 percent of its population during the 1950s, another twenty percent during the 60s and seventeen percent during each of the two ensuing decades. This population implosion left behind empty houses and vacant storefronts—two of the factors that helped in the growth of whitewater rafting and other recreation industries that have changed the Gorge from a transportation barrier into a tourist attraction. Cheap housing made it possible for rafters and other sportspersons attracted to the Gorge to become settlers, while the fine old houses in the center of town, once the homes of bankers and coal company lawyers, became bed-and-breakfast inns serving recreational tourists.

Only the law firms fronting the courthouse square remain from the old days. Otherwise hardware and drug stores have given way to recreational outfitters, crafts and art galleries, an organic grocery, and—between 1994 and 1999—a restaurant, the Sedona Grille, that served southwestern-style food so good that it attracted not only the whitewater crowd but also local diners from as far away as Charleston and Beckley. Started by a Pennsylvania couple who had come to Fayetteville mainly because of the low cost there of starting up their own place, Sedona became one of the flashpoints of native reactions to change when it applied for a liquor license in 1995, and again in 1999 when the owners tried to expand from their crowded storefront into one of the nearby inns. The owners won the first contest after a lengthy and dispiriting court battle but lost the second, moving instead into another location on the outskirts of town. Meanwhile, new flashpoints have emerged in controversies over school consolidation and the enforcement of preservation regulations in the recently-established Fayetteville Historic District.[13]

13. Interview with Virginia Price and Brian Levine, Fayetteville WV, February 1, 2001; *Fayette Tribune*, March 29, April 12, 21, May 17, 31, August 30, September 23, December 6, 1999, January 17, April 18, August 21, October 9, 2000. January 15, 2001.

The cumulative effect of these changes had a positive effect on West Virginia's image, both at home and abroad. With automobile license plates officially proclaiming the "wild and wonderful" character of its scenic attractions and with the appeal of Snowshoe, Mountain Stage, Augusta Heritage, and the dozens of refurbishment projects that transformed Main Streets from Bramwell to Shepherdstown, West Virginians were no longer caught "in a limelight that showed only blemishes." (196) And yet the fundamental contradiction between mountainous terrain and the intensive use of resources by modern society remains. Snowshoe, for example, was threatened at the century's end with a nearby quarrying operation whose expansion investors and homeowners opposed because of its impact on the resort area's scenic values.

On a larger scale, the demographic geography of the state is trending back toward the profile that existed when the state was originally created. In 1870 West Virginia's population and wealth were concentrated on the northern and western edges of the state and in the Kanawha Valley around and below Charleston. The mushroom growth of extractive industry during the half-century or so that followed filled central and southern West Virginia and the Allegheny Highlands along the eastern border with mines, lumber and coal camps, and railroad and mill towns, and in general summoned a larger population than this territory had supported during pre-industrial times. During the past half-century the "interior," as nineteenth century people called it, has been emptying out. Twenty-three of 33 central and southern West Virginia counties recorded further population declines in the 2000 census. The ski industry in Pocahontas County or recreational tourism in Fayette have provided some relief from what would have been an even worse population implosion. Nevertheless, if you ask a long-time resident of such counties what has changed most about their communities, they will usually say something about all the people who are gone.

All this was predictable. In fact experts at WVU determined back in 1968 that the state needed to lose between a quarter and a third of its people if it wanted to achieve parity with national indicators of economic well-being such as per-capita income or the proportion of persons on welfare. They did not shout this from the rooftops, however, and if they had, who would have heard them? For as another expert pointed out with respect to the entire Appalachian region in 1967, "What banker, what real estate owner, what school administrator wishes to aid in the depopulation of his community and thus weaken the basis of his business and of the community's social institutions?"[14] Rather than planning to meet such a future, state and local leaders developed a standard set of procedures which might almost be termed rituals: highly publicized "industrial recruitment" trips by governors to New York or California—or, somewhat later, Frankfurt or Tokyo—the creation of industrial parks, the publishing of brochures, the coinage of slogans.

During the 1980s, deindustrialization spread from the coalfields to the manufacturing zones along the Ohio, Monongahela and Kanawha rivers. Previously there had been "two West Virginias," as the *New York Times* reported during the 1960 presidential primary: an impoverished interior and a "prosperous, growing" urban West Virginia whose citizens resented the "painful shadow" that the coalfields cast over their "rapidly expanding industrial base."[15] Then seemingly almost overnight, the Manufacturing Belt of which northern and western West Virginia was a part became a Rustbelt, its blue-collar jobs transferred overseas or vanished due to technological unemployment. No one had predicted this, and so West Virginians joined with others in the Midwest and Northeast to ask what went wrong and what could be done about it, while at the federal level President Ronald Reagan assured citizens that government was part of the problem, not the solution to these woes.

Actually, Reagan spoke truer than he knew, for scholars have since demonstrated that the federal government, primarily through its defense spending, had decisively reshaped the American economy's regional contours, transferring jobs and

14. Rupert B. Vance, "The Region's Future: A National Challenge," in Thomas R. Ford, ed., *The Southern Appalachian Region: A Survey* (Lexington: University of Kentucky Press, 1967), 293-99.

15. *New York Times*, May 2, 1960, p. 14.

economic growth from the Manufacturing Belt to the Sunbelt. So influential was the military-industrial complex in shaping national growth, one team of experts concluded that "Gunbelt" rather than "Sunbelt" was a more appropriate term for the states and localities that benefited from this shift and that defense spending amounted to "a kind of underground regional policy" far larger in scope and impact than explicit regional redevelopment strategies, such as those of the Appalachian Regional Commission. Although West Virginia met its full share of the Cold War's manpower requirements —and more than its share judged by its disproportionately high number of Congressional Medal of Honor winners in Korea and Vietnam—the state missed out on the economic benefits of the Gunbelt economy.[16]

An examination of the federal budget since 1983, the first year that consolidated spending reports were made available for all federal agencies, shows that while West Virginians got a steadily increasing share of transfer payments—social security, welfare, and regular and special disability payments such as the "black lung" checks that started arriving in disabled miners' mailboxes after 1969—the state consistently ranked near the bottom in direct defense expenditures—the operations of military installations such as airbases and arsenals or the paychecks and pensions of active and retired military personnel. It ranked even lower in terms of defense contracts, the privatized system of procurement that the military came to favor during the Cold War. The state also ranked low in terms of federal loan guarantees, an indicator of dynamism in local economies since the guarantees represent the volume of home mortgages and small business loans. Perhaps most crucial of all, the state received few of the "spin off" benefits that accrued to Gunbelt communities. "The military and its surrogates acting in the name of national security . . . . nurtured leading industries, steered migration, financed physical infrastructure, expanded higher

16. Ann Markusen, Peter Hall, Scott Campbell and Sabina Deitrick, *The Rise of the Gunbelt: The Military Remapping of Industrial America* (New York: Oxford University Press, 1991), 244. I deal with these issues at greater length in *Appalachia: A History* (Chapel Hill: University of North Carolina Press, 2002).

education, and promoted the births and deaths of regional economies."[17] Federally-funded defense or aerospace research led to commercial "spin-offs" comprising whole new industries: semi-conductors, computers, a range of electronic communications applications, and civilian nuclear power, for example.

There was nothing predictable or inevitable about West Virginia's starvation diet at the military-industrial banquet. The "Arsenal of Democracy" during two world wars had been the same Manufacturing Belt of which West Virginia's steel mills and chemical and glass plants were a part and which turned into the Rustbelt as the Cold War neared its climax during the Reagan years. Experts who examined the matter have concluded that "passive attributes" such as climate or terrain were not decisive in defense locational decisions, except of course in the case of naval bases which are necessarily close to deep water. Politicians had a significant, though not always a decisive, impact on the location of defense facilities. Two West Virginian senators, Matthew M. Neely and Harley M. Kilgore, were both influential during the Truman adminstration (1945-53) when many key Cold War decisions were made; in addition, Truman's second secretary of defense, Louis Johnson, was from Clarksburg. However, politicians were not the only players involved. A team of regional scientists who investigated the locational impacts of defense spending and procurement concluded that "it is not the passive attributes of places that determine the location of defense-related activity in the economy, but the active involvement of many participants, each with distinctive motivations, choosing among a number of potential sites. Whether boosters, colonels, generals, firm managers, or elected representatives, selected groups have mattered a great deal in shaping America's military-production geography."[18] Secretary Johnson, for example, presided over the decision to locate the U.S. Air Force Academy in Colorado, but his choices were limited by a panel

17. Bruce J. Schulman, *From Cotton Belt to Sunbelt: Federal Policy, Economic Development, and the Transformation of the South, 1938-1980* (New York: Oxford University Press, 1991), 137.

18. Markusen, Hall, Campbell, and Deitrick, *Rise of the Gunbelt*, 3-4, 239.

of experts who had narrowed all the possible locations to this location and two others, one in Wisconsin, the other in Illinois.

Perhaps West Virginia was done in by its unfavorable image—the legacy of feuds and mine wars and the popular media's fascination with comic book hillbillies. Perhaps John L. Lewis was to blame, for his controversial series of wartime miners'strikes had inflamed military leaders. Perhaps it was simply a matter of luck or initiative. Consider the cases of The Greenbrier in White Sulphur Springs and The Broadmoor, its equally luxurious competitor in Colorado Springs. Both hotels were well-known to the military, The Greenbrier as a wartime internment center and military hospital, The Broadmoor as a place where generals and other top brass and such could come for rest and relaxation, with expenses mostly on the house. Where in these facts do we find the clue that tells us why Colorado Springs got so much more out of its military connection than did White Sulphur? The Greenbrier got a secret underground bunker that would have served as Congress's home had a nuclear attack threatened Washington. Colorado Springs also got a bunker, the NORAD headquarters deep inside Cheyenne Mountain. But while the Greenbrier bunker was maintained by a handful of undercover agents until the prospect of Armageddon faded, Colorado Springs got payroll after payroll—the Air Force Academy, an expanded air base and a refurbished army base, plus eventually a number of private defense contractors and non-defense electronics and communications firms who located branch operations there to escape the escalating cost of doing business in California. The population of this western resort, roughly the size of Wheeling in 1950, expanded to around 400,000 by the end of the century, while the population and employment bases of Wheeling and other West Virginia cities continued to shrink. With a bit more luck, or more insightful leadership, or a better image, could things have turned out differently?, Such questions can't now be answered given the current state of research, but it seems important to pose them.

I must admit that it would not have occurred to investigate defense spending as a potential stimulus to economic growth back in 1976. The regionalist assumptions that I adhered to then did not accommodate comparisons of the breadth required to understand one state's place in a global economy. Yet regionalism illuminates well enough the trade-offs involved between coal mining and tourism, and it correctly identifies the likely winners from intensified resource development. The patterns of a colonial economy, which prevail as much as ever where extractive industries are concerned, mean that beneficiaries that actually live in West Virginia are comparatively few, confined to at most a few thousand landowners, investors, lawyers, bankers, engineers, consultants, and equipment distributors. What is new in comparison to 1976 is the relatively small number of mining jobs involved: A total of 16,500 miners worked in the state in 2001, compared with 55,000 in 1975 and 120,000 in 1950. Even allowing for the multiplier effects derived from wage and non-wage expenditures claimed by the coal industry, it is clear that the vast majority of West Virginians have no personal stake in the matter and in fact may end up as losers if environmentalists are right about the impact of coal on the state's future chances of creating a more sustainable economy.

Yet it is still true that "the coal industry retains much of its old-time political power in West Virginia and can readily deploy it to defend immediate and specific economic concerns" (202). Or as the retired Logan County politician Raymond Chafin puts it, "These coal companies and big businesses are all the same. Their money people ask, 'Which man is going to let me dump the most in the creek?,' 'Who's going to let me strip coal and scrape the trees over the hillside the way I want?,' or 'Who'll let me get by this law or that one?' They donate [campaign funds] to the fellow who lets them get away with more."[19] A study of interest groups in all fifty states found that West Virginia is one of nine states where the growth of citizens' groups, single-issue lobbies and other manifestation of expanded participation in policy determination at the state level has had the least impact. Similarly, another national study examined the efficacy of ethics

19. Raymond Chafin and Topper Sherwood, *Just Good Politics: The Life of Raymond Chafin, Appalachian Boss* (Pittsburgh: University of Pittsburgh Press, 1994), 175.

legislation adopted in West Virginia in 1989, in the wake of corruption scandals that sent not only ex-governor Moore but several prominent legislators to prison. This study rated West
Virginia's public disclosure laws, designed to identify potential
conflicts of interest and to illuminate the various means by
which lobbyists wield influence in Charleston, 43rd in the
nation. An investigative reporter for the Charleston *Sunday
Gazette-Mail* compared West Virginia's laws to those of neighboring Maryland, where a tough and comprehensive law disclosed that lobbyists had spent $23, 000,000 in 1999 attempting
to influence state legislators and agencies. Had West Virginia's
laws been in effect instead, Maryland lobbyists would have had
to disclose only $757,356 of this sum.[20] It is important in this
regard to note that the corruption convictions of recent years
came about through federal, rather than state prosecutions, with
penalties handed down by federal rather than state courts. Thus
comments made earlier in this volume about a tradition of official cynicism in West Virginia were unfortunately not invalidated by recent events.

The battle over mountaintop removal mining (MTR) brings
other long standing patterns in West Virginia history once again
to the fore. Most West Virginians believed that federal legislation enacted in 1977 brought strip mining under control. The
new law, enforced by the state Department of Environmental
Protection (DEP) under regulations written by DEP but subject
to the oversight of federal officials, eliminated some of the
abuses that drove the 1970s movement to abolish strip mining. It
became more difficult for coal companies to pass on to the public "externalities" (the economist's term for unprofitable actions
that are nevertheless part of the cost of doing business in a particular industry) such as unreclaimed land, polluted streams,
torn-up roads and damaged communities. Reclamation was
defined as restoring stripped land to its "approximate original
contour," unless specific conditions were met, such as the
submission of realistic plans for using a specific piece of

---

20. Scott Finn, "Ethics law falling short of promise to clean up government, critics
say," Charleston *Sunday Gazette-Mail*, July 23, 2000.

stripped land for the development of businesses, residences or public facilities. The controversy over MTR disclosed that the DEP had enforced its regulations erractically, if at all, while this new method of stripping brought most of the old abuses back to life in a gargantuan form. Whereas formerly strip mining chewed along the slopes of mountains, mining companies now treat the entire mountaintop as "overburden" to be removed in order to get at the coal seams beneath and nearby watersheds as convenient places to dump "spoil," as the industry refers to the soil and rock removed from a ridgetop or from the layers between coal seams. This practice creates "valley fills" extending for miles along the length of a stream. Notwithstanding rhetorical claims made about the state's need for flat land constructed by lopping off mountains and dumping the spoil into adjacent streambeds, investigation shows that no such land has been used for development purposes, while the only public facilities to materialize in this fashion were a high school near Welch, an air strip near Logan, and the new state penitentiary in Fayette County.

Surface mining now accounts for roughly a third of West Virginia coal production, as compared with around a fifth when this book was originally published. Its growth is driven by several factors. One is competition from coal from Wyoming, Montana and other western states. Western coal, considered "lignite" a century ago because of its relatively low thermal value and high transportation costs, now dominates the Midwestern coal market and is becoming competitive—in terms of its cost per b.t.u.— with Appalachian coal, due to lowered transportation costs and the greater efficiency of modern boilers that turn coal into electricity by means of steam generation. A second change is that, thanks to the hard won victories of the United Mine Workers, Miners for Democracy and the Black Lung Association, coal companies now have to assume externalities—the costs of protecting the safety and health of miners and of paying them good wages and benefits—that had previously been burdens on the public or, more commonly, the miners themselves. This factor in turn drove another impulse to rely more on technology than on labor, which has meant costly new equipment, vastly increased in scale and capacity, requiring fewer workers to operate it than the equipment it replaced but at the same creating a relentless drive for its efficient and continuous use in order to amortize the cost of acquiring it. Mountaintop removal allows fewer workers to produce a volume of coal than the same volume produced by conventional strip-mining methods and far fewer compared to the same volume produced underground. The new method increased southern West Virginia coal's competitiveness vis a vis coal from Wyoming, but at a fearful cost in terms of disrupting the region's familiar landscape.

The issue came to a head in 1998, when the West Virginia Highlands Conservancy, joined by several citizens of affected communities, filed suit in federal court to force the state DEP to enforce its rules on stream protection against the practice of valley fills. In March 1999, U.S.district judge Charles H. Haden II sided with the plaintiffs, issuing an injunction against a DEP permit expanding an Arch Coal MTR operation on Blair Mountain in Logan County, then ruling in October that MTR valley fills permitted by DEP violate federal clean water laws. If nothing else, the furious outcry that Haden's decision elicited from West Virginia politicians—led by Senator Byrd and the entire congressional delegation but also embracing Governor Cecil Underwood and most state legislators and all UMWA officials— showed how little has changed with respect to the industry's power in West Virginia. The same unanimity of official opinion prevailed in April 2001, when a federal appeals panel invalidated the Haden decision on the technical grounds that the suit should have been brought in state rather than federal court. This would seem to put the issue squarely before state authorities during the coming decade, but it is also possible that still higher federal courts will accept Haden's argument that state regulations mandated and approved by federal authority can properly be enforced by a federal court.

As this epilogue is written, coal is on the cusp of another boom, with the price per ton soaring while industry leaders anticipate the dividends to be earned from their support of a friendly federal administration. Mountaintop removal is again moving forward on a larger-than-ever scale. At the same time, another energy crisis promises to divert public attention from environmental concerns. As with previous booms, the major beneficiaries will claim that a new and permanent level of prosperity is at hand in the coalfields. To which, as a historian, I can only reply with a paraphrase of an Auden poem remembered from college:

What they're saying may be so.
Is it likely?
No.

What about another central theme asserted in Chapter 8: "an enduring and complex sectionalism?" In the past sectionalism created an expectation that West Virginia's limited public resources would be scattered among localities rather than concentrated; the most recent example cited in the first edition was the creation of two new medical schools in Huntington and Lewisburg to compete for students and funds with the existing school at Morgantown at a time when only the most populous states supported more than one such establishment. How much did sectionalism shape West Virginia's response to the problems and opportunities of the past twenty-five years? The answer: not as much as I would have predicted back in 1976.

One reason for the decline of sectionalism is the pervasive influence of the federal government. New highways are the most obvious manifestation of this impact. Interstate 79—awarded to West Virginia by the administration of John F. Kennedy after the original interstate routes bypassed everything but the Kanawha Valley and the tips of the two panhandles—has been supplemented by the Appalachian development corridors that now extend to every corner of the state. It is now possible to drive from Bluefield to Morgantown in under four hours; a trip from Martinsburg to Huntington takes longer, but can be made entirely on expressways, avoiding the traffic lights that are still found in places on U.S. 19 or 50 (now incorporated into ARC corridors L and D.) Just as the completion of the rail network had done in the early decades of the twentieth century, the interstate and Appalachian highways built in West Virginia since the 1960s had a unifying impact on the people of the state. Perhaps the most remarkable evidence of this impact was the emergence of Flatwoods as a kind of universal meeting place. Sensing opportunity as I-79 neared completion, developer John Skidmore bought land near this Braxton County interchange during the late 1970s and created a small conference center conveniently located between population centers of the Monongahela and Kanawha valleys. In two decades, Skidmore's enterprises multiplied to include restaurants and fast food franchises, an expanded hotel and conference center, and a shopping mall modeled on Thomas Jefferson's design for the University of Virginia. In December 2000, plans were announced for Flatwoods's first modern residential development, complete with an 18-hole golf course. While Charleston remains the meeting place for official state business and the state's upper echelon still loves to congregate at White Sulphur Springs, Flatwoods has become the gathering place for nearly everyone else, hosting conferences ranging from working lunches to week-long training sessions, involving subjects and organizations representing the full spectrum of civic activity in the state.

Senator Robert C. Byrd emerged during the 1980s and 90s as the most influential single individual in directing federal tax dollars to West Virginia, especially after he exchanged the position of Senate majority leader for the chairmanship of the Senate committee on appropriations in 1988. From this point on, Byrd set out to remedy the dearth of prior federal investments in the state. While transfer payments grew with the proportion of elderly and disabled people, Byrd made the state a venue for federal government operations far beyond the level to be expected in a small state without a major urban administrative center. Federal installations in Beckley, Clarksburg, Fairmont and especially the Eastern Panhandle testify to Byrd's success in directing federal agencies where to site their facilities and spend their funds. Among the state's colleges and universities, Shepherd, Concord, and Davis and Elkins colleges and Wheeling Jesuit University received research and demonstration projects funded by federal agencies and earmarked for West Virginia by Byrd, as did Marshall University and West Virginia University. In addition to helping keep the Appalachian Regional

Commission program alive under the hostile Reagan and Bush I administrations, Byrd presided over the building of bridges in Huntington and Williamson and a splendid new federal building in downtown Charleston. Through his influence, the National Aeronautics and Space Administration built a "software testing" facility near Fairmont that, according to the senator, will lead to more "high technology coming into West Virginia."[21] The new Robert C. Byrd High School in Clarksburg, with its internet-based model curriculum, will presumably train the technologically-sophisticated work force that such "high tech" enterprises will require.

Byrd's critics, especially those in the metropolitan Washington area, denounce him as a "prince of pork" and note the frequency with which his name is chiseled onto the buildings that this largesse makes possible. But it is just as reasonable—given West Virginia's long history of exploitation by non-resident energy corporations and its failure to gain much from the federal defense and aerospace budgets of the Cold War years—to regard Byrd's efforts as reparations, not pork barrel. And while Byrd is not the first senator to be accused of having an outsized ego, the satisfaction he gets from seeing his name on a plaque or façade is about all that he gets for his efforts, for as he pointed out in a 1994 interview, critics "can't lay a glove on me" in terms of personal benefits from his work. "Everything according to the rules, everything according to the book. I have brought billions to West Virginia. What little my wife and I have, we've earned it. . . ." He and his wife even clean their own house, as Byrd playfully informed West Virginia's wealthy junior senator during a ceremonial occasion in Charleston in 1998.[22] Given some of the less fortunate traditions of West Virginia politics, Byrd's combination of senatorial pomp and power and personal abstemiousness is itself historic.

The decline of sectionalism was further fostered by the gubernatorial administration of Gaston Caperton, who defeated

21. "Transcript of interview with Robert C. Byrd for the film 'West Virginia,' September 7, 1994," roll 256. (http://129.71.134.132/wvinter.htm)

22. Ibid., roll 258.

Moore's fourth run for the governorship in 1988. A wealthy businessman with limited prior experience in politics, Caperton proved to be, according to a friendly critic, an "imperfect politician" who nonetheless racked up a record of solid achievement.[23] During his two terms (1989-1997), West Virginia benefited economically from a prosperous national economy as well as from Byrd's infusions of federal billions. Caperton made improving education and government reorganization his principal goals. Although voters turned down the constitutional changes he wanted to eliminate independently-elected state officials such as secretary of state or commissioner of agriculture, he was able to streamline state administration and to enact other reforms, such as selling off the unprofitable system of state-owned liquor stores. Since the liquor stores had been a mainstay of local patronage since the 1930s, courthouse politicians bitterly opposed this change, which further eroded the political basis of sectionalism.

During his first term, Caperton pushed for educational reform without taking the demands of teachers into his reform equation. The result was the first statewide teachers' strike in West Virginia history. For eleven days in March 1990, three-quarters of the state's 21,000 teachers stayed off the job, affecting schools in 47 of the 55 counties. After communication between the governor and the teachers' union broke down, union representatives and legislative leaders negotiated an end to the strike. Teachers got improved pay and benefits and a greater role in what Caperton insisted were necessary changes required to make the state more competitive in the new postindustrial economy. West Virginia's ranking in terms of teachers salaries moved the state from 49th to 31st nationally during the Caperton years, while a more streamlined but also more centralized bureaucracy in Charleston equipped classrooms with new instructional technology and software. How effectively these changes will lead to the desired results is impossible to tell in the short term. Since many other states were adopting similar reforms during these

23. Jennifer Bundy, "Economic Progress, Personal Turmoil Dominate Caperton's 8 Years in Office," *Charleston Gazette*, November 28, 1996, p. 1B.

years, the state's relative standing generally did not change dramatically. For example, the American Electronics Association (AeA) state-by-state comparison of "high tech" employment, wages and production shows that West Virginia held its own between 1996 and 2001, but still ranks 46th among the states in terms of high-tech employment and 49th in average wages (which nevertheless are 50 percent higher than the average private sector wage in other industries.) High-tech products—by which is generally meant communications equipment, software and other computer-related products, and other types of electronic hardware wherein the most critical input consists of scientific or technical information—accounted for roughly one percent of the state's "exports," according to AeA. In this regard, the long-term goals of the Byrd-Caperton strategy may run up against a new type of regionalism, for as several studies of the new economy have shown, the highly educated workers on which this economy depends are attracted not so much to the Sunbelt or Gunbelt as to zones of amenity—localities with an enhanced quality of life, which may be defined by any number of factors, among them diversity, tolerance, cosmopolitan culture and convenient access to outdoor recreation and beautiful scenery. West Virginia, of course, has these last resources in abundance, but as long as they remain under the threat of strip mining, clearcutting and industrial pollution, their potential appeal to high tech scientists and engineers may be compromised.

In any case, sectionalism has not vanished from the West Virginia scene. That much was clear when a new dispute broke out in 1998 over a proposed regional airport located between Charleston, Huntington and Parkersburg. The supporters of the plan pointed to the role that air freight and passenger business play in the postindustrial economy. Defenders of Charleston's space-constricted Yeager Airport disputed these assertions and claimed that a regional airport would render Charleston the only state capital in the nation without its own airport (a piece of disinformation that presumably represented geographical ignorance rather than outright mendacity). The point here is not to pass judgment on the merit of the regional airport scheme. The point is that the kind of thinking that scatters resources in order to appease local or sectional feeling almost always leads to a situation where more turns out to be less. That kind of thinking in West Virginia is by no means dead.

The twentieth century ended, as it began, with Americans reading best-selling books about Appalachia. Two of the non-fiction best-sellers were written by former West Virginians. Homer Hickam, Jr., a retired rocket engineer living in Huntsville, Alabama captivated readers with *Rocket Boys*, a memoir of youthful intellectual adventure set against the 1950s backdrop of a dying McDowell County coal town. This book reached an even wider audience as a Hollywood film, *October Sky*, although it is worth pointing out that the producers chose to avoid unionized West Virginia as a location and filmed the story in non-union Tennessee. Hickam followed his success in 2000 with an elaboration of his memoir, entitled *The Coalwood Way* and in May 2001 signed up with the West Virginia Port Authority to star in television commercials touting the regional airport.

Whereas *Rocket Boys* views the nadir of the postwar crisis in the coalfields through an optimistic lens, Jedediah Purdy's *For Common Things* suggests that the worst may be yet to come. The son of back-to-the-landers who schooled him at home before sending him off to prep school and Harvard, Purdy uses his home state as one of two touchstones—the other being the former Soviet satellite nations of east central Europe—by which to argue against his generation's ironic detachment from politics. "When I think of responsibility or foolishness, preservation or destruction, generosity or greed, they take the forms of Appalachia. They come to me as green slopes and shattered hills, good and poor farms, faces firm with practiced concern, contorted with outrage, or slack and ruddy with indifference." In the face of environmental degradation such as mountaintop removal, Purdy's book is above all else a stand against indifference. "The destruction of Appalachia is a terrible symptom of a blinkered economic logic that needs changing," he concludes.[24]

24. Purdy, *For Common Things*, 132, 149, 159.

Whether or not this message gets through will determine much of West Virginia's future and also shape the historical reputation of Purdy's peers. The results of the 2000 election in West Virginia were not encouraging in this regard. Another writer, Denise Giardina, mounted an independent campaign for the governorship based on the single issue of her opposition to mountaintop removal. She won less than two percent of the vote. In the presidential campaign, heavy coal industry campaign contributions and resentment against environmentalism on the part of rank-and-file miners put West Virginia's five electoral votes into the Republican column for only the third time since 1928. Since the Republican presidential candidate had only a one-vote edge in the electoral college, West Virginia's defection from the Democrats proved decisive.[25] This was perhaps the greatest impact the state has had in national politics since the 1960 primary. Whether that influence was for good or ill must remain for future historians to decide.

25. A comprehensive overview of the environmental and political implications of energy policy in West Virginia can be found in Jeff Goodell, "Blasts from the Past. Thanks to the Bush Administration, Big Coal is Back. But Can It be Taught to Behave?" The New York Times Magazine, July 22, 2001, 30–37, 44, 62–63.

ACKNOWLEDGMENTS

No matter how I might organize the list of people who helped me make this book, George Parkinson's name would come first. It was through him that I first learned of the series of which this volume is a part. As curator of the West Virginia Collection in the West Virginia University Library, he placed at my disposal all of the resources of the state's finest archive, and he contributed to the writing of the book both as critic and friend.

Other archivists contributed to the research on which much of the book is based. Rodney Pyles, assistant curator of the West Virginia Collection, was always ready to assist with his abundant knowledge of the Collection's holdings, and I enjoyed the further assistance of Golda Riggs and Martha Neville of the Collection staff. Mrs. Pearl M. Rogers of the West Virginia Department of Archives and History in Charleston was graciously supportive in her role as archivist and also, as publisher of *West Virginia History*, granted me permission to reproduce in chapters 2 and 3 parts of my article, "The Old Dominion and the New," that appeared in that journal in July 1972.

Researching the landscapes of West Virginia history took me on weekend jaunts around the state from Weirton to Welch and Harpers Ferry to Huntington, enjoying at every stop hospitality, advice, and insights provided by many kind people. I especially want to thank Merle Moore of Clarksburg, Ann and Dan Fisher of Martinsburg, Alice Waugh of Marlinton, Mike Williams of Lewisburg, Anne and Evan Buck of Charleston, George King of Harpers Ferry, and Judge C. W. Ferguson of Wayne.

My colleagues Arthur Donovan, John C. Super, and John A. Maxwell of the department of history at West Virginia University each read one or more versions of the manuscript and contributed valuable suggestions for its improvement. William T. Doherty, chairman of the department, made available a variety of institutional supports to the project. Jane Yeager and Lois Brennan of the department staff handled the typing.

All of these people deserve credit for the strengths of this volume; none of them shares responsibility for its defects.

Index